JLA CLASSIFIED

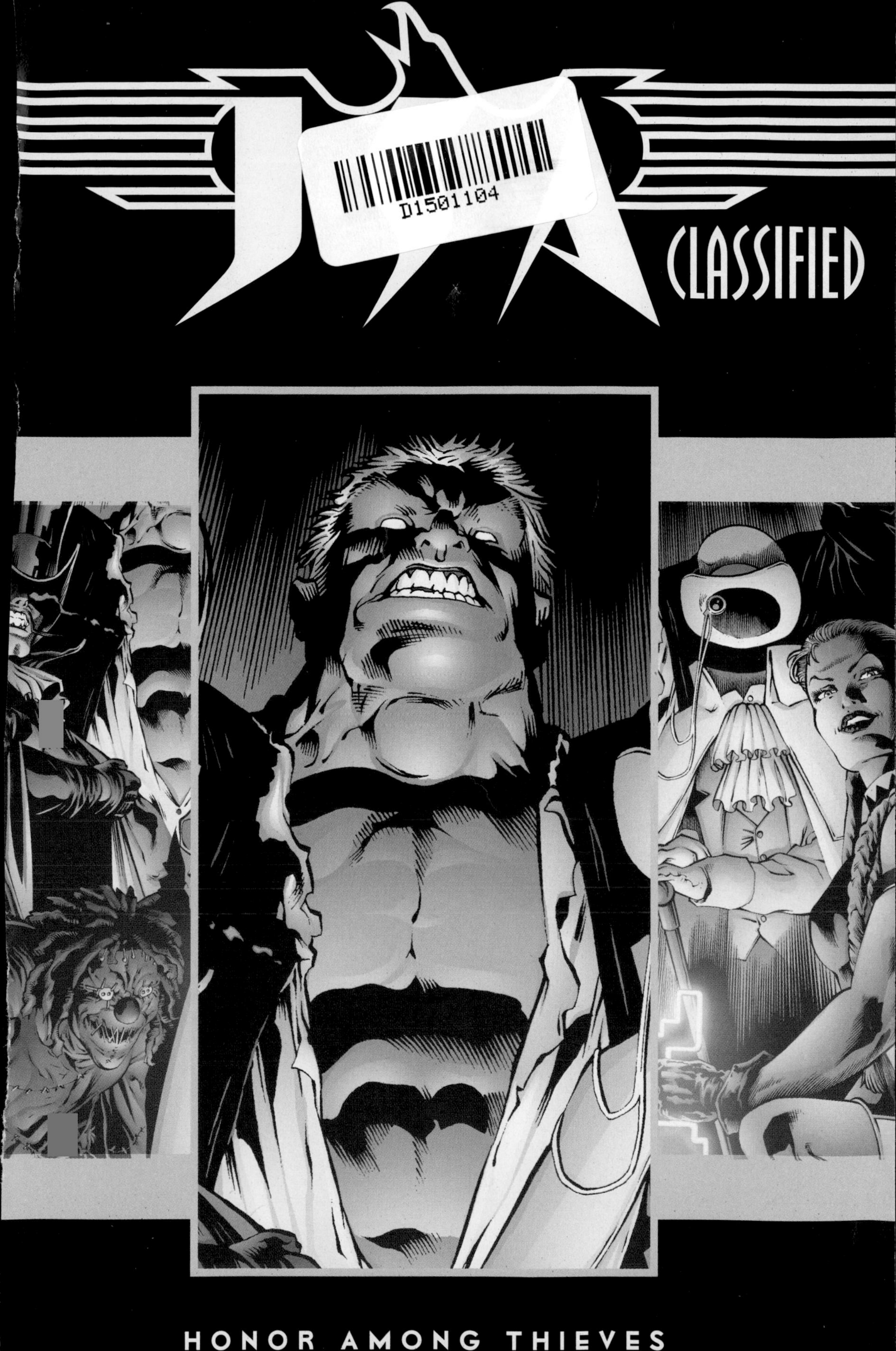

HONOR AMONG THIEVES

JSA CLASSIFIED

HONOR AMONG THIEVES

DAN DIDIO SENIOR VP-EXECUTIVE EDITOR

STEPHEN WACKER EDITOR-ORIGINAL SERIES

HARVEY RICHARDS ASSISTANT EDITOR-ORIGINAL SERIES

ANTON KAWASAKI EDITOR-COLLECTED EDITION

ROBBIN BROSTERMAN SENIOR ART DIRECTOR

PAUL LEVITZ PRESIDENT & PUBLISHER

GEORG BREWER VP-DESIGN & DC DIRECT CREATIVE

RICHARD BRUNING SENIOR VP-CREATIVE DIRECTOR

PATRICK CALDON EXECUTIVE VP-FINANCE & OPERATIONS

CHRIS CARAMALIS VP-FINANCE

JOHN CUNNINGHAM VP-MARKETING

TERRI CUNNINGHAM VP-MANAGING EDITOR

STEPHANIE FIERMAN SENIOR VP-SALES & MARKETING

ALISON GILL VP-MANUFACTURING

HANK KANALZ VP-GENERAL MANAGER, WILDSTORM

JIM LEE EDITORIAL DIRECTOR-WILDSTORM

PAULA LOWITT SENIOR VP-BUSINESS & LEGAL AFFAIRS

MARYELLEN MCLAUGHLIN VP-ADVERTISING & CUSTOM PUBLISHING

JOHN NEE VP-BUSINESS DEVELOPMENT

GREGORY NOVECK SENIOR VP-CREATIVE AFFAIRS

CHERYL RUBIN SENIOR VP-BRAND MANAGEMENT

JEFF TROJAN VP-BUSINESS DEVELOPMENT, DC DIRECT

BOB WAYNE VP-SALES

Cover by Joe Bennett & Ruy Jose with Tanya & Richard Horie
Publication design by Robbie Biederman

JSA CLASSIFIED: HONOR AMONG THIEVES

DC Comics, 1700 Broadway, New York, NY 10019
A Warner Bros. Entertainment Company
Printed in Canada. First Printing.
ISBN: 1-4012-1218-2
ISBN 13: 978-1-4012-1218-6

Jen Van Meter
Peter J. Tomasi
Writers

Patrick Olliffe
Don Kramer
Pencillers

Ruy Jose
Drew Geraci
Keith Champagne
Inkers

Nathan Eyring
John Kalisz
Colorists

Jared K. Fletcher
Nick J. Napolitano
Rob Leigh
Letterers

Joe Bennett & Ruy Jose
Jose Marzan, Jr.
Original Covers

JUSTICE SOCIETY OF AMERICA

DR. MID-NITE
A medical prodigy, Pieter Anton Cross refused to work within the system. Treating people on his own, he came into contact with a dangerous drug that altered his body chemistry, letting him see light in the infrared spectrum. Although he was blinded in a car accident that was meant to kill him, he continues to protect the weak in the assumed identity of Dr. Mid-Nite.

JAKEEM THUNDER
Young Jakeem Williams came into possession of a pen that was actually the vessel for a 5th-Dimensional being known as the Thunderbolt. Jakeem became his new partner and is now learning how best to use his position of power despite chafing at being treated like a kid.

THE FLASH
The first in a long line of super-speedsters, Jay Garrick is capable of running at velocities near the speed of light. A scientist, Garrick has also served as mentor to other speedsters and heroes over several generations.

MR. TERRIFIC
Haunted by the death of his wife, Olympic gold medal-winning decathlete Michael Holt was ready to take his own life. Instead, inspired by the Spectre's story of the original Mr. Terrific, he rededicated himself to ensuring fair play among the street youth using his wealth and technical skills.

SAND
The ward of original Sandman Wesley Dodds, Sandy Hawkins was transformed through a bizarre experiment and became a geomorph — able to transform his body into sand and to control silicon to a limited degree.

STARGIRL
When Courtney Whitmore discovered the cosmic converter belt once worn by the JSA's original Star-Spangled Kid, she saw it as an opportunity to cut class and kick some butt. Now, she is slowly beginning to learn about the awesome legacy she has become a part of. She has quickly become the team's conscience.

WILDCAT
A former heavyweight boxing champ, Ted Grant, a.k.a. Wildcat, prowls the mean streets defending the helpless. One of the world's foremost hand-to-hand combatants, he has trained many of today's best fighters — including Black Canary, Catwoman, and the Batman.

THE INJUSTICE SOCIETY

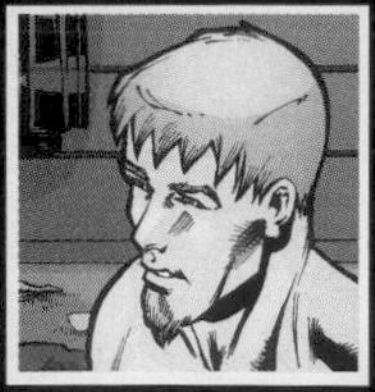

ICICLE

Cameron Mahkent is the son of the original Icicle, who was an adversary of the Justice Society — especially Green Lantern Alan Scott. Unlike his father who used a "cold gun" weapon, Cameron has actual cold powers that allow him to freeze objects and people.

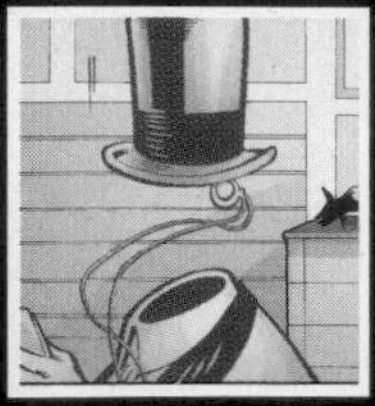

GENTLEMAN GHOST

"Gentleman Jim" Craddock was a criminal in 1800s England, but after moving to America he encountered gunslingers Nighthawk and Cinnamon, who captured him and sentenced him to be hanged. Craddock then transcended death, coming back as a phantom, and has haunted the Earth ever since.

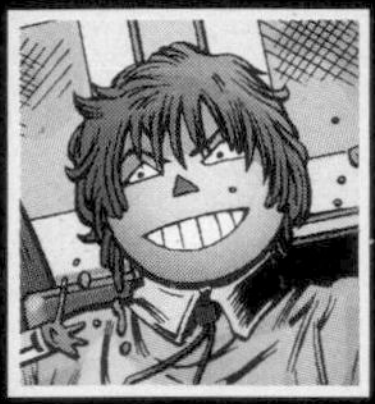

RAG DOLL

Peter Merkel was born with the unique condition of "triple-jointedness," allowing him to twist and contort his body in a number of ways, making it extremely difficult to be caught. He has often eluded the original Flash, Jay Garrick.

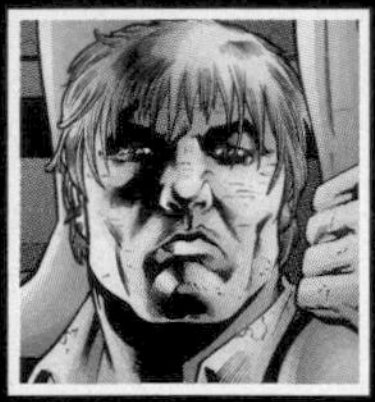

SOLOMON GRUNDY

Cyrus Gold was a wealthy merchant in the late 19th century whose murdered body was disposed of in Slaughter Swamp. Fifty years later, his corpse was reanimated into a large, shambling creature with no memory of his past. The super-strong monster has wandered the Earth ever since, often coming into combat with the Justice Society.

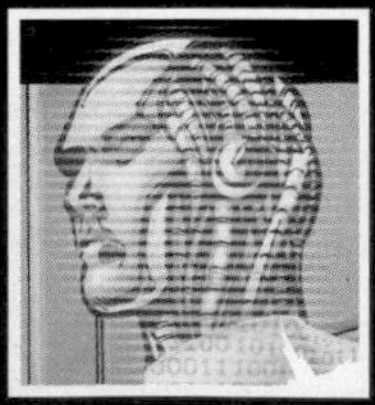

THE THINKER

The original Thinker was a nemesis of the JSA who used his mental-powered "Thinking Cap" to commit crimes before dying. Later, the cap's technology gained consciousness and took on a visual "hologram" form as the new Thinker — a deadly artificial intelligence.

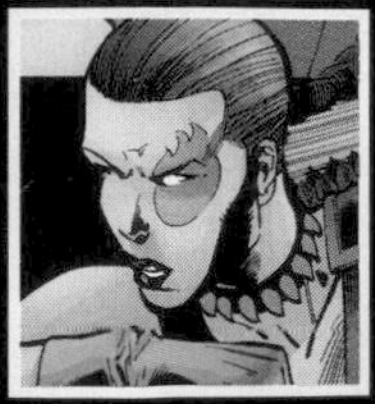

TIGRESS

Artemis Crock is the daughter of the original Tigress and the Sportsmaster — two villains who frequently combatted the JSA. An extraordinary athlete and hand-to-hand combatant, Artemis has mastered the use of many weapons — most especially the crossbow.

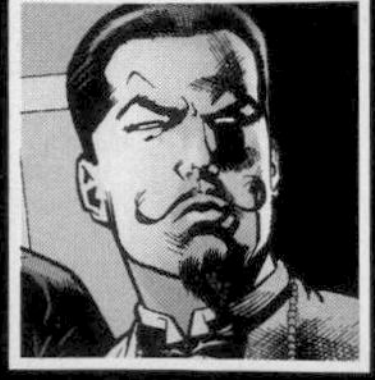

THE WIZARD

Formerly a gunman for various crime bosses, William Zard tired of working for others and moved to Tibet where he trained in the mystic arts. After mastering the powers of illusion and deception, Zard returned to the U.S. to embark a new life as a criminal magician.

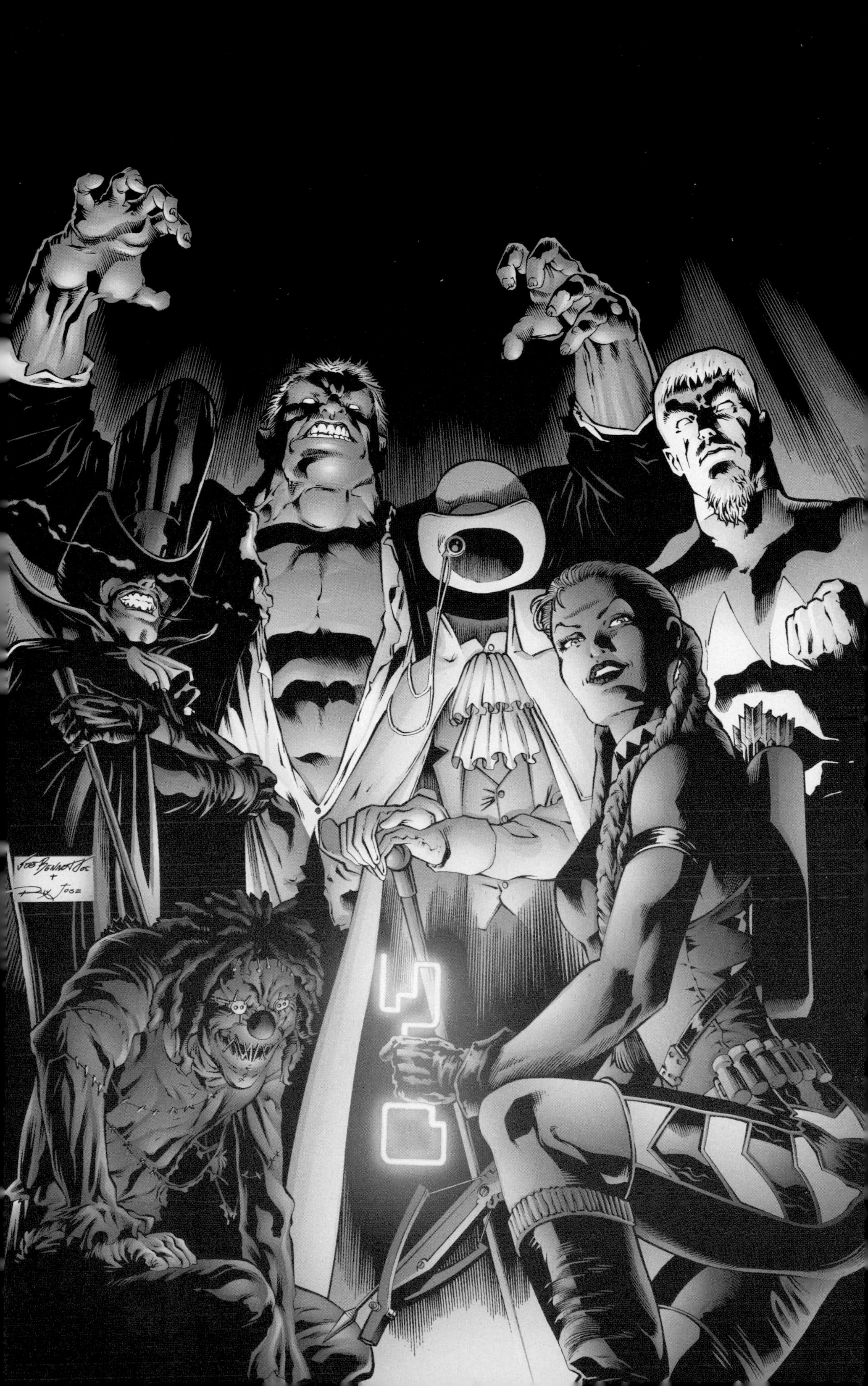

HONOR AMONG THIEVES

Jen Van Meter **Writer**
Patrick Olliffe **Penciller**
Ruy Jose & Drew Geraci **Inkers**
Nathan Eyring **Colorist**

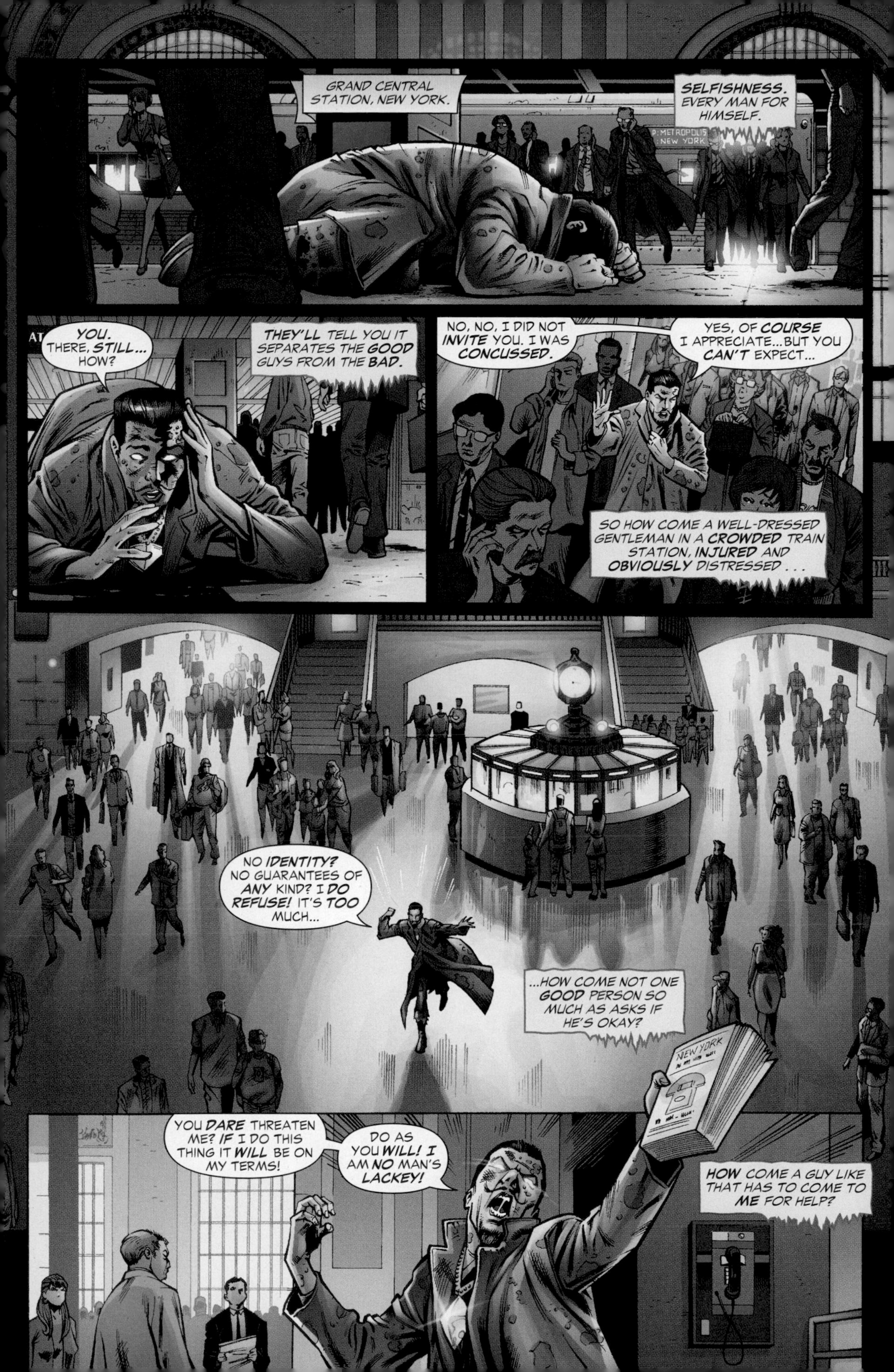
GRAND CENTRAL STATION, NEW YORK.
SELFISHNESS. EVERY MAN FOR HIMSELF.
P: METROPOLIS : NEW YORK
YOU. THERE, STILL... HOW?
THEY'LL TELL YOU IT SEPARATES THE GOOD GUYS FROM THE BAD.
NO, NO, I DID NOT INVITE YOU. I WAS CONCUSSED.
YES, OF COURSE I APPRECIATE...BUT YOU CAN'T EXPECT...
SO HOW COME A WELL-DRESSED GENTLEMAN IN A CROWDED TRAIN STATION, INJURED AND OBVIOUSLY DISTRESSED . . .
NO IDENTITY? NO GUARANTEES OF ANY KIND? I DO REFUSE! IT'S TOO MUCH...
...HOW COME NOT ONE GOOD PERSON SO MUCH AS ASKS IF HE'S OKAY?
NEW YORK
YOU DARE THREATEN ME? IF I DO THIS THING IT WILL BE ON MY TERMS!
DO AS YOU WILL! I AM NO MAN'S LACKEY!
HOW COME A GUY LIKE THAT HAS TO COME TO ME FOR HELP?

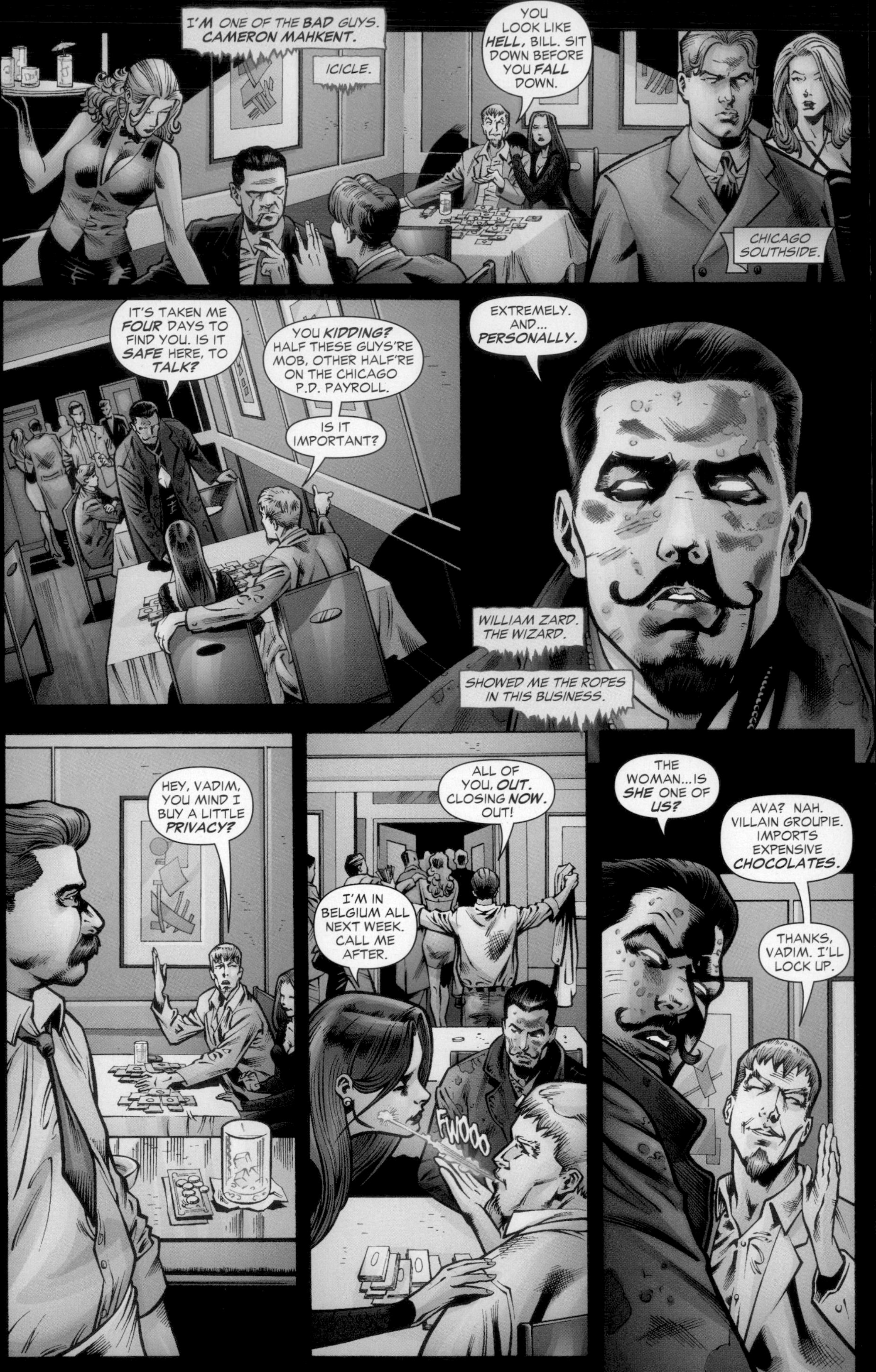

I'M ONE OF THE BAD GUYS. CAMERON MAHKENT.
ICICLE.
YOU LOOK LIKE HELL, BILL. SIT DOWN BEFORE YOU FALL DOWN.
CHICAGO SOUTHSIDE.
IT'S TAKEN ME FOUR DAYS TO FIND YOU. IS IT SAFE HERE, TO TALK?
YOU KIDDING? HALF THESE GUYS'RE MOB, OTHER HALF'RE ON THE CHICAGO P.D. PAYROLL.
IS IT IMPORTANT?
EXTREMELY. AND... PERSONALLY.
WILLIAM ZARD. THE WIZARD.
SHOWED ME THE ROPES IN THIS BUSINESS.
HEY, VADIM, YOU MIND I BUY A LITTLE PRIVACY?
ALL OF YOU, OUT. CLOSING NOW. OUT!
I'M IN BELGIUM ALL NEXT WEEK. CALL ME AFTER.
FWOOO
THE WOMAN...IS SHE ONE OF US?
AVA? NAH. VILLAIN GROUPIE. IMPORTS EXPENSIVE CHOCOLATES.
THANKS, VADIM. I'LL LOCK UP.

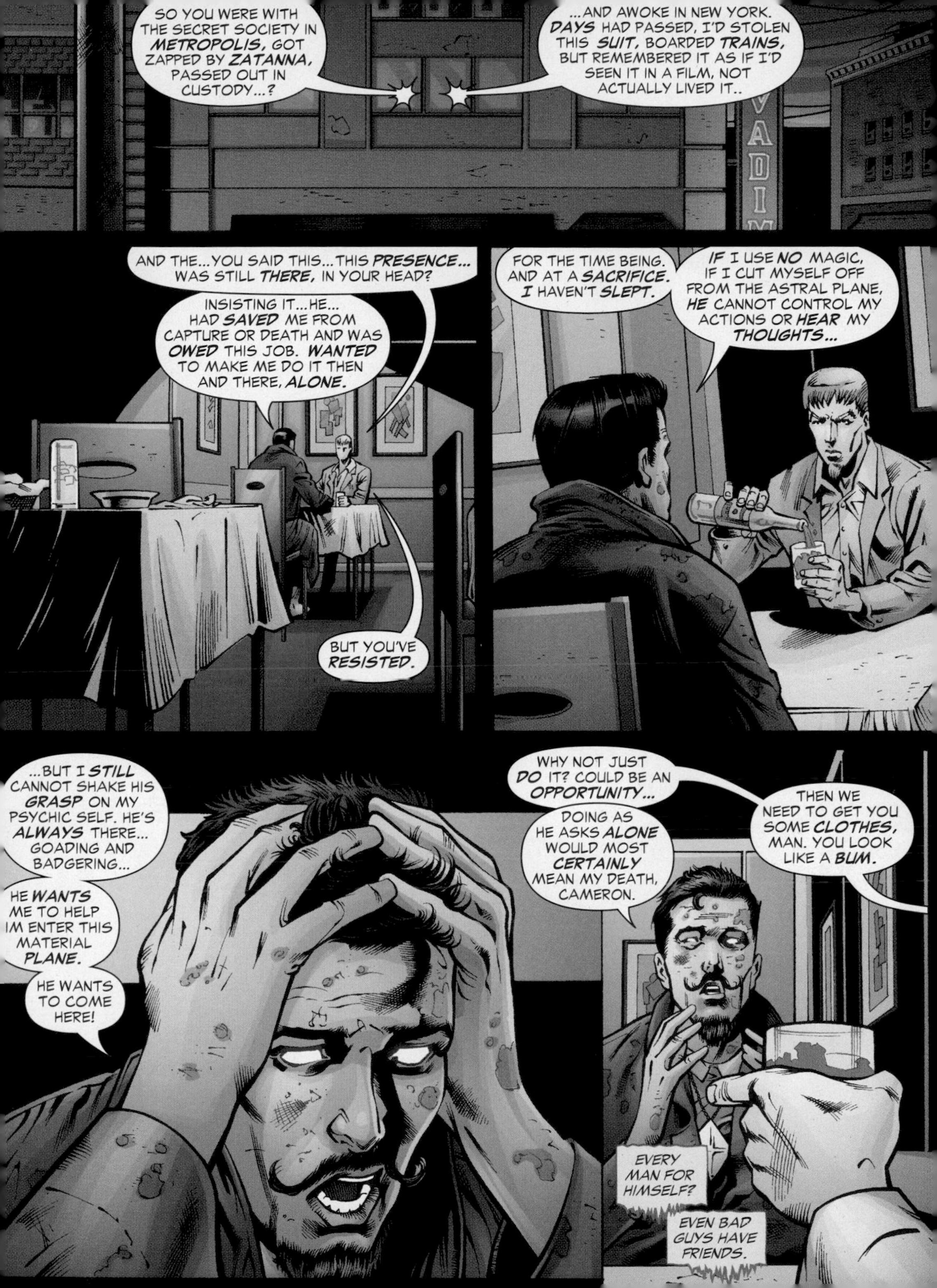
SO YOU WERE WITH THE SECRET SOCIETY IN METROPOLIS, GOT ZAPPED BY ZATANNA, PASSED OUT IN CUSTODY...?
...AND AWOKE IN NEW YORK. DAYS HAD PASSED, I'D STOLEN THIS SUIT, BOARDED TRAINS, BUT REMEMBERED IT AS IF I'D SEEN IT IN A FILM, NOT ACTUALLY LIVED IT..
AND THE...YOU SAID THIS...THIS PRESENCE... WAS STILL THERE, IN YOUR HEAD?
INSISTING IT...HE... HAD SAVED ME FROM CAPTURE OR DEATH AND WAS OWED THIS JOB. WANTED TO MAKE ME DO IT THEN AND THERE, ALONE.
BUT YOU'VE RESISTED.
FOR THE TIME BEING. AND AT A SACRIFICE. I HAVEN'T SLEPT.
IF I USE NO MAGIC, IF I CUT MYSELF OFF FROM THE ASTRAL PLANE, HE CANNOT CONTROL MY ACTIONS OR HEAR MY THOUGHTS...
...BUT I STILL CANNOT SHAKE HIS GRASP ON MY PSYCHIC SELF. HE'S ALWAYS THERE... GOADING AND BADGERING...
HE WANTS ME TO HELP IM ENTER THIS MATERIAL PLANE.
HE WANTS TO COME HERE!
WHY NOT JUST DO IT? COULD BE AN OPPORTUNITY...
DOING AS HE ASKS ALONE WOULD MOST CERTAINLY MEAN MY DEATH, CAMERON.
THEN WE NEED TO GET YOU SOME CLOTHES, MAN. YOU LOOK LIKE A BUM.
EVERY MAN FOR HIMSELF?
EVEN BAD GUYS HAVE FRIENDS.

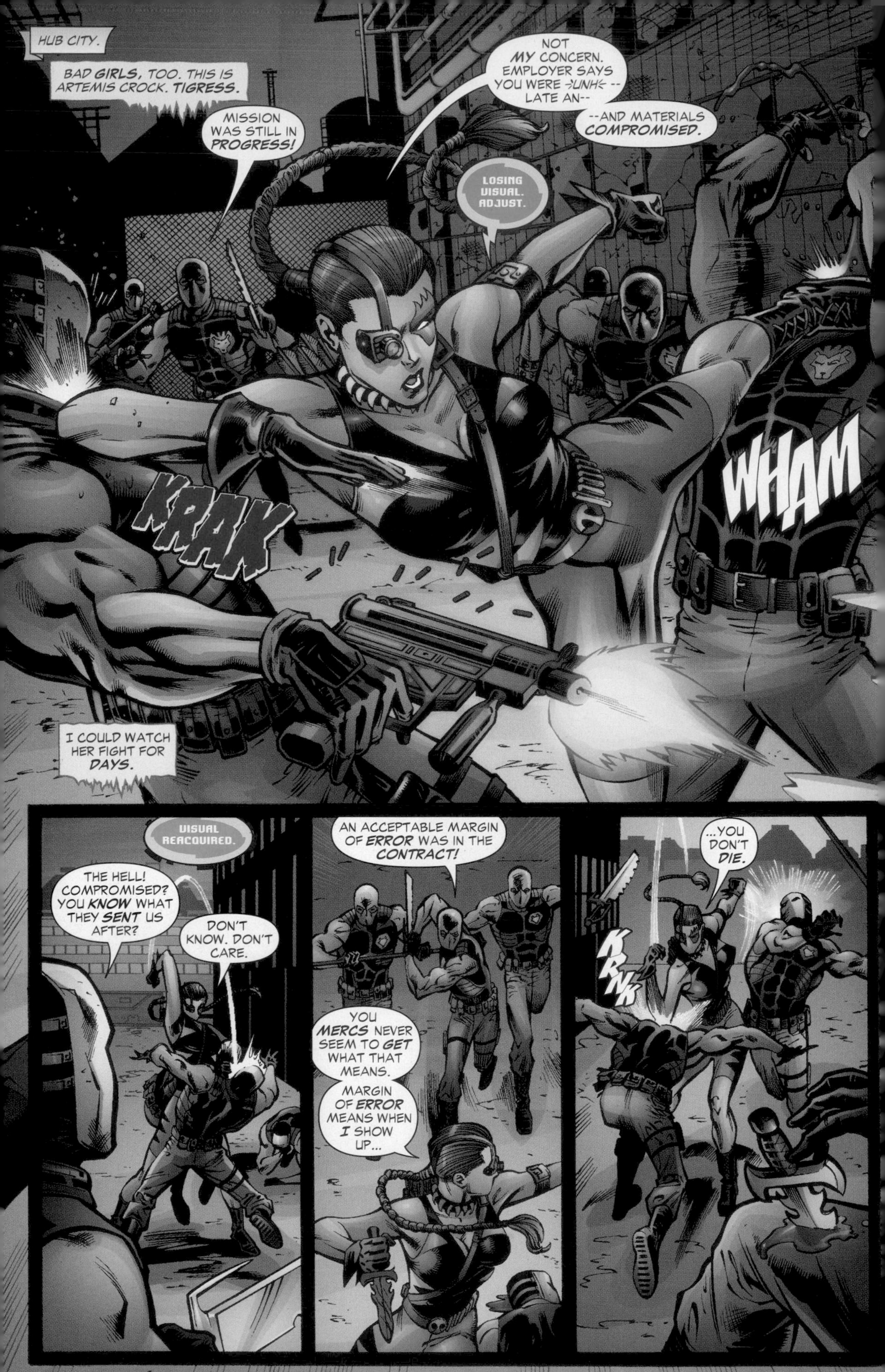
HUB CITY.
BAD GIRLS, TOO. THIS IS ARTEMIS CROCK. TIGRESS.
MISSION WAS STILL IN PROGRESS!
NOT MY CONCERN. EMPLOYER SAYS YOU WERE UNH -- LATE AN--
--AND MATERIALS COMPROMISED.
LOSING VISUAL. ADJUST.
KRAK
WHAM
I COULD WATCH HER FIGHT FOR DAYS.
VISUAL REACQUIRED.
THE HELL! COMPROMISED? YOU KNOW WHAT THEY SENT US AFTER?
DON'T KNOW. DON'T CARE.
AN ACCEPTABLE MARGIN OF ERROR WAS IN THE CONTRACT!
YOU MERCS NEVER SEEM TO GET WHAT THAT MEANS.
MARGIN OF ERROR MEANS WHEN I SHOW UP...
...YOU DON'T DIE.
KRNK

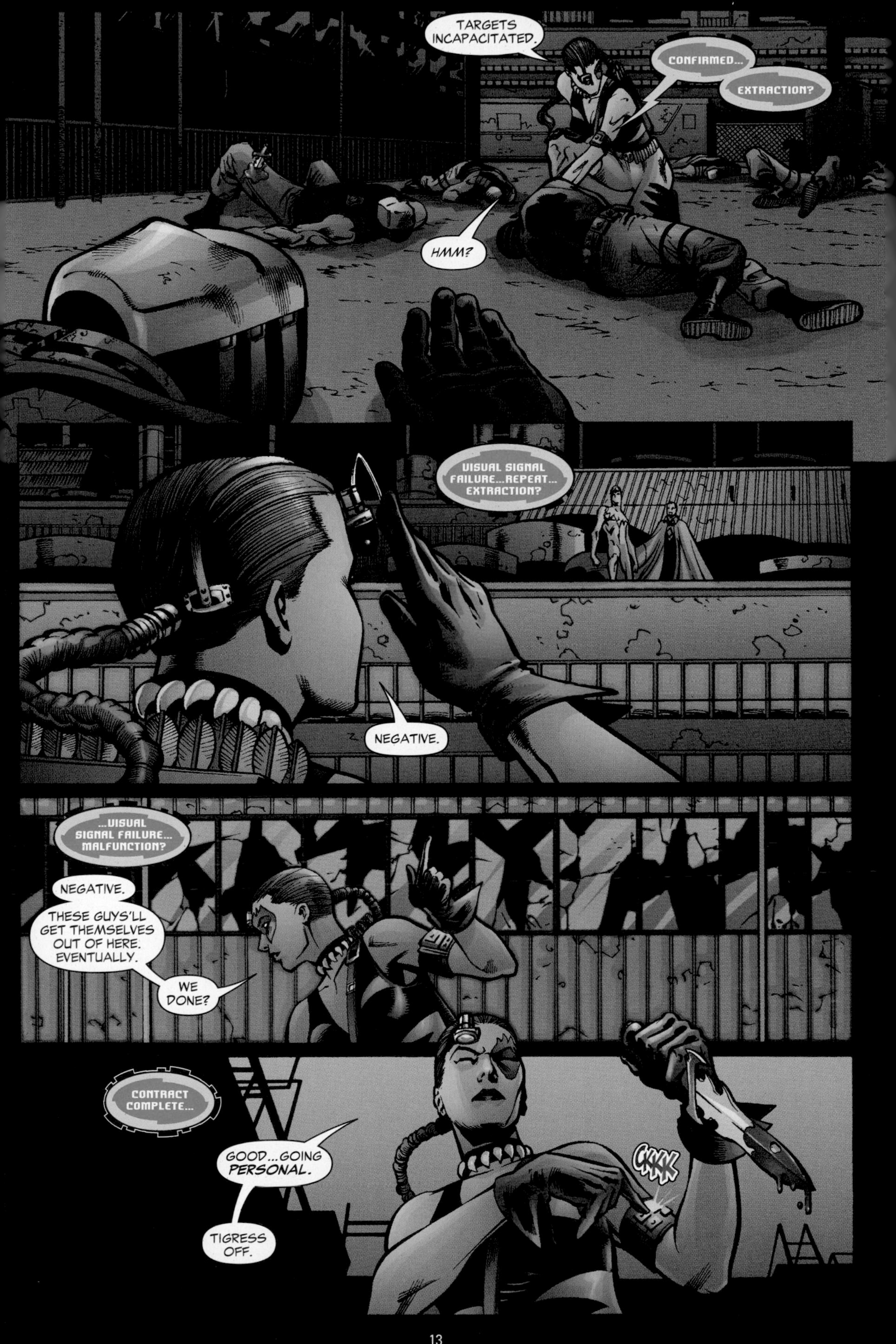
TARGETS INCAPACITATED.
CONFIRMED...
EXTRACTION?
HMM?
VISUAL SIGNAL FAILURE...REPEAT... EXTRACTION?
NEGATIVE.
...VISUAL SIGNAL FAILURE... MALFUNCTION?
NEGATIVE.
THESE GUYS'LL GET THEMSELVES OUT OF HERE. EVENTUALLY.
WE DONE?
CONTRACT COMPLETE...
GOOD...GOING PERSONAL.
TIGRESS OFF.
CKKK

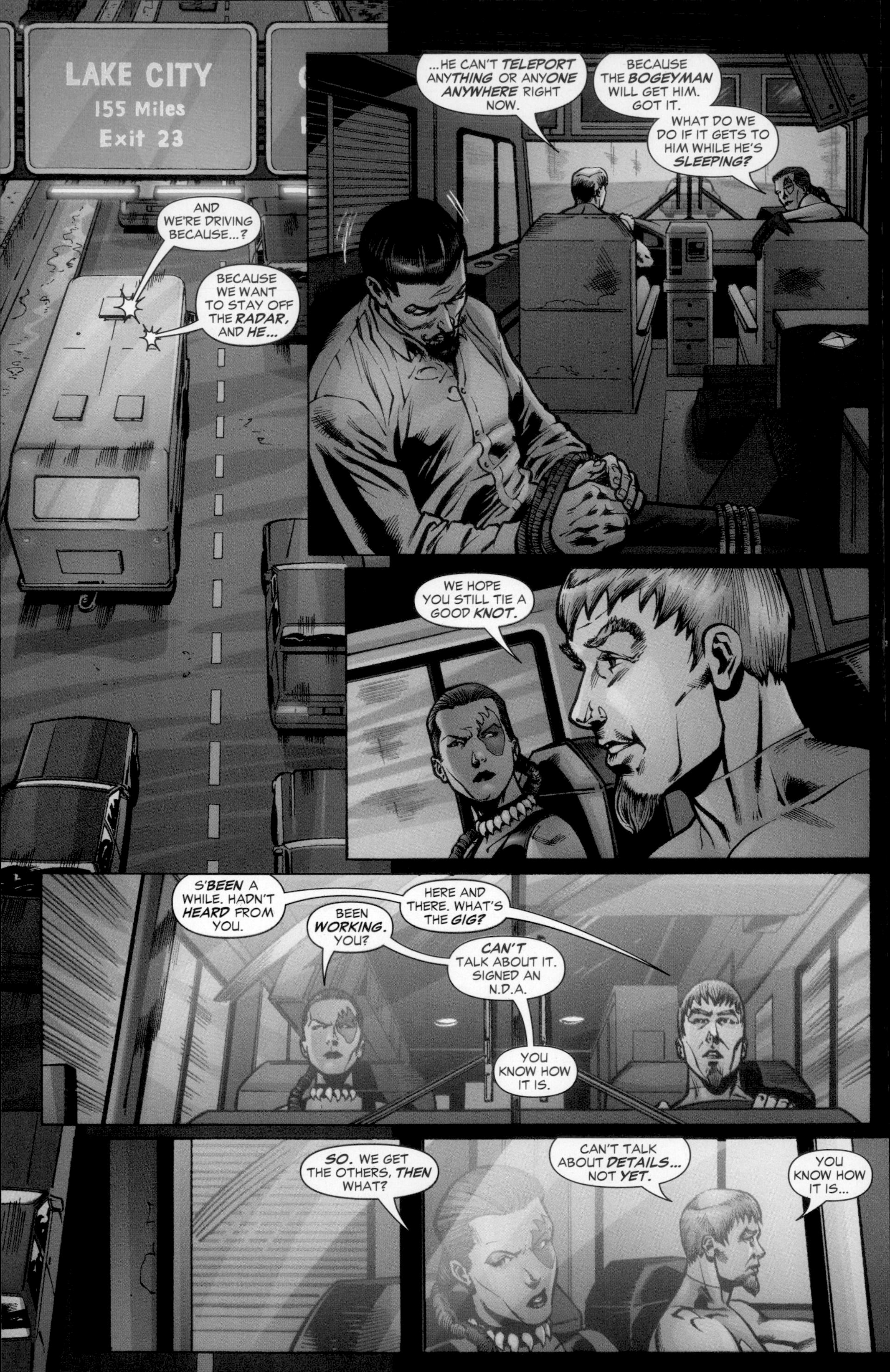
LAKE CITY
155 Miles
Exit 23
AND WE'RE DRIVING BECAUSE...?
BECAUSE WE WANT TO STAY OFF THE RADAR, AND HE...
...HE CAN'T TELEPORT ANYTHING OR ANYONE ANYWHERE RIGHT NOW.
BECAUSE THE BOGEYMAN WILL GET HIM. GOT IT.
WHAT DO WE DO IF IT GETS TO HIM WHILE HE'S SLEEPING?
WE HOPE YOU STILL TIE A GOOD KNOT.
S'BEEN A WHILE. HADN'T HEARD FROM YOU.
BEEN WORKING. YOU?
HERE AND THERE. WHAT'S THE GIG?
CAN'T TALK ABOUT IT. SIGNED AN N.D.A.
YOU KNOW HOW IT IS.
SO. WE GET THE OTHERS, THEN WHAT?
CAN'T TALK ABOUT DETAILS... NOT YET.
YOU KNOW HOW IT IS...

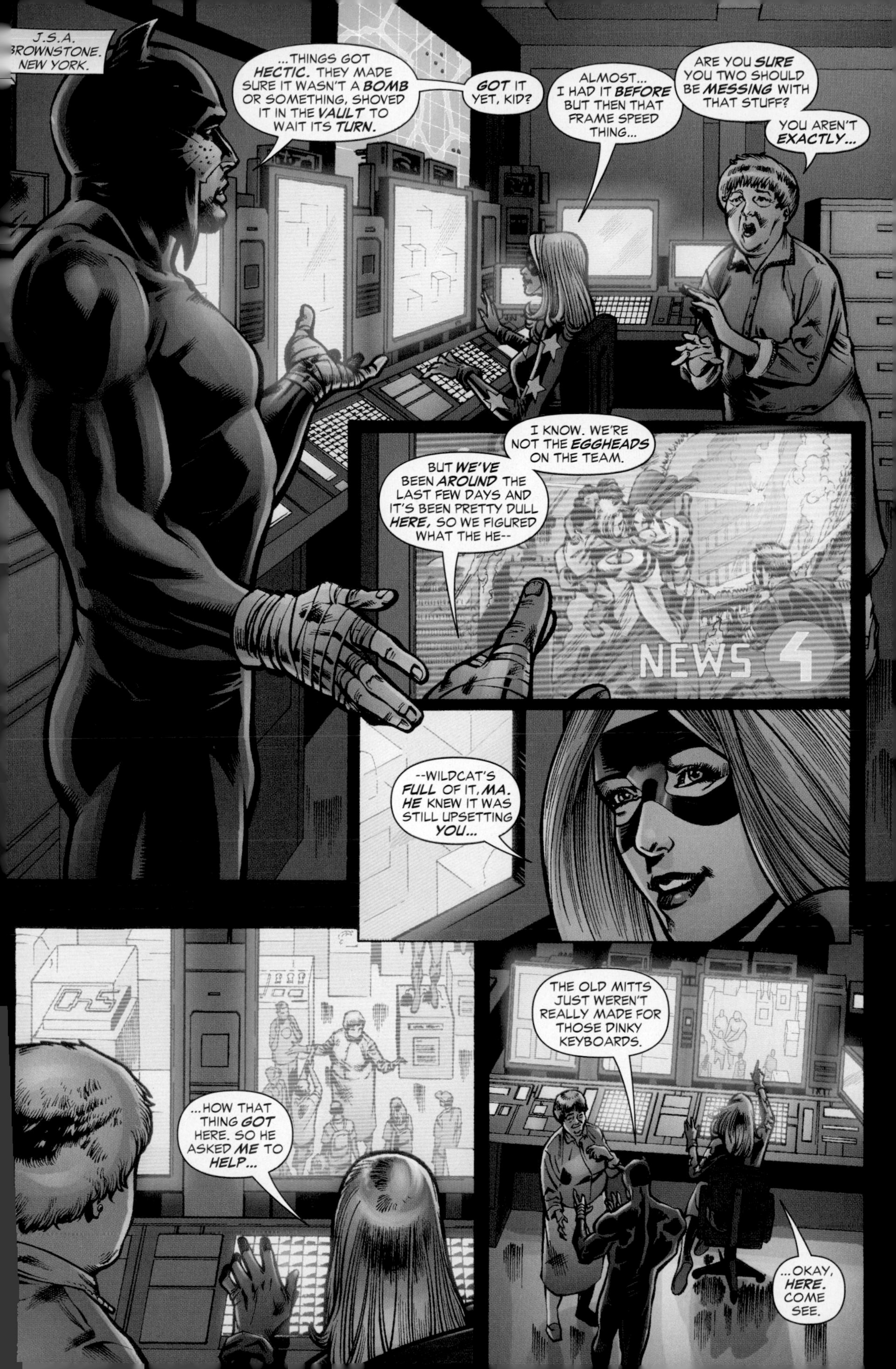
J.S.A. BROWNSTONE. NEW YORK.
...THINGS GOT HECTIC. THEY MADE SURE IT WASN'T A BOMB OR SOMETHING, SHOVED IT IN THE VAULT TO WAIT ITS TURN.
GOT IT YET, KID?
ALMOST... I HAD IT BEFORE BUT THEN THAT FRAME SPEED THING...
ARE YOU SURE YOU TWO SHOULD BE MESSING WITH THAT STUFF?
YOU AREN'T EXACTLY...
I KNOW. WE'RE NOT THE EGGHEADS ON THE TEAM.
BUT WE'VE BEEN AROUND THE LAST FEW DAYS AND IT'S BEEN PRETTY DULL HERE, SO WE FIGURED WHAT THE HE--
NEWS 4
--WILDCAT'S FULL OF IT, MA. HE KNEW IT WAS STILL UPSETTING YOU...
...HOW THAT THING GOT HERE. SO HE ASKED ME TO HELP...
THE OLD MITTS JUST WEREN'T REALLY MADE FOR THOSE DINKY KEYBOARDS.
...OKAY, HERE. COME SEE.

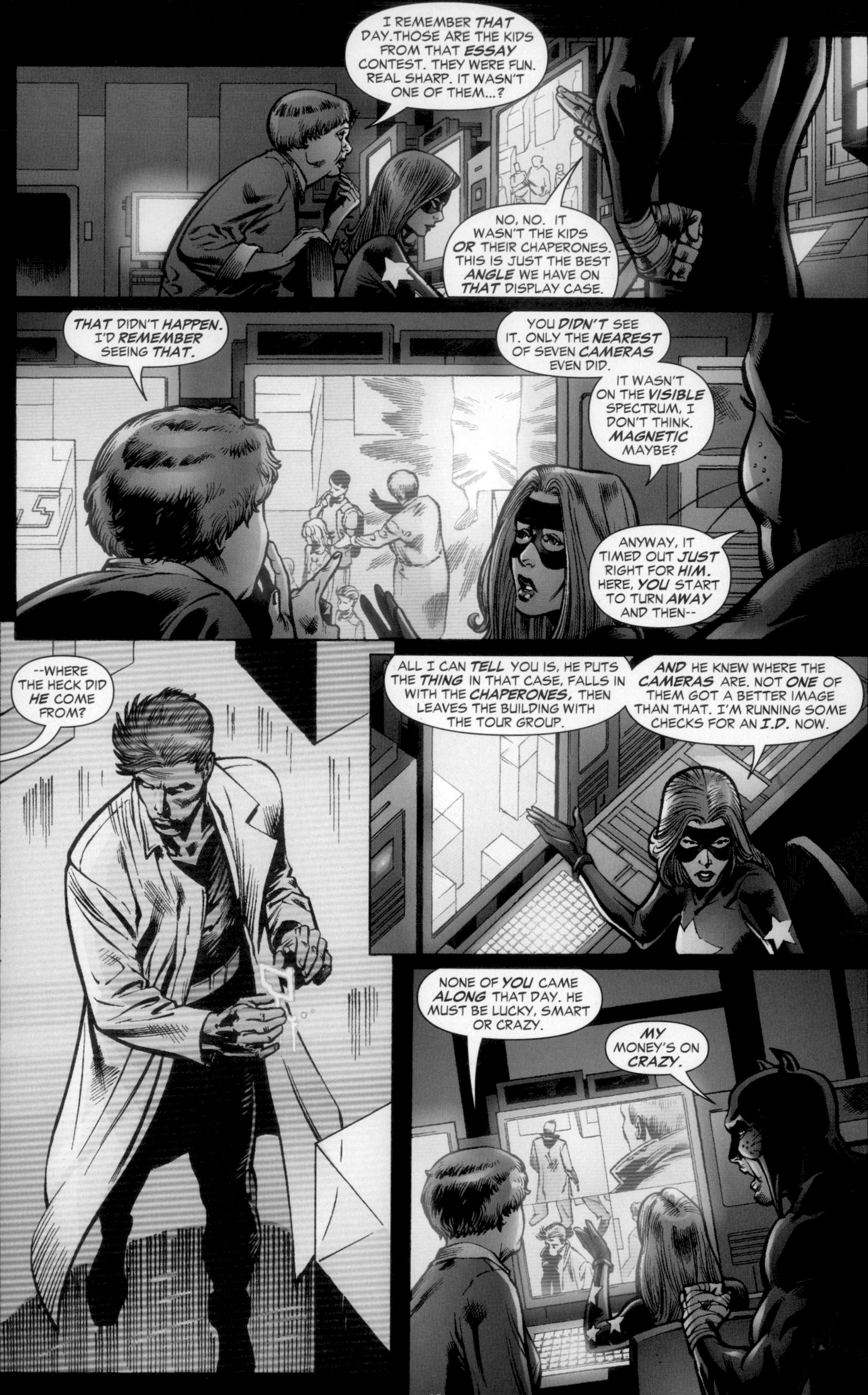
I REMEMBER THAT DAY. THOSE ARE THE KIDS FROM THAT ESSAY CONTEST. THEY WERE FUN. REAL SHARP. IT WASN'T ONE OF THEM...?
NO, NO. IT WASN'T THE KIDS OR THEIR CHAPERONES. THIS IS JUST THE BEST ANGLE WE HAVE ON THAT DISPLAY CASE.
THAT DIDN'T HAPPEN. I'D REMEMBER SEEING THAT.
YOU DIDN'T SEE IT. ONLY THE NEAREST OF SEVEN CAMERAS EVEN DID.
IT WASN'T ON THE VISIBLE SPECTRUM, I DON'T THINK. MAGNETIC MAYBE?
ANYWAY, IT TIMED OUT JUST RIGHT FOR HIM. HERE, YOU START TO TURN AWAY AND THEN--
--WHERE THE HECK DID HE COME FROM?
ALL I CAN TELL YOU IS, HE PUTS THE THING IN THAT CASE, FALLS IN WITH THE CHAPERONES, THEN LEAVES THE BUILDING WITH THE TOUR GROUP.
AND HE KNEW WHERE THE CAMERAS ARE. NOT ONE OF THEM GOT A BETTER IMAGE THAN THAT. I'M RUNNING SOME CHECKS FOR AN I.D. NOW.
NONE OF YOU CAME ALONG THAT DAY. HE MUST BE LUCKY, SMART OR CRAZY.
MY MONEY'S ON CRAZY.

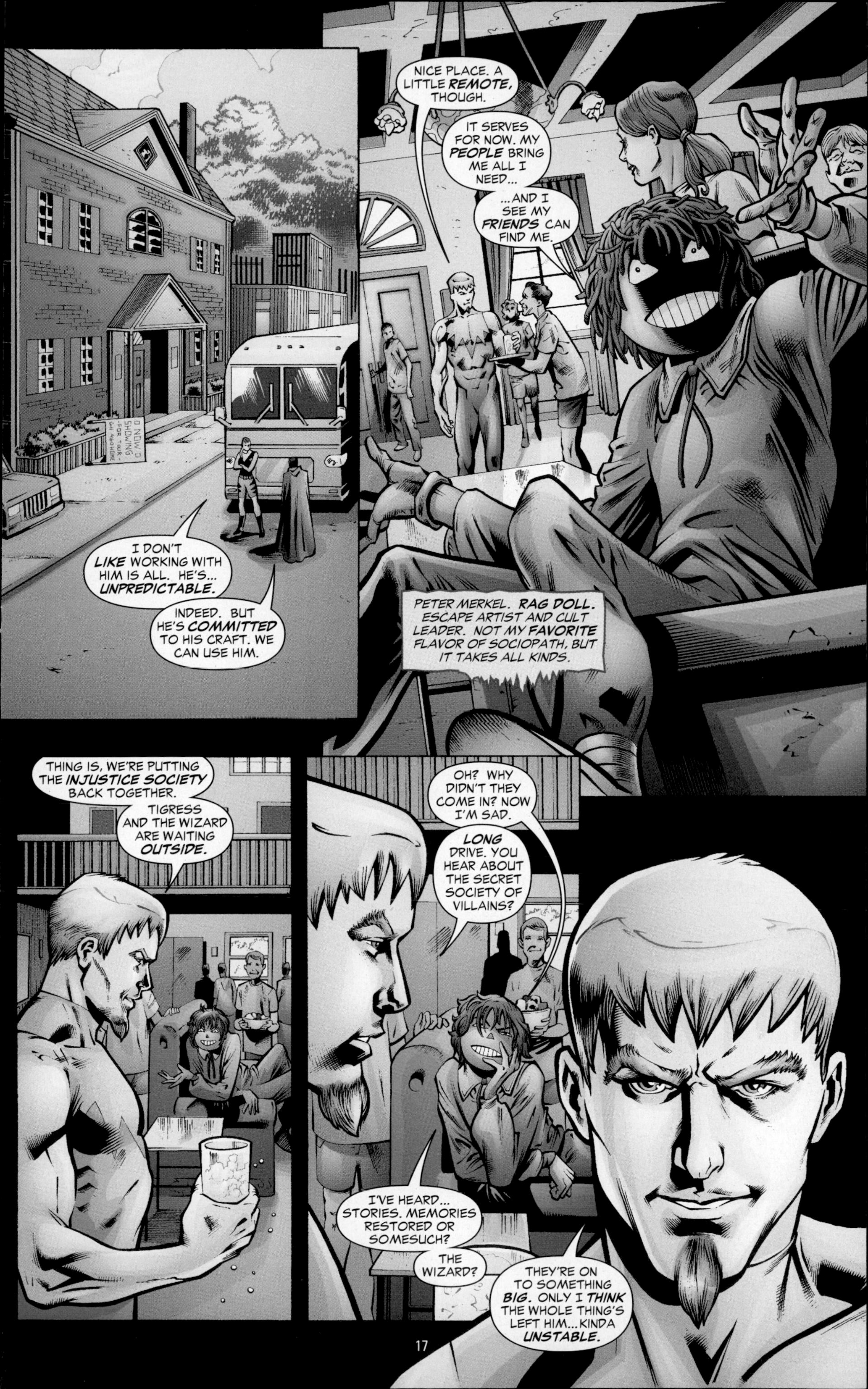
I DON'T LIKE WORKING WITH HIM IS ALL. HE'S... UNPREDICTABLE.
INDEED. BUT HE'S COMMITTED TO HIS CRAFT. WE CAN USE HIM.
NICE PLACE. A LITTLE REMOTE, THOUGH.
IT SERVES FOR NOW. MY PEOPLE BRING ME ALL I NEED...
...AND I SEE MY FRIENDS CAN FIND ME.
PETER MERKEL. RAG DOLL. ESCAPE ARTIST AND CULT LEADER. NOT MY FAVORITE FLAVOR OF SOCIOPATH, BUT IT TAKES ALL KINDS.
THING IS, WE'RE PUTTING THE INJUSTICE SOCIETY BACK TOGETHER.
TIGRESS AND THE WIZARD ARE WAITING OUTSIDE.
OH? WHY DIDN'T THEY COME IN? NOW I'M SAD.
LONG DRIVE. YOU HEAR ABOUT THE SECRET SOCIETY OF VILLAINS?
I'VE HEARD... STORIES. MEMORIES RESTORED OR SOMESUCH?
THE WIZARD?
THEY'RE ON TO SOMETHING BIG. ONLY I THINK THE WHOLE THING'S LEFT HIM...KINDA UNSTABLE.

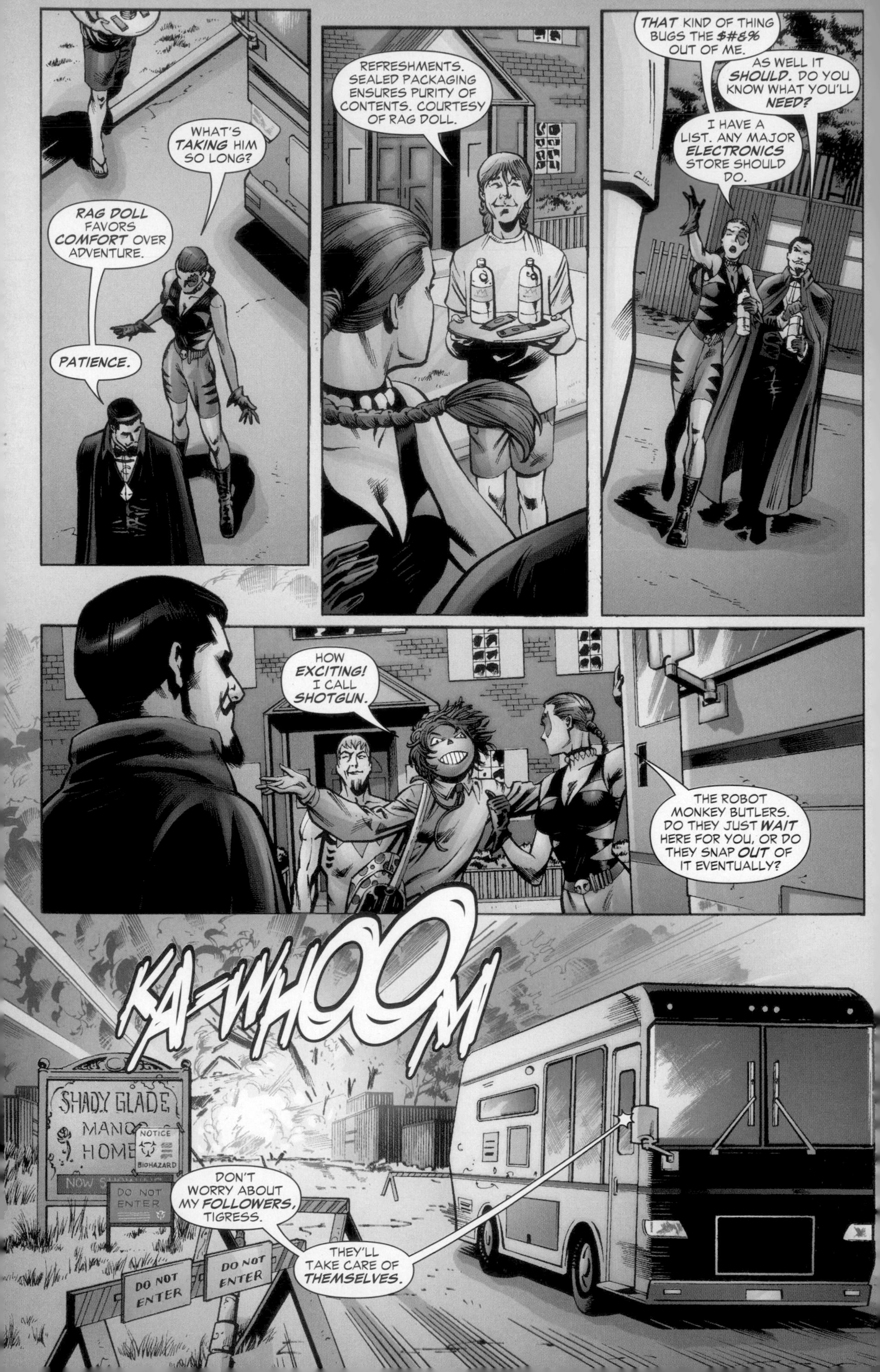
WHAT'S TAKING HIM SO LONG?
RAG DOLL FAVORS COMFORT OVER ADVENTURE.
PATIENCE.
REFRESHMENTS. SEALED PACKAGING ENSURES PURITY OF CONTENTS. COURTESY OF RAG DOLL.
THAT KIND OF THING BUGS THE $#&% OUT OF ME.
AS WELL IT SHOULD. DO YOU KNOW WHAT YOU'LL NEED?
I HAVE A LIST. ANY MAJOR ELECTRONICS STORE SHOULD DO.
HOW EXCITING! I CALL SHOTGUN.
THE ROBOT MONKEY BUTLERS. DO THEY JUST WAIT HERE FOR YOU, OR DO THEY SNAP OUT OF IT EVENTUALLY?
KA-WHOOM
SHADY GLADE MANOR HOME
NOTICE
BIOHAZARD
DO NOT ENTER
DON'T WORRY ABOUT MY FOLLOWERS, TIGRESS.
THEY'LL TAKE CARE OF THEMSELVES.
DO NOT ENTER
DO NOT ENTER

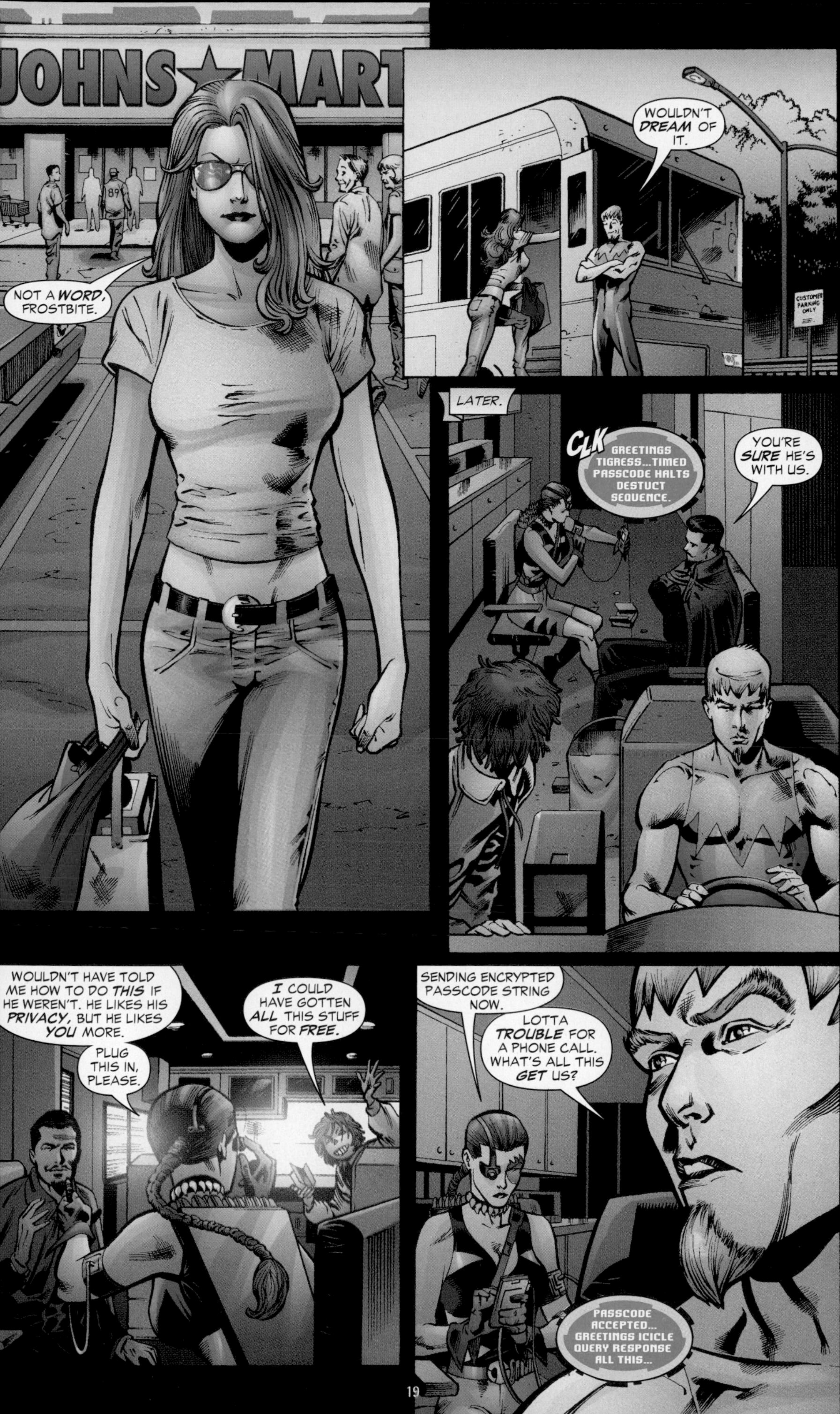
JOHNS MART
NOT A WORD, FROSTBITE.
WOULDN'T DREAM OF IT.
CUSTOMER PARKING ONLY
LATER.
CLK
GREETINGS TIGRESS...TIMED PASSCODE HALTS DESTUCT SEQUENCE.
YOU'RE SURE HE'S WITH US.
WOULDN'T HAVE TOLD ME HOW TO DO THIS IF HE WEREN'T. HE LIKES HIS PRIVACY, BUT HE LIKES YOU MORE.
PLUG THIS IN, PLEASE.
I COULD HAVE GOTTEN ALL THIS STUFF FOR FREE.
SENDING ENCRYPTED PASSCODE STRING NOW.
LOTTA TROUBLE FOR A PHONE CALL. WHAT'S ALL THIS GET US?
PASSCODE ACCEPTED... GREETINGS ICICLE QUERY RESPONSE ALL THIS...

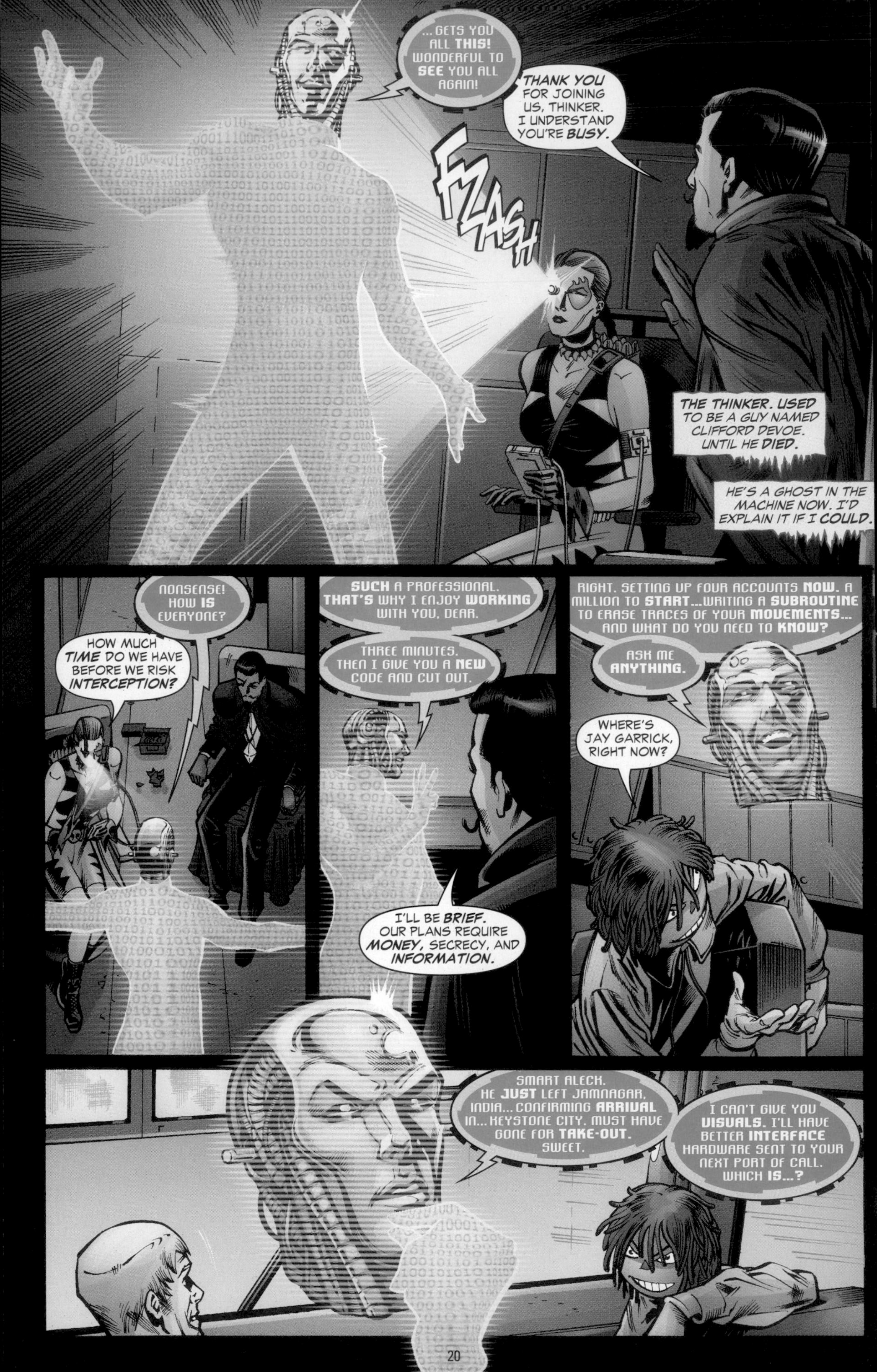
...GETS YOU ALL THIS! WONDERFUL TO SEE YOU ALL AGAIN!
THANK YOU FOR JOINING US, THINKER. I UNDERSTAND YOU'RE BUSY.
FZZASH
THE THINKER. USED TO BE A GUY NAMED CLIFFORD DEVOE. UNTIL HE DIED.
HE'S A GHOST IN THE MACHINE NOW. I'D EXPLAIN IT IF I COULD.
NONSENSE! HOW IS EVERYONE?
HOW MUCH TIME DO WE HAVE BEFORE WE RISK INTERCEPTION?
SUCH A PROFESSIONAL. THAT'S WHY I ENJOY WORKING WITH YOU, DEAR.
THREE MINUTES. THEN I GIVE YOU A NEW CODE AND CUT OUT.
I'LL BE BRIEF. OUR PLANS REQUIRE MONEY, SECRECY, AND INFORMATION.
RIGHT. SETTING UP FOUR ACCOUNTS NOW. A MILLION TO START...WRITING A SUBROUTINE TO ERASE TRACES OF YOUR MOVEMENTS... AND WHAT DO YOU NEED TO KNOW?
ASK ME ANYTHING.
WHERE'S JAY GARRICK, RIGHT NOW?
SMART ALECK. HE JUST LEFT JAMNAGAR, INDIA... CONFIRMING ARRIVAL IN... KEYSTONE CITY. MUST HAVE GONE FOR TAKE-OUT. SWEET.
I CAN'T GIVE YOU VISUALS. I'LL HAVE BETTER INTERFACE HARDWARE SENT TO YOUR NEXT PORT OF CALL. WHICH IS...?

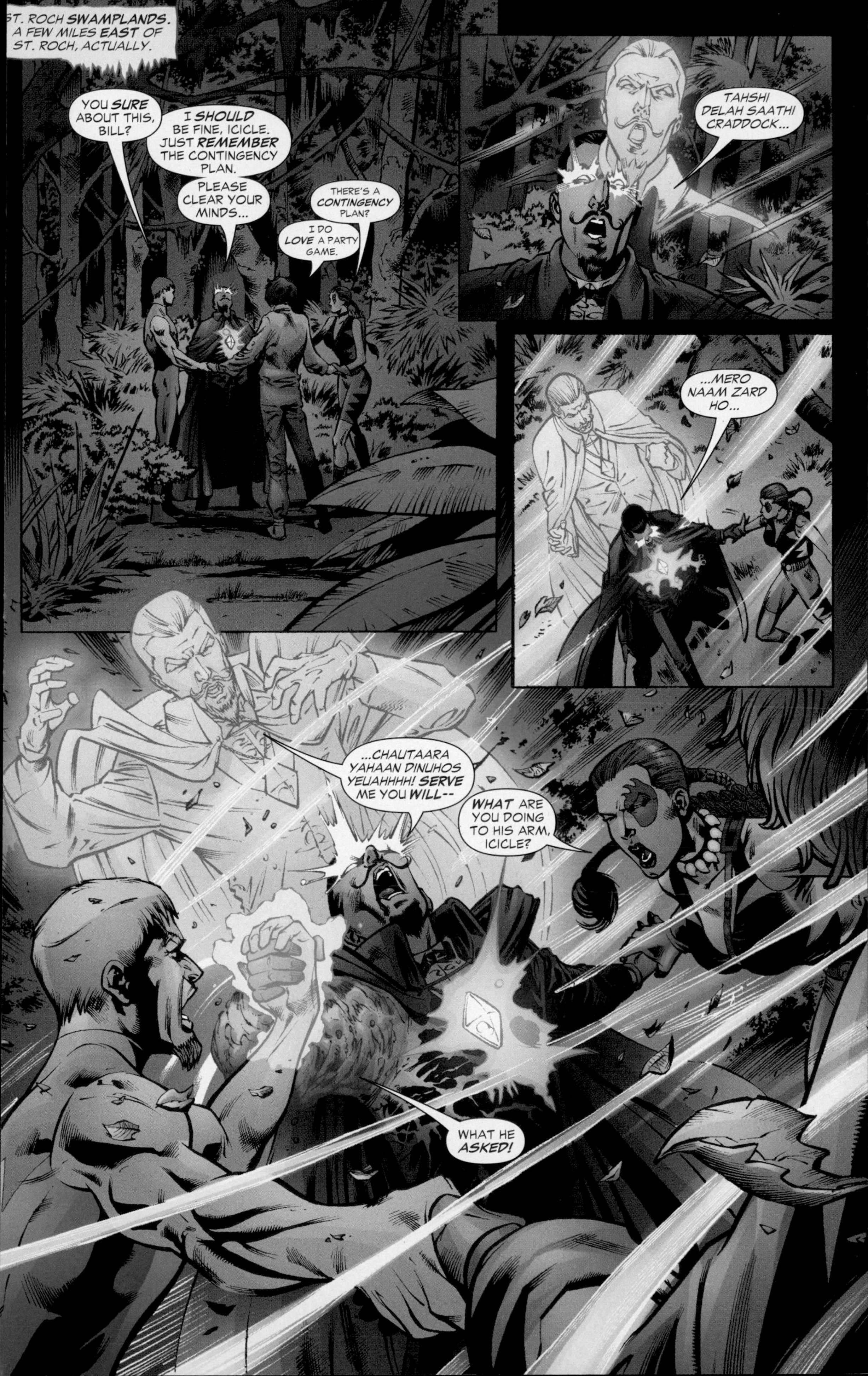
ST. ROCH SWAMPLANDS. A FEW MILES EAST OF ST. ROCH, ACTUALLY.
YOU SURE ABOUT THIS, BILL?
I SHOULD BE FINE, ICICLE. JUST REMEMBER THE CONTINGENCY PLAN.
PLEASE CLEAR YOUR MINDS...
THERE'S A CONTINGENCY PLAN?
I DO LOVE A PARTY GAME.
TAHSHI DELAH SAATHI CRADDOCK...
...MERO NAAM ZARD HO...
...CHAUTAARA YAHAAN DINUHOS YEUAHHHH! SERVE ME YOU WILL--
WHAT ARE YOU DOING TO HIS ARM, ICICLE?
WHAT HE ASKED!

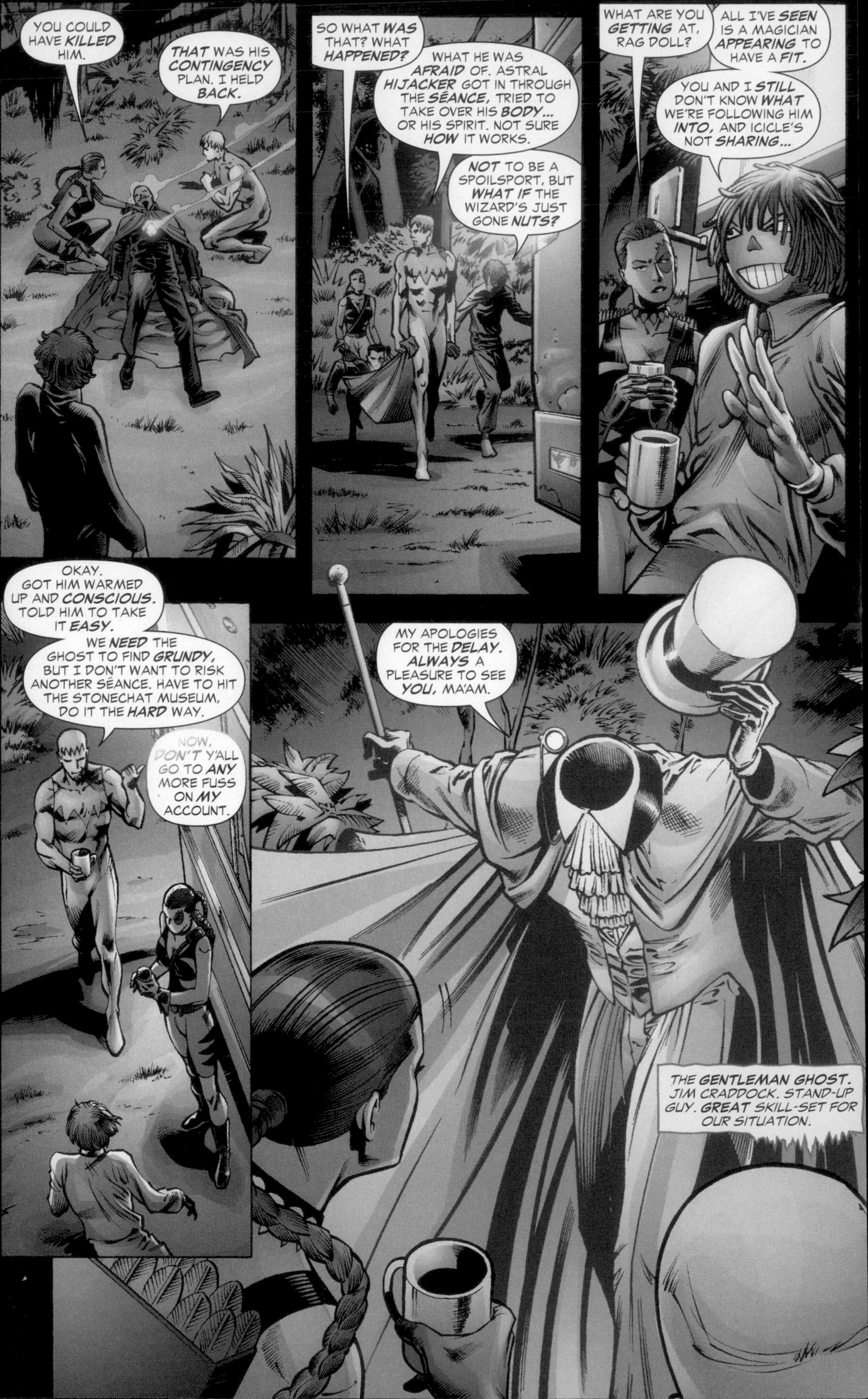
YOU COULD HAVE KILLED HIM.
THAT WAS HIS CONTINGENCY PLAN. I HELD BACK.
SO WHAT WAS THAT? WHAT HAPPENED?
WHAT HE WAS AFRAID OF. ASTRAL HIJACKER GOT IN THROUGH THE SÉANCE, TRIED TO TAKE OVER HIS BODY... OR HIS SPIRIT. NOT SURE HOW IT WORKS.
NOT TO BE A SPOILSPORT, BUT WHAT IF THE WIZARD'S JUST GONE NUTS?
WHAT ARE YOU GETTING AT, RAG DOLL?
ALL I'VE SEEN IS A MAGICIAN APPEARING TO HAVE A FIT.
YOU AND I STILL DON'T KNOW WHAT WE'RE FOLLOWING HIM INTO, AND ICICLE'S NOT SHARING...
OKAY. GOT HIM WARMED UP AND CONSCIOUS. TOLD HIM TO TAKE IT EASY.
WE NEED THE GHOST TO FIND GRUNDY, BUT I DON'T WANT TO RISK ANOTHER SÉANCE. HAVE TO HIT THE STONECHAT MUSEUM, DO IT THE HARD WAY.
NOW, DON'T Y'ALL GO TO ANY MORE FUSS ON MY ACCOUNT.
MY APOLOGIES FOR THE DELAY. ALWAYS A PLEASURE TO SEE YOU, MA'AM.
THE GENTLEMAN GHOST. JIM CRADDOCK. STAND-UP GUY. GREAT SKILL-SET FOR OUR SITUATION.

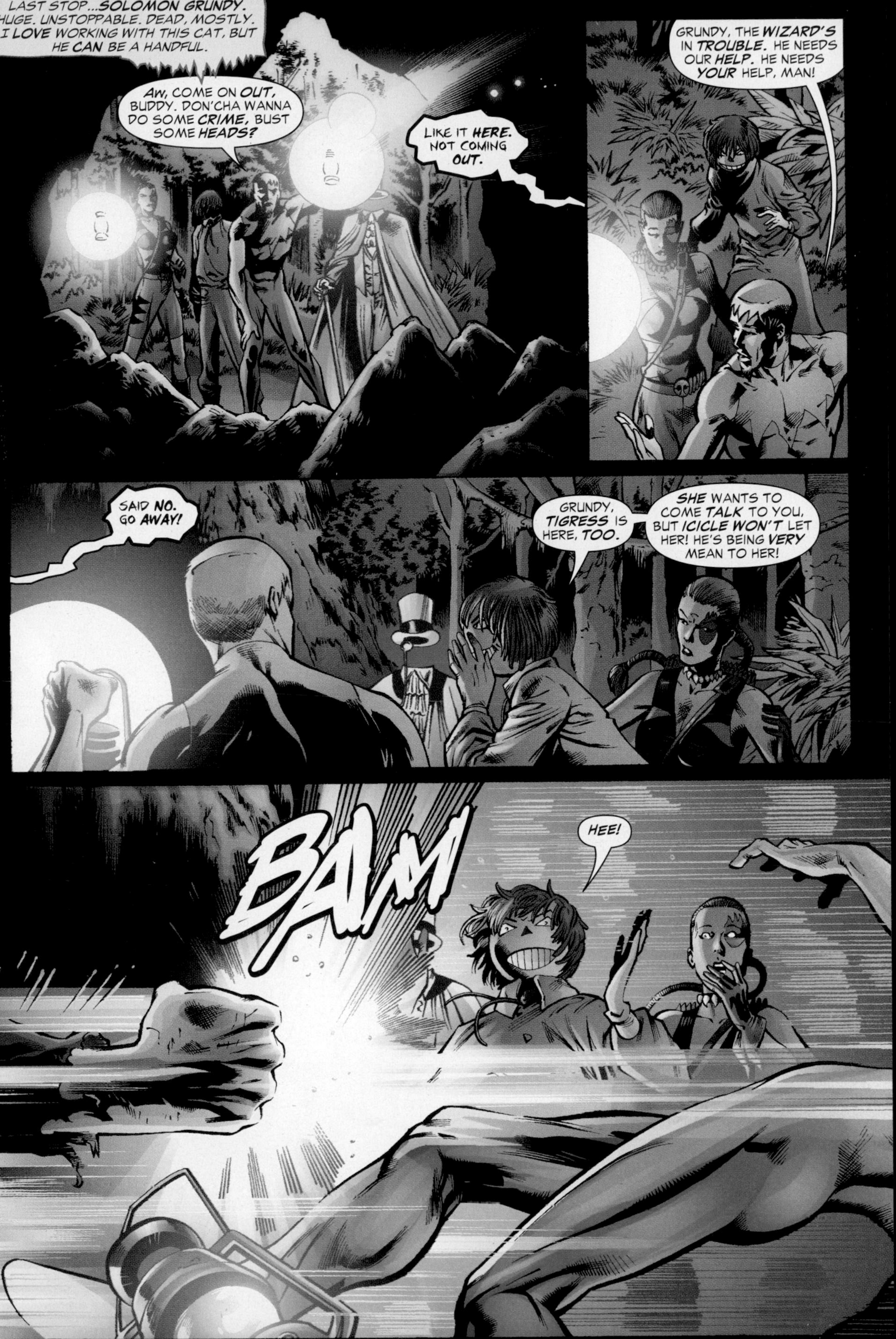
LAST STOP...SOLOMON GRUNDY. HUGE. UNSTOPPABLE. DEAD, MOSTLY. I LOVE WORKING WITH THIS CAT, BUT HE CAN BE A HANDFUL.
AW, COME ON OUT, BUDDY. DON'CHA WANNA DO SOME CRIME, BUST SOME HEADS?
LIKE IT HERE. NOT COMING OUT.
GRUNDY, THE WIZARD'S IN TROUBLE. HE NEEDS OUR HELP. HE NEEDS YOUR HELP, MAN!
SAID NO. GO AWAY!
GRUNDY, TIGRESS IS HERE, TOO.
SHE WANTS TO COME TALK TO YOU, BUT ICICLE WON'T LET HER! HE'S BEING VERY MEAN TO HER!
BAM
HEE!

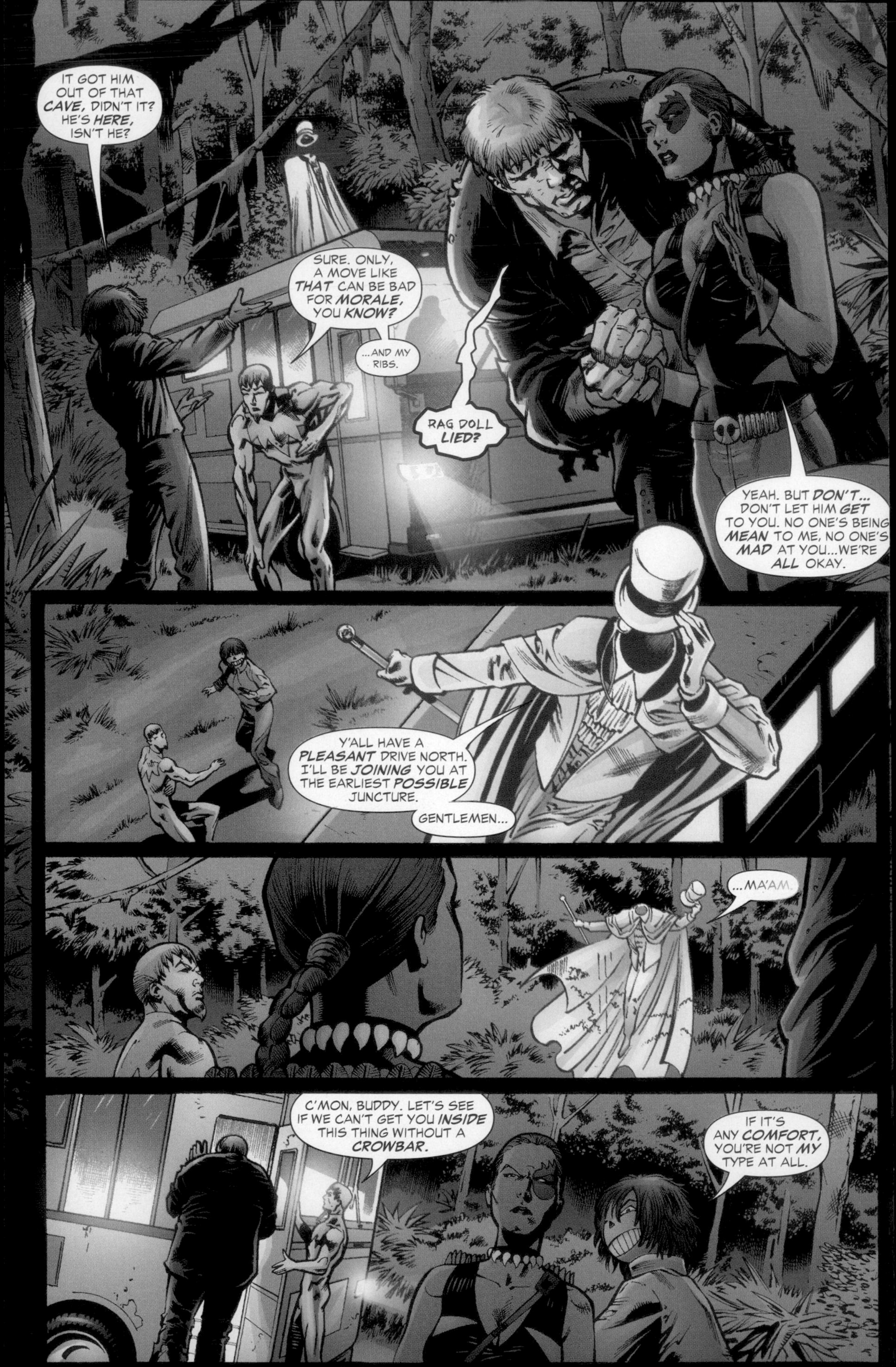

IT GOT HIM OUT OF THAT CAVE, DIDN'T IT? HE'S HERE, ISN'T HE?
SURE. ONLY, A MOVE LIKE THAT CAN BE BAD FOR MORALE, YOU KNOW?
...AND MY RIBS.
RAG DOLL LIED?
YEAH. BUT DON'T... DON'T LET HIM GET TO YOU. NO ONE'S BEING MEAN TO ME, NO ONE'S MAD AT YOU...WE'RE ALL OKAY.
Y'ALL HAVE A PLEASANT DRIVE NORTH. I'LL BE JOINING YOU AT THE EARLIEST POSSIBLE JUNCTURE.
GENTLEMEN...
...MA'AM.
C'MON, BUDDY. LET'S SEE IF WE CAN'T GET YOU INSIDE THIS THING WITHOUT A CROWBAR.
IF IT'S ANY COMFORT, YOU'RE NOT MY TYPE AT ALL.

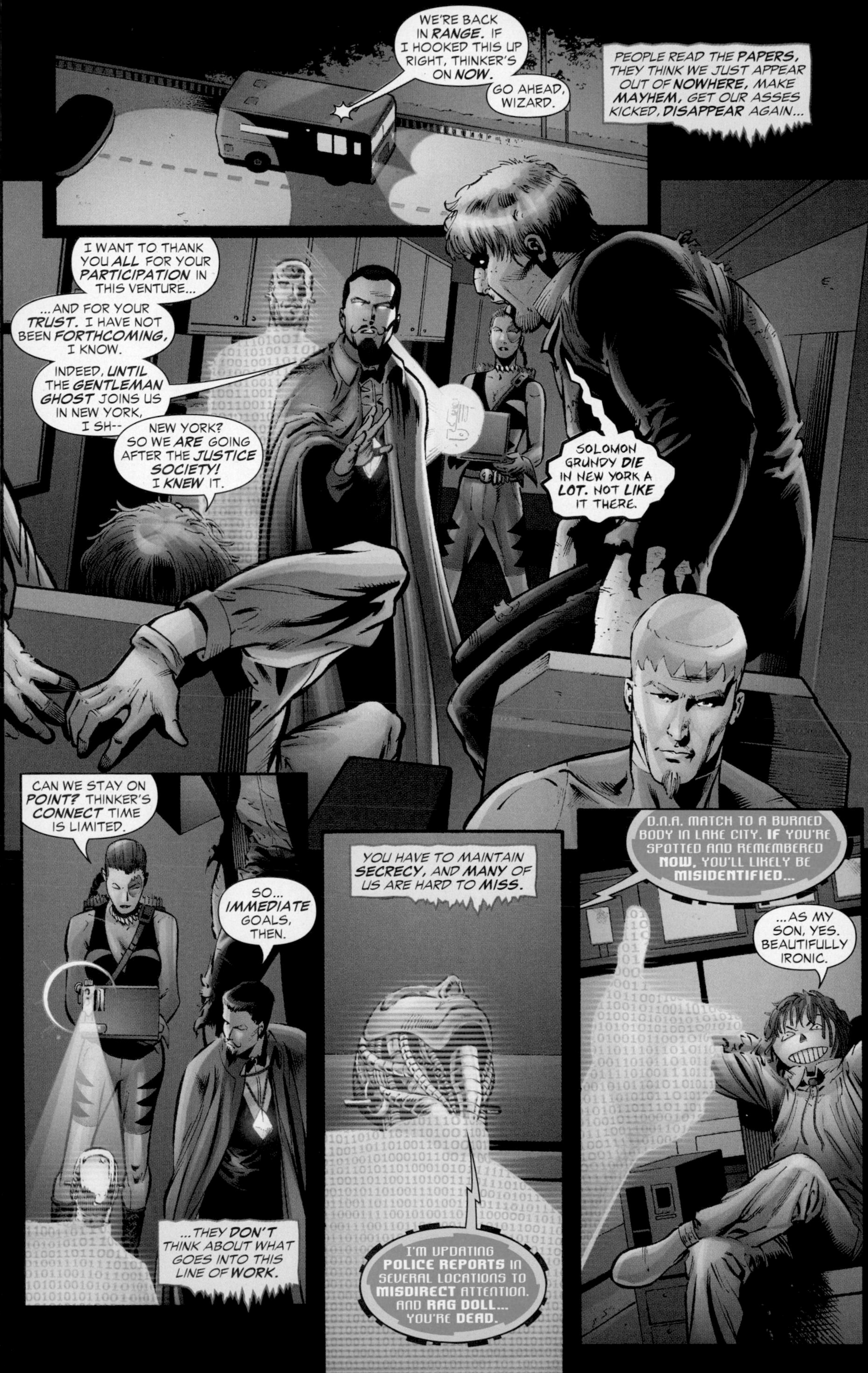

WE'RE BACK IN RANGE. IF I HOOKED THIS UP RIGHT, THINKER'S ON NOW.
GO AHEAD, WIZARD.
PEOPLE READ THE PAPERS, THEY THINK WE JUST APPEAR OUT OF NOWHERE, MAKE MAYHEM, GET OUR ASSES KICKED, DISAPPEAR AGAIN...
I WANT TO THANK YOU ALL FOR YOUR PARTICIPATION IN THIS VENTURE...
...AND FOR YOUR TRUST. I HAVE NOT BEEN FORTHCOMING, I KNOW.
INDEED, UNTIL THE GENTLEMAN GHOST JOINS US IN NEW YORK, I SH--
NEW YORK? SO WE ARE GOING AFTER THE JUSTICE SOCIETY! I KNEW IT.
SOLOMON GRUNDY DIE IN NEW YORK A LOT. NOT LIKE IT THERE.
CAN WE STAY ON POINT? THINKER'S CONNECT TIME IS LIMITED.
SO... IMMEDIATE GOALS, THEN.
...THEY DON'T THINK ABOUT WHAT GOES INTO THIS LINE OF WORK.
YOU HAVE TO MAINTAIN SECRECY, AND MANY OF US ARE HARD TO MISS.
I'M UPDATING POLICE REPORTS IN SEVERAL LOCATIONS TO MISDIRECT ATTENTION. AND RAG DOLL... YOU'RE DEAD.
D.N.A. MATCH TO A BURNED BODY IN LAKE CITY. IF YOU'RE SPOTTED AND REMEMBERED NOW, YOU'LL LIKELY BE MISIDENTIFIED...
...AS MY SON, YES. BEAUTIFULLY IRONIC.

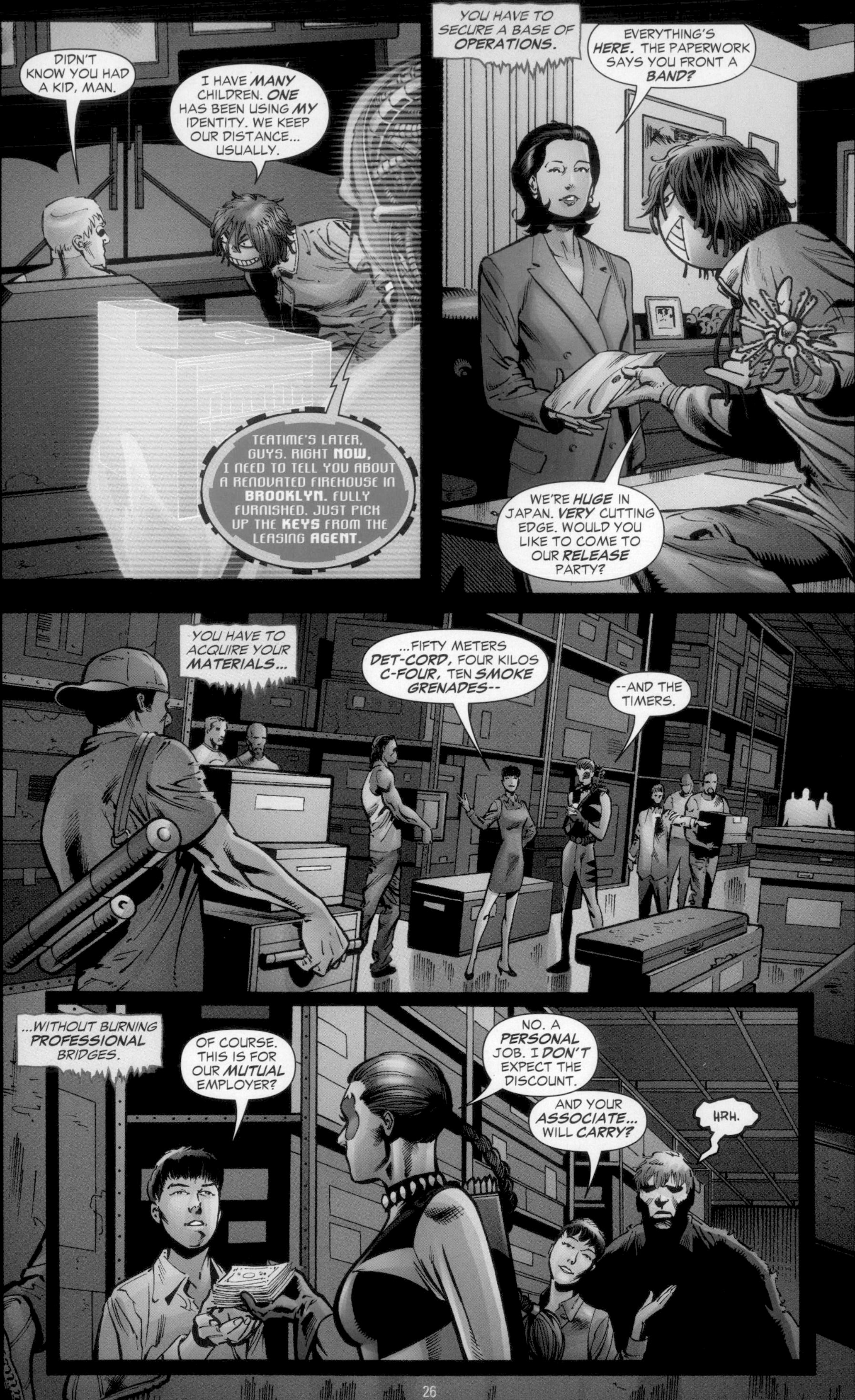

DIDN'T KNOW YOU HAD A KID, MAN.
I HAVE MANY CHILDREN. ONE HAS BEEN USING MY IDENTITY. WE KEEP OUR DISTANCE... USUALLY.
TEATIME'S LATER, GUYS. RIGHT NOW, I NEED TO TELL YOU ABOUT A RENOVATED FIREHOUSE IN BROOKLYN. FULLY FURNISHED. JUST PICK UP THE KEYS FROM THE LEASING AGENT.
YOU HAVE TO SECURE A BASE OF OPERATIONS.
EVERYTHING'S HERE. THE PAPERWORK SAYS YOU FRONT A BAND?
WE'RE HUGE IN JAPAN. VERY CUTTING EDGE. WOULD YOU LIKE TO COME TO OUR RELEASE PARTY?
YOU HAVE TO ACQUIRE YOUR MATERIALS...
...FIFTY METERS DET-CORD, FOUR KILOS C-FOUR, TEN SMOKE GRENADES--
--AND THE TIMERS.
...WITHOUT BURNING PROFESSIONAL BRIDGES.
OF COURSE. THIS IS FOR OUR MUTUAL EMPLOYER?
NO. A PERSONAL JOB. I DON'T EXPECT THE DISCOUNT.
AND YOUR ASSOCIATE... WILL CARRY?
HRH.

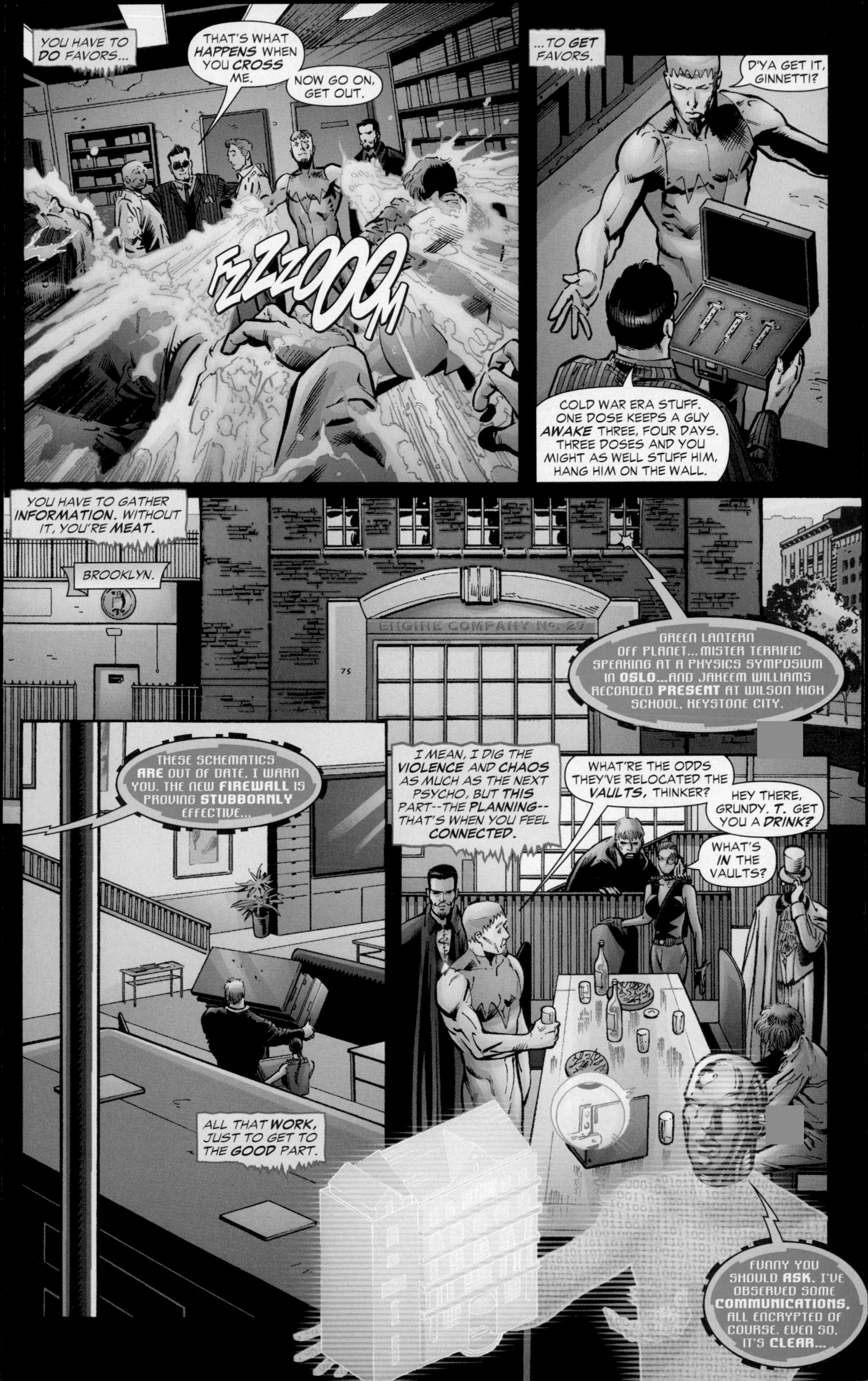
YOU HAVE TO DO FAVORS...
THAT'S WHAT HAPPENS WHEN YOU CROSS ME.
NOW GO ON, GET OUT.
FZZZOOOM
...TO GET FAVORS.
D'YA GET IT, GINNETTI?
COLD WAR ERA STUFF. ONE DOSE KEEPS A GUY AWAKE THREE, FOUR DAYS. THREE DOSES AND YOU MIGHT AS WELL STUFF HIM, HANG HIM ON THE WALL.
YOU HAVE TO GATHER INFORMATION. WITHOUT IT, YOU'RE MEAT.
BROOKLYN.
ENGINE COMPANY No. 27
75
GREEN LANTERN OFF PLANET...MISTER TERRIFIC SPEAKING AT A PHYSICS SYMPOSIUM IN OSLO...AND JAKEEM WILLIAMS RECORDED PRESENT AT WILSON HIGH SCHOOL, KEYSTONE CITY.
THESE SCHEMATICS ARE OUT OF DATE, I WARN YOU. THE NEW FIREWALL IS PROVING STUBBORNLY EFFECTIVE...
ALL THAT WORK, JUST TO GET TO THE GOOD PART.
I MEAN, I DIG THE VIOLENCE AND CHAOS AS MUCH AS THE NEXT PSYCHO, BUT THIS PART--THE PLANNING--THAT'S WHEN YOU FEEL CONNECTED.
WHAT'RE THE ODDS THEY'VE RELOCATED THE VAULTS, THINKER?
HEY THERE, GRUNDY. T. GET YOU A DRINK?
WHAT'S IN THE VAULTS?
FUNNY YOU SHOULD ASK. I'VE OBSERVED SOME COMMUNICATIONS, ALL ENCRYPTED OF COURSE. EVEN SO, IT'S CLEAR...

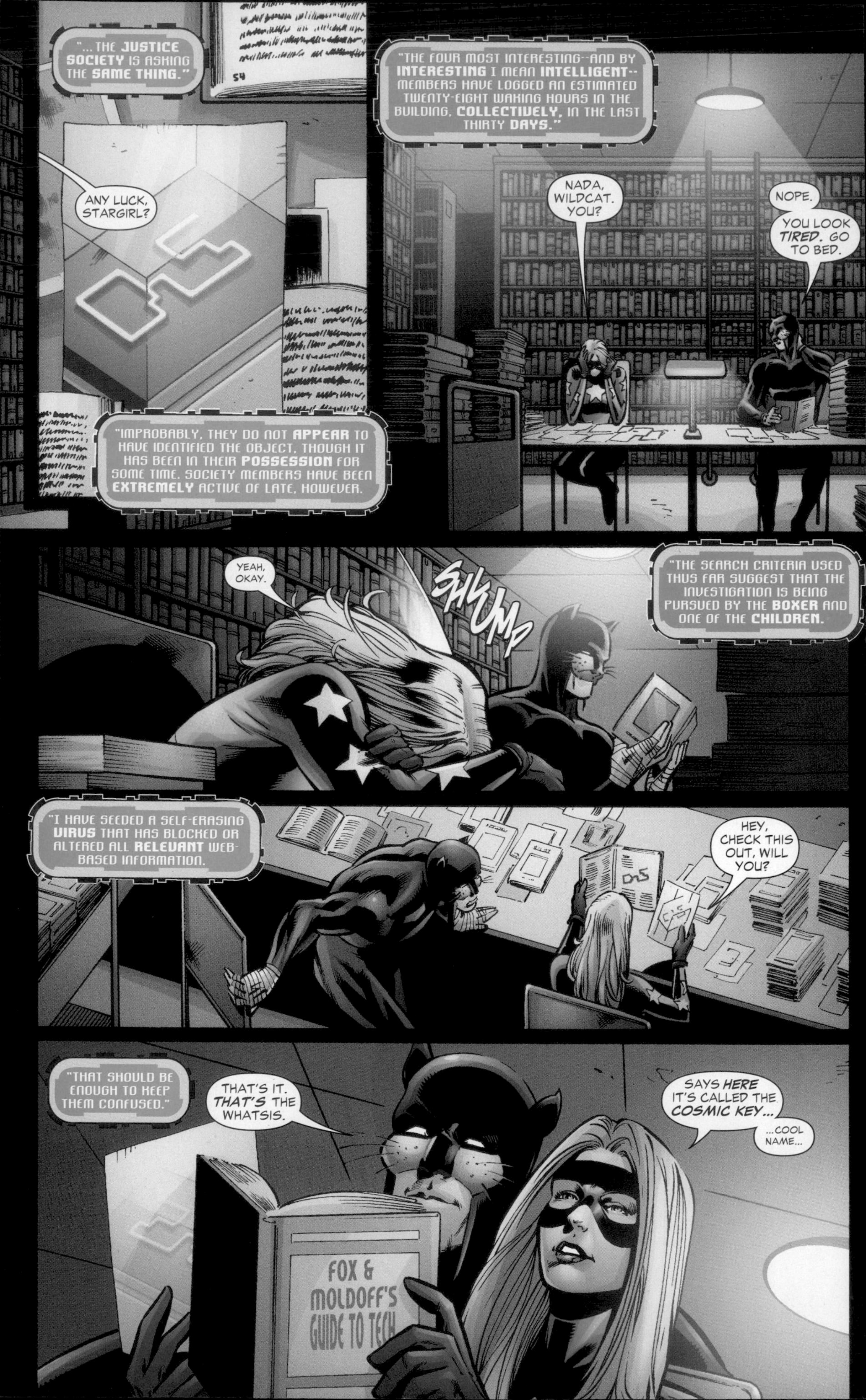
"... THE JUSTICE SOCIETY IS ASKING THE SAME THING."
ANY LUCK, STARGIRL?
"IMPROBABLY, THEY DO NOT APPEAR TO HAVE IDENTIFIED THE OBJECT, THOUGH IT HAS BEEN IN THEIR POSSESSION FOR SOME TIME. SOCIETY MEMBERS HAVE BEEN EXTREMELY ACTIVE OF LATE, HOWEVER.
"THE FOUR MOST INTERESTING--AND BY INTERESTING I MEAN INTELLIGENT--MEMBERS HAVE LOGGED AN ESTIMATED TWENTY-EIGHT WAKING HOURS IN THE BUILDING, COLLECTIVELY, IN THE LAST THIRTY DAYS."
NADA, WILDCAT. YOU?
NOPE.
YOU LOOK TIRED. GO TO BED.
YEAH, OKAY.
SHLUMP
"THE SEARCH CRITERIA USED THUS FAR SUGGEST THAT THE INVESTIGATION IS BEING PURSUED BY THE BOXER AND ONE OF THE CHILDREN.
"I HAVE SEEDED A SELF-ERASING VIRUS THAT HAS BLOCKED OR ALTERED ALL RELEVANT WEB-BASED INFORMATION.
HEY, CHECK THIS OUT, WILL YOU?
"THAT SHOULD BE ENOUGH TO KEEP THEM CONFUSED."
THAT'S IT. THAT'S THE WHATSIS.
SAYS HERE IT'S CALLED THE COSMIC KEY...
...COOL NAME...
FOX & MOLDOFF'S GUIDE TO TECH

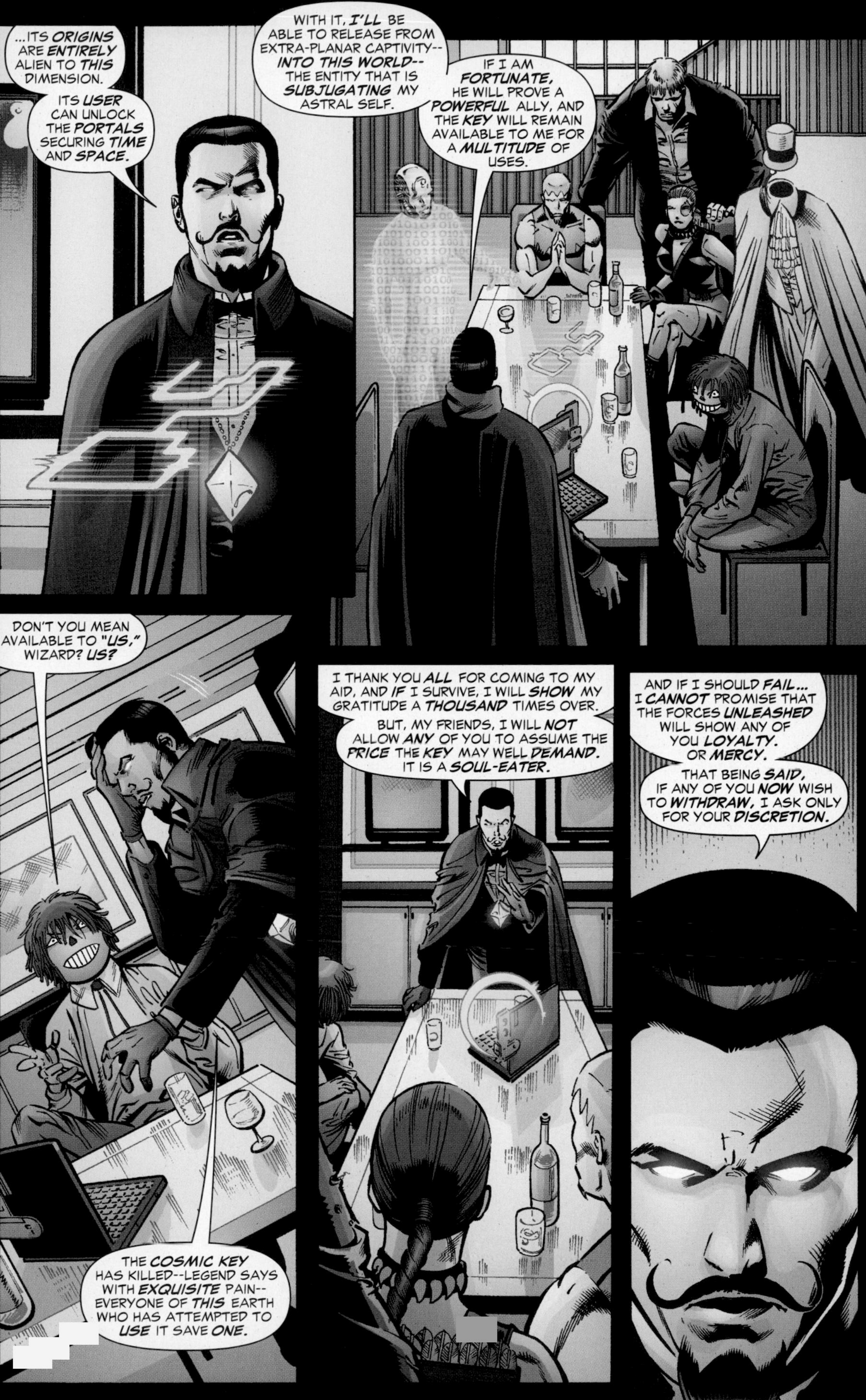
...ITS ORIGINS ARE ENTIRELY ALIEN TO THIS DIMENSION.
ITS USER CAN UNLOCK THE PORTALS SECURING TIME AND SPACE.
WITH IT, I'LL BE ABLE TO RELEASE FROM EXTRA-PLANAR CAPTIVITY-- INTO THIS WORLD-- THE ENTITY THAT IS SUBJUGATING MY ASTRAL SELF.
IF I AM FORTUNATE, HE WILL PROVE A POWERFUL ALLY, AND THE KEY WILL REMAIN AVAILABLE TO ME FOR A MULTITUDE OF USES.
DON'T YOU MEAN AVAILABLE TO "US," WIZARD? US?
THE COSMIC KEY HAS KILLED--LEGEND SAYS WITH EXQUISITE PAIN-- EVERYONE OF THIS EARTH WHO HAS ATTEMPTED TO USE IT SAVE ONE.
I THANK YOU ALL FOR COMING TO MY AID, AND IF I SURVIVE, I WILL SHOW MY GRATITUDE A THOUSAND TIMES OVER.
BUT, MY FRIENDS, I WILL NOT ALLOW ANY OF YOU TO ASSUME THE PRICE THE KEY MAY WELL DEMAND. IT IS A SOUL-EATER.
AND IF I SHOULD FAIL... I CANNOT PROMISE THAT THE FORCES UNLEASHED WILL SHOW ANY OF YOU LOYALTY. OR MERCY.
THAT BEING SAID, IF ANY OF YOU NOW WISH TO WITHDRAW, I ASK ONLY FOR YOUR DISCRETION.

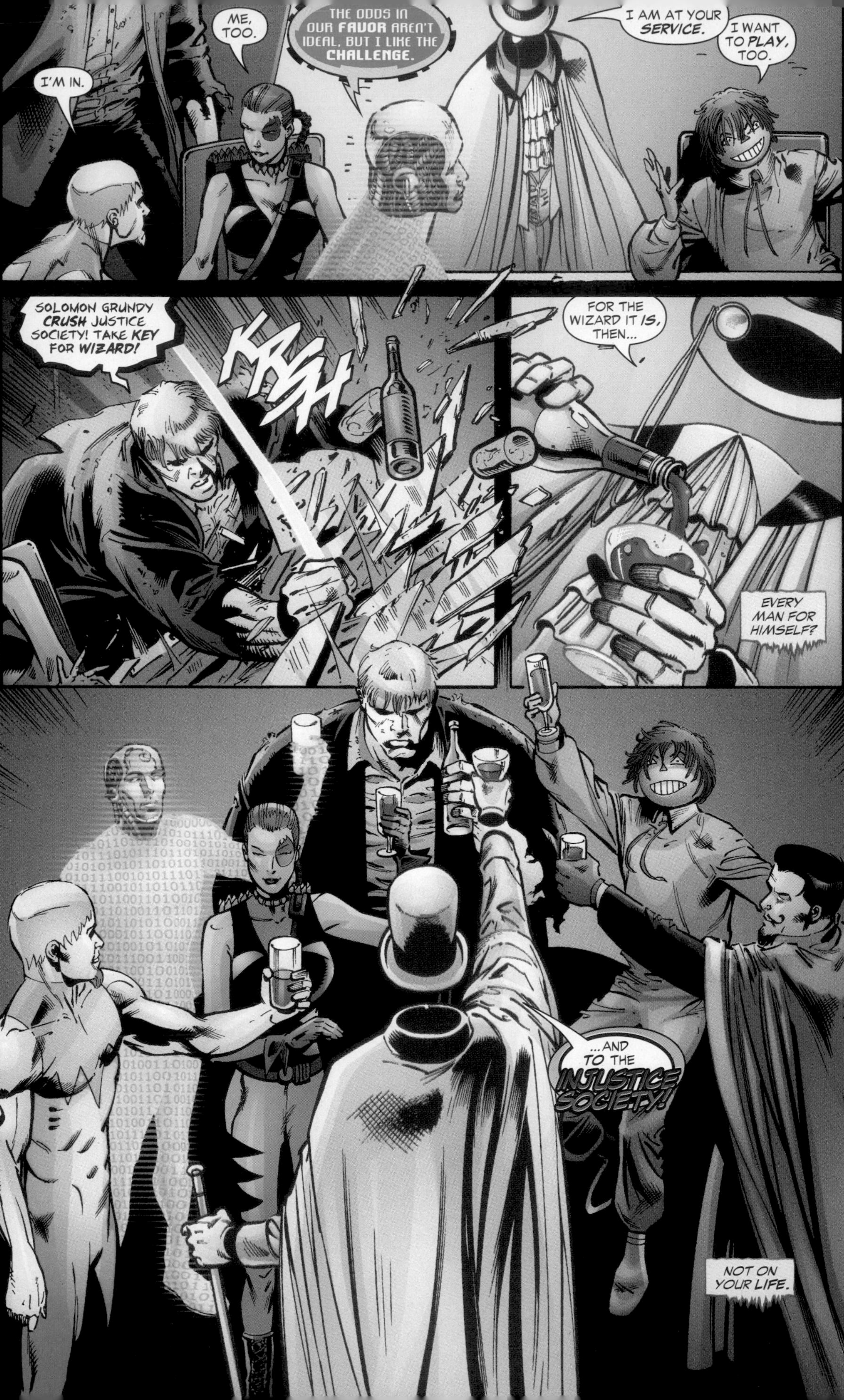
I'M IN.
ME, TOO.
THE ODDS IN OUR FAVOR AREN'T IDEAL, BUT I LIKE THE CHALLENGE.
I AM AT YOUR SERVICE.
I WANT TO PLAY, TOO.
SOLOMON GRUNDY CRUSH JUSTICE SOCIETY! TAKE KEY FOR WIZARD!
KRASH
FOR THE WIZARD IT IS, THEN...
EVERY MAN FOR HIMSELF?
...AND TO THE INJUSTICE SOCIETY!
NOT ON YOUR LIFE.

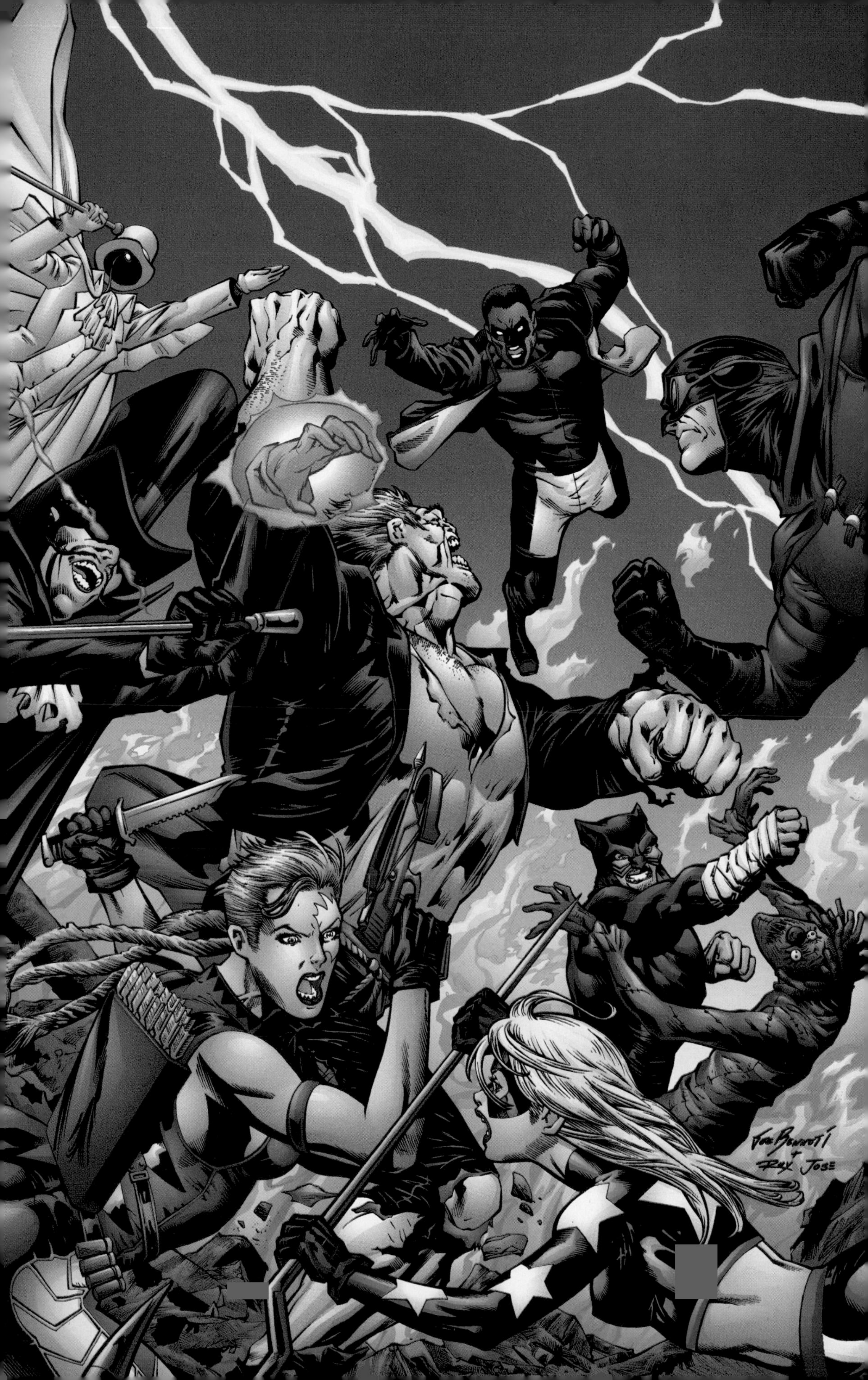

SOME CATS LIKE WORKING ALONE... IDIOTS AND LUNATICS, YOU ASK ME.

DOESN'T LOOK LOAD-BEARING TO ME.

I KNOW, FROM THE OUTSIDE IT LOOKS LIKE WE'RE ALL A BUNCH OF BACKSTABBING PSYCHOS, BUT FROM THE INSIDE...

WE'RE UNDERGROUND. EVERYTHING'S HOLDING SOMETHING UP, RAG DOLL.

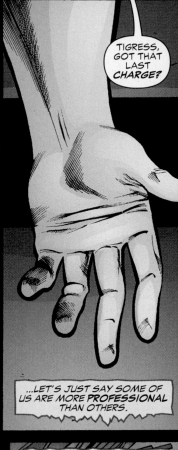

TIGRESS, GOT THAT LAST CHARGE?

...LET'S JUST SAY SOME OF US ARE MORE PROFESSIONAL THAN OTHERS.

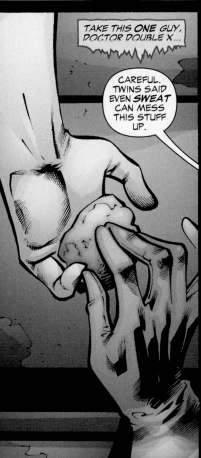

TAKE THIS ONE GUY, DOCTOR DOUBLE X...

CAREFUL. TWINS SAID EVEN SWEAT CAN MESS THIS STUFF UP.

...IN AND OUT OF THE SLAB LIKE IT'S THE JOHN. EVER WONDER WHY?

MESS IT UP, NO BOOM...?

I'LL TELL YOU WHY, AND IT'S NOT BECAUSE BATMAN IS SUCH A FREAKIN' GENIUS, EITHER. DUDE CHEAPS HIMSELF ON MANPOWER AND MATERIAL EVERY TIME.

...OR MESS IT UP, BOOM?

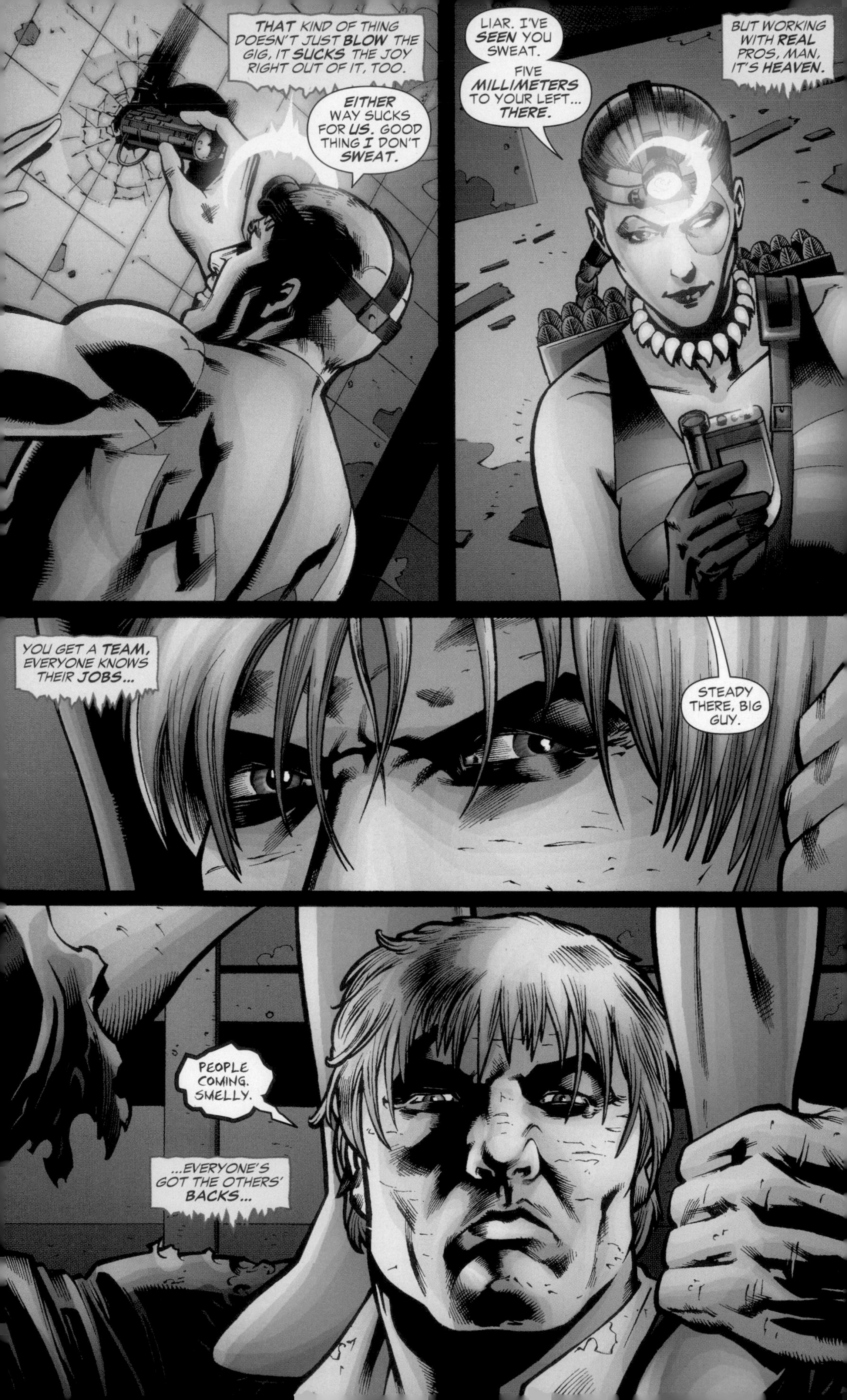
THAT KIND OF THING DOESN'T JUST BLOW THE GIG, IT SUCKS THE JOY RIGHT OUT OF IT, TOO.
EITHER WAY SUCKS FOR US. GOOD THING I DON'T SWEAT.
LIAR. I'VE SEEN YOU SWEAT.
FIVE MILLIMETERS TO YOUR LEFT... THERE.
BUT WORKING WITH REAL PROS, MAN, IT'S HEAVEN.
YOU GET A TEAM, EVERYONE KNOWS THEIR JOBS...
STEADY THERE, BIG GUY.
PEOPLE COMING. SMELLY.
...EVERYONE'S GOT THE OTHERS' BACKS...

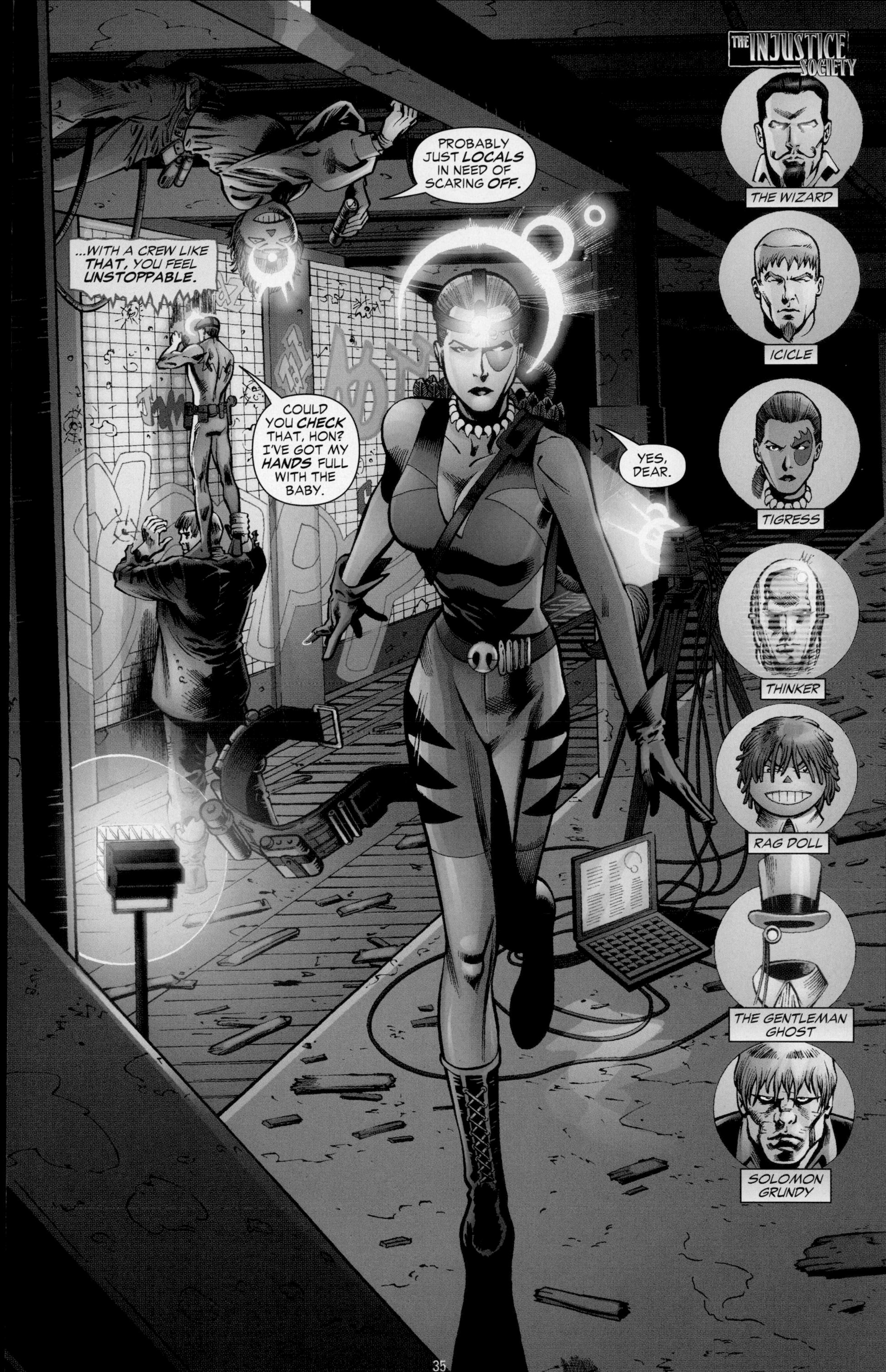
THE INJUSTICE SOCIETY
PROBABLY JUST LOCALS IN NEED OF SCARING OFF.
...WITH A CREW LIKE THAT, YOU FEEL UNSTOPPABLE.
COULD YOU CHECK THAT, HON? I'VE GOT MY HANDS FULL WITH THE BABY.
YES, DEAR.
THE WIZARD
ICICLE
TIGRESS
THINKER
RAG DOLL
THE GENTLEMAN GHOST
SOLOMON GRUNDY

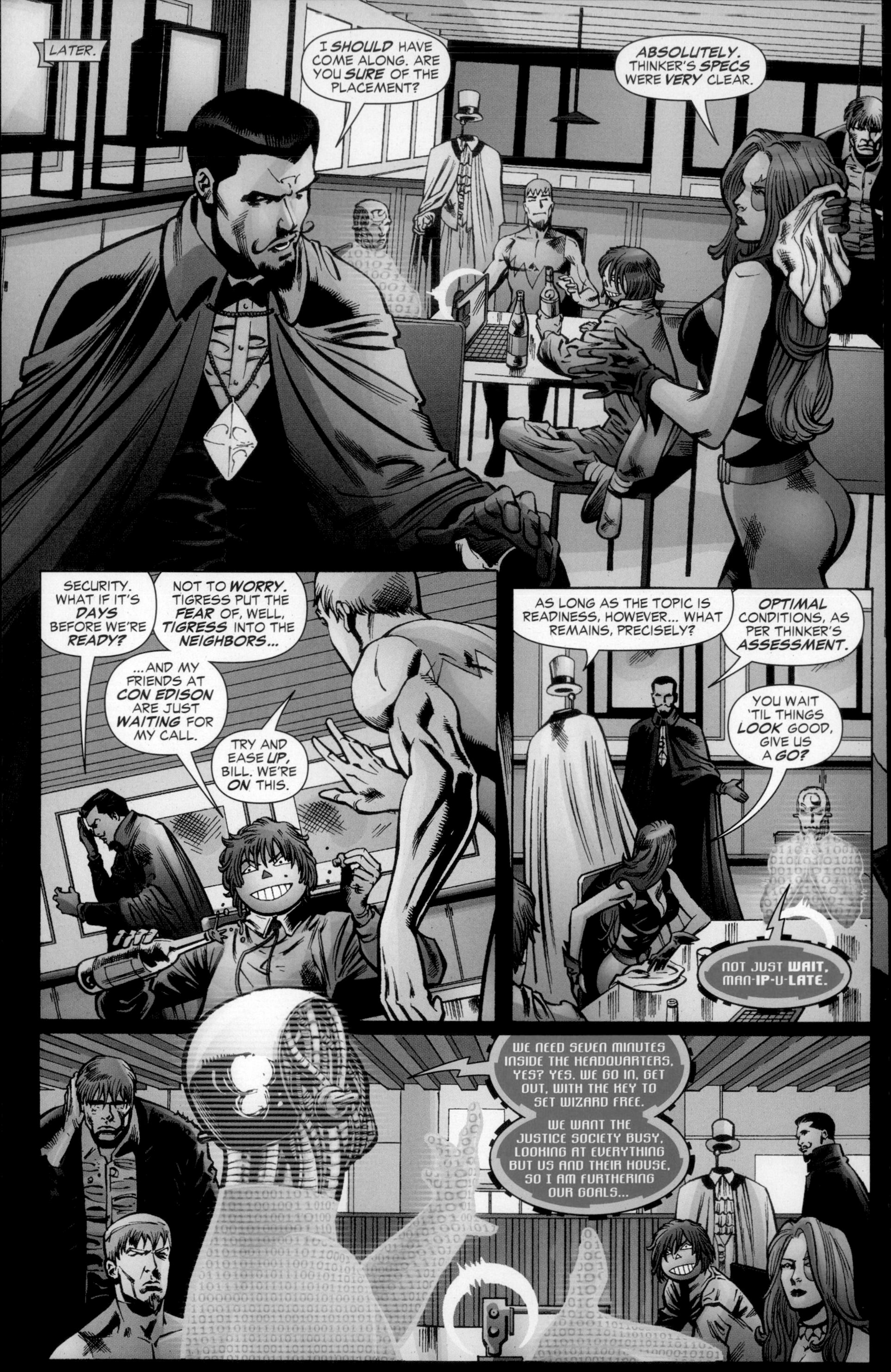
LATER.
I SHOULD HAVE COME ALONG. ARE YOU SURE OF THE PLACEMENT?
ABSOLUTELY. THINKER'S SPECS WERE VERY CLEAR.
SECURITY. WHAT IF IT'S DAYS BEFORE WE'RE READY?
NOT TO WORRY. TIGRESS PUT THE FEAR OF, WELL, TIGRESS INTO THE NEIGHBORS...
...AND MY FRIENDS AT CON EDISON ARE JUST WAITING FOR MY CALL.
TRY AND EASE UP, BILL. WE'RE ON THIS.
AS LONG AS THE TOPIC IS READINESS, HOWEVER... WHAT REMAINS, PRECISELY?
OPTIMAL CONDITIONS, AS PER THINKER'S ASSESSMENT.
YOU WAIT 'TIL THINGS LOOK GOOD, GIVE US A GO?
NOT JUST WAIT, MAN-IP-U-LATE.
WE NEED SEVEN MINUTES INSIDE THE HEADQUARTERS, YES? YES. WE GO IN, GET OUT, WITH THE KEY TO SET WIZARD FREE.
WE WANT THE JUSTICE SOCIETY BUSY, LOOKING AT EVERYTHING BUT US AND THEIR HOUSE, SO I AM FURTHERING OUR GOALS...

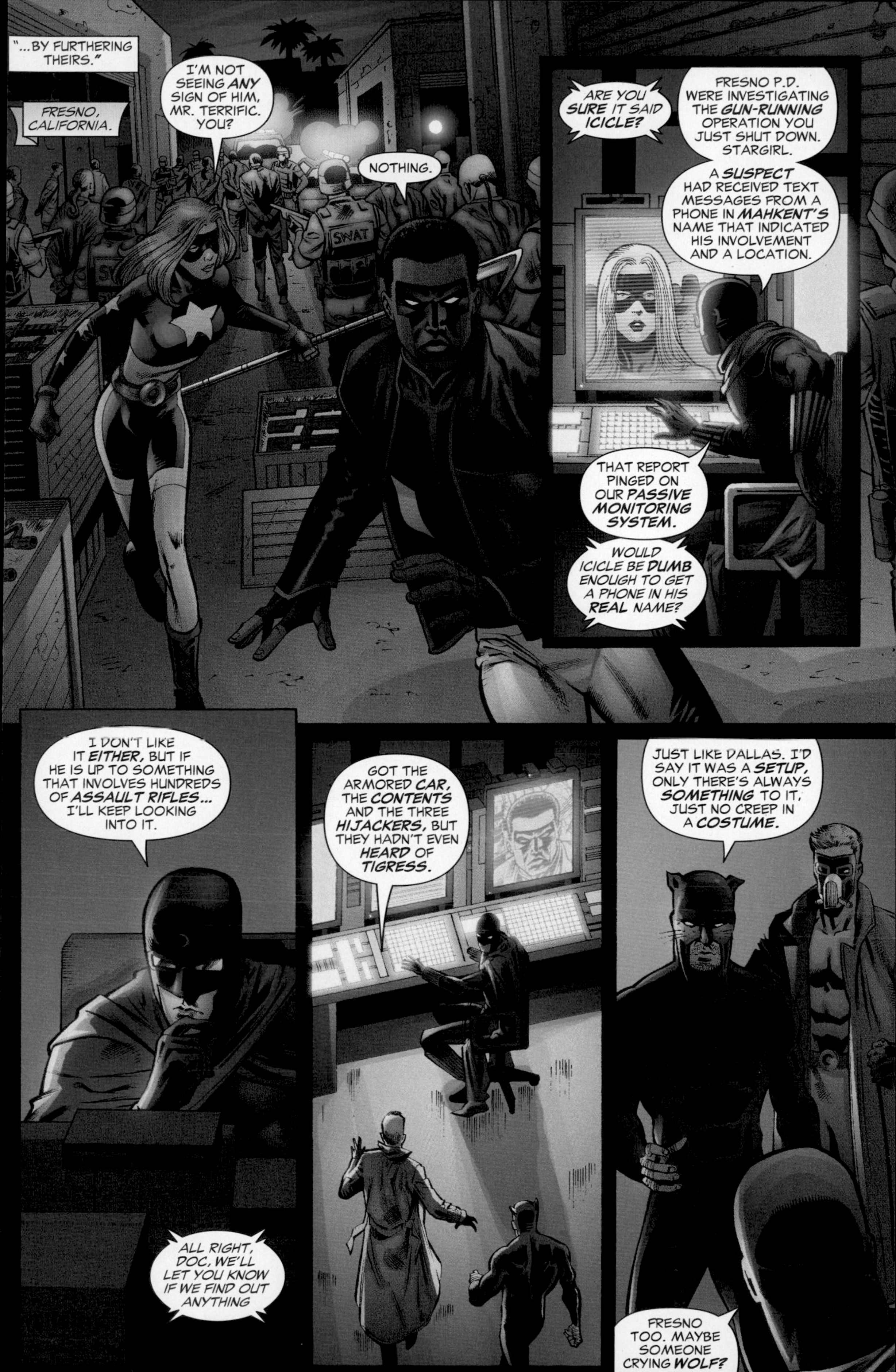
"...BY FURTHERING THEIRS."
FRESNO, CALIFORNIA.
I'M NOT SEEING ANY SIGN OF HIM, MR. TERRIFIC. YOU?
NOTHING.
ARE YOU SURE IT SAID ICICLE?
FRESNO P.D. WERE INVESTIGATING THE GUN-RUNNING OPERATION YOU JUST SHUT DOWN. STARGIRL.
A SUSPECT HAD RECEIVED TEXT MESSAGES FROM A PHONE IN MAHKENT'S NAME THAT INDICATED HIS INVOLVEMENT AND A LOCATION.
THAT REPORT PINGED ON OUR PASSIVE MONITORING SYSTEM.
WOULD ICICLE BE DUMB ENOUGH TO GET A PHONE IN HIS REAL NAME?
I DON'T LIKE IT EITHER, BUT IF HE IS UP TO SOMETHING THAT INVOLVES HUNDREDS OF ASSAULT RIFLES... I'LL KEEP LOOKING INTO IT.
ALL RIGHT, DOC, WE'LL LET YOU KNOW IF WE FIND OUT ANYTHING
GOT THE ARMORED CAR, THE CONTENTS AND THE THREE HIJACKERS, BUT THEY HADN'T EVEN HEARD OF TIGRESS.
JUST LIKE DALLAS. I'D SAY IT WAS A SETUP, ONLY THERE'S ALWAYS SOMETHING TO IT, JUST NO CREEP IN A COSTUME.
FRESNO TOO. MAYBE SOMEONE CRYING WOLF?

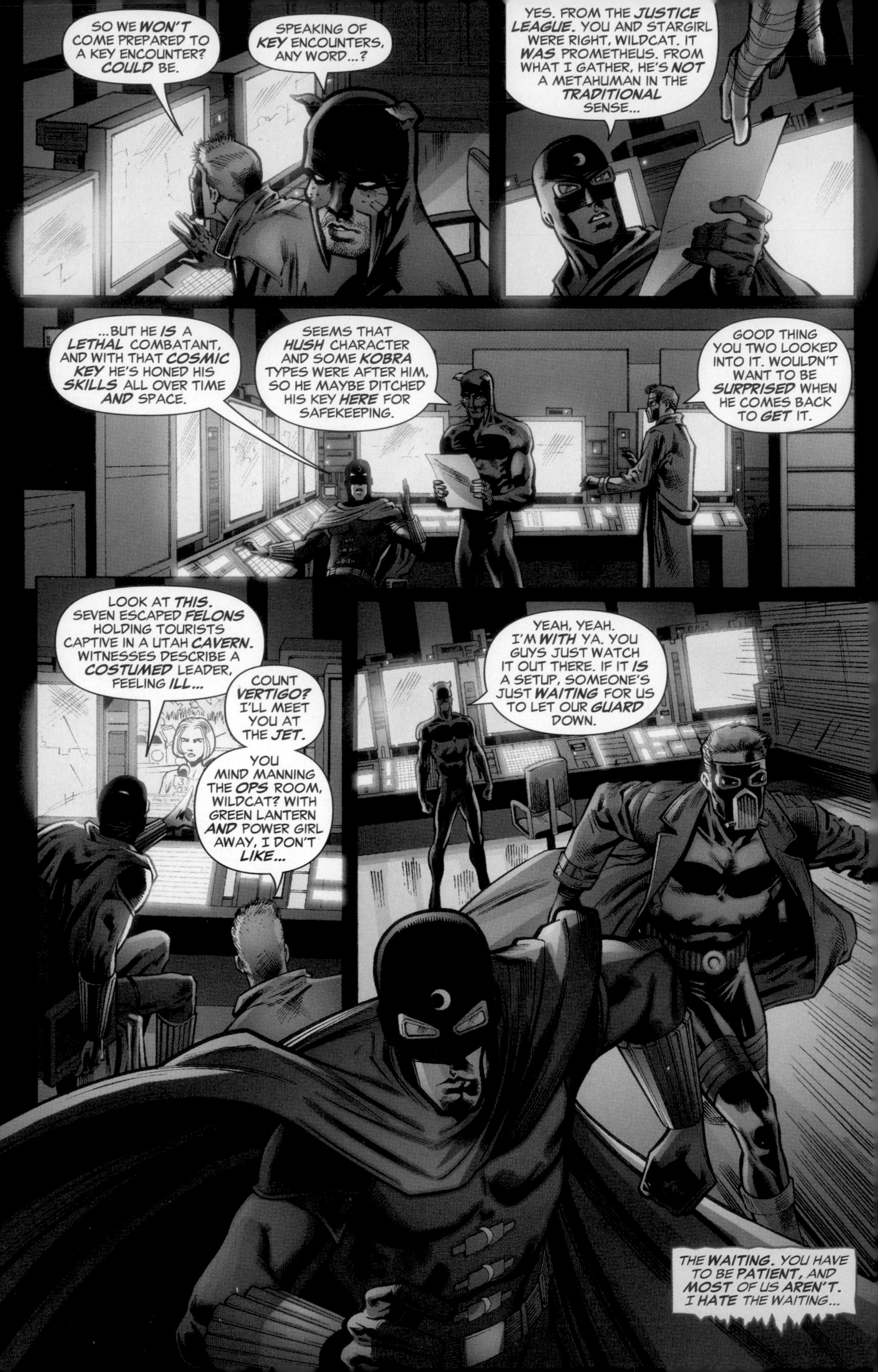
SO WE WON'T COME PREPARED TO A KEY ENCOUNTER? COULD BE.
SPEAKING OF KEY ENCOUNTERS, ANY WORD...?
YES. FROM THE JUSTICE LEAGUE. YOU AND STARGIRL WERE RIGHT, WILDCAT. IT WAS PROMETHEUS. FROM WHAT I GATHER, HE'S NOT A METAHUMAN IN THE TRADITIONAL SENSE...
...BUT HE IS A LETHAL COMBATANT, AND WITH THAT COSMIC KEY HE'S HONED HIS SKILLS ALL OVER TIME AND SPACE.
SEEMS THAT HUSH CHARACTER AND SOME KOBRA TYPES WERE AFTER HIM, SO HE MAYBE DITCHED HIS KEY HERE FOR SAFEKEEPING.
GOOD THING YOU TWO LOOKED INTO IT. WOULDN'T WANT TO BE SURPRISED WHEN HE COMES BACK TO GET IT.
LOOK AT THIS. SEVEN ESCAPED FELONS HOLDING TOURISTS CAPTIVE IN A UTAH CAVERN. WITNESSES DESCRIBE A COSTUMED LEADER, FEELING ILL...
COUNT VERTIGO? I'LL MEET YOU AT THE JET.
YOU MIND MANNING THE OPS ROOM, WILDCAT? WITH GREEN LANTERN AND POWER GIRL AWAY, I DON'T LIKE...
YEAH, YEAH. I'M WITH YA. YOU GUYS JUST WATCH IT OUT THERE. IF IT IS A SETUP, SOMEONE'S JUST WAITING FOR US TO LET OUR GUARD DOWN.
THE WAITING. YOU HAVE TO BE PATIENT, AND MOST OF US AREN'T. I HATE THE WAITING...

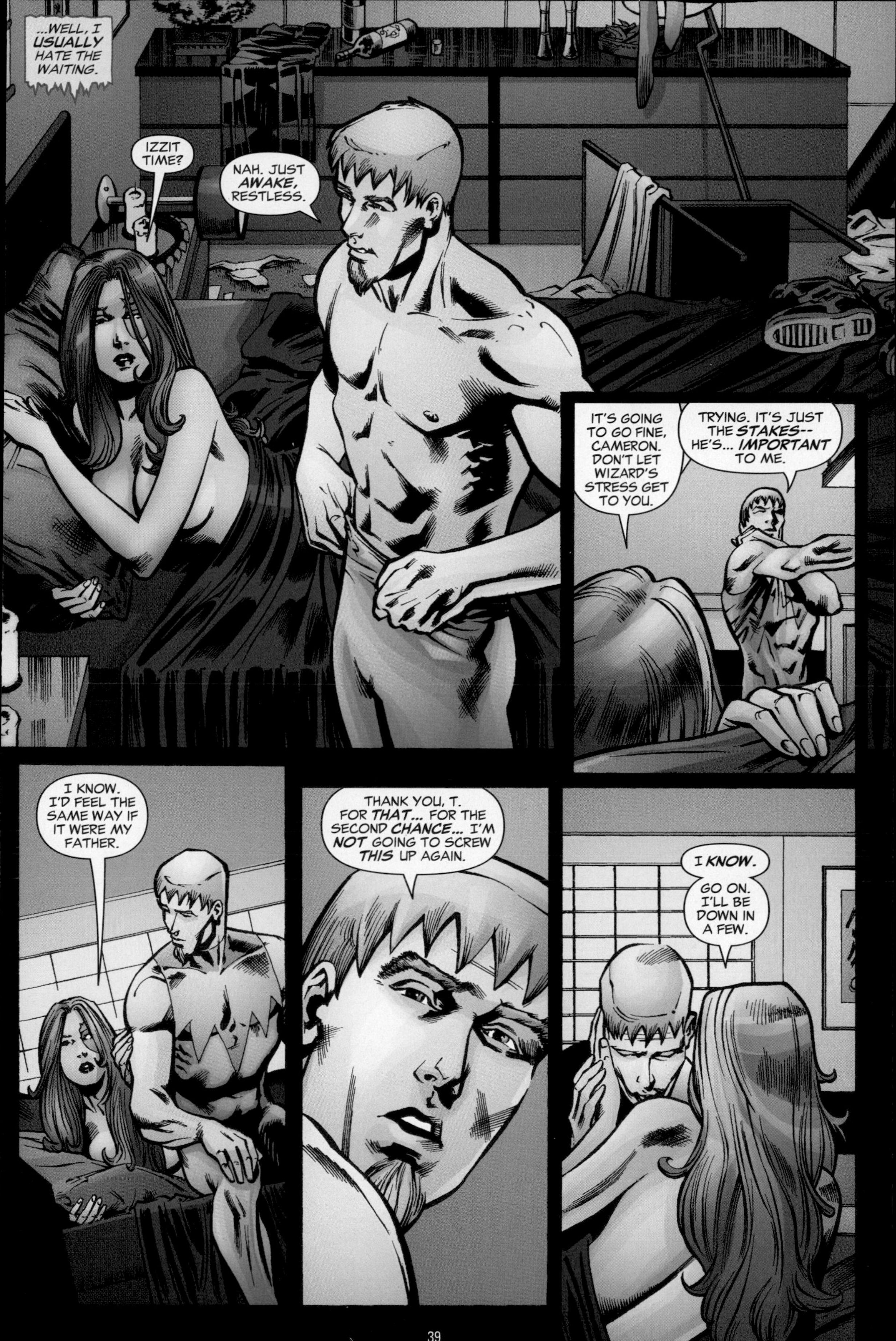
...WELL, I USUALLY HATE THE WAITING.
IZZIT TIME?
NAH. JUST AWAKE, RESTLESS.
IT'S GOING TO GO FINE, CAMERON. DON'T LET WIZARD'S STRESS GET TO YOU.
TRYING. IT'S JUST THE STAKES-- HE'S... IMPORTANT TO ME.
I KNOW. I'D FEEL THE SAME WAY IF IT WERE MY FATHER.
THANK YOU, T. FOR THAT... FOR THE SECOND CHANCE... I'M NOT GOING TO SCREW THIS UP AGAIN.
I KNOW.
GO ON. I'LL BE DOWN IN A FEW.

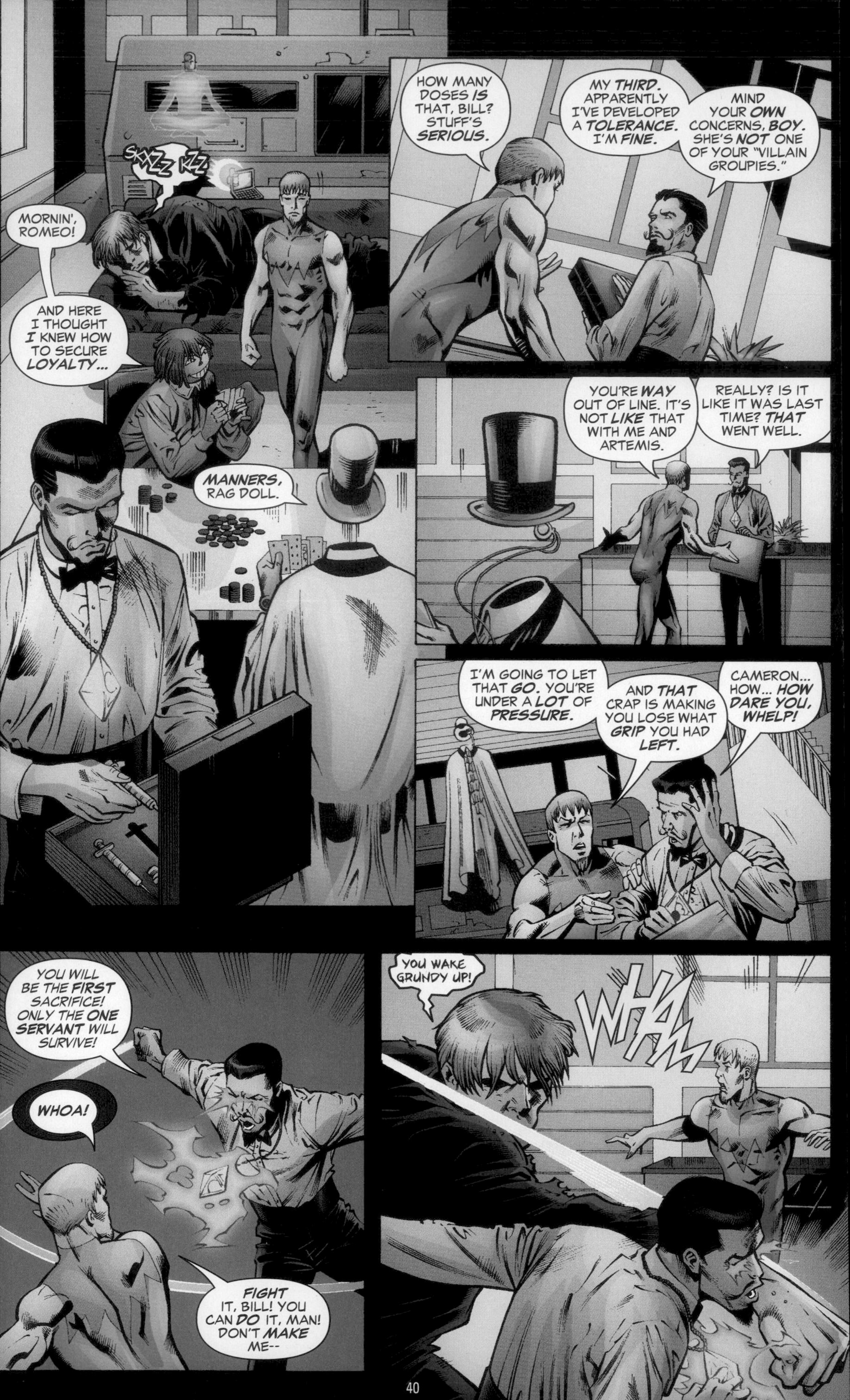

SKXZZ KZZ
MORNIN', ROMEO!
AND HERE I THOUGHT I KNEW HOW TO SECURE LOYALTY...
MANNERS, RAG DOLL.
HOW MANY DOSES IS THAT, BILL? STUFF'S SERIOUS.
MY THIRD. APPARENTLY I'VE DEVELOPED A TOLERANCE. I'M FINE.
MIND YOUR OWN CONCERNS, BOY. SHE'S NOT ONE OF YOUR "VILLAIN GROUPIES."
YOU'RE WAY OUT OF LINE. IT'S NOT LIKE THAT WITH ME AND ARTEMIS.
REALLY? IS IT LIKE IT WAS LAST TIME? THAT WENT WELL.
I'M GOING TO LET THAT GO. YOU'RE UNDER A LOT OF PRESSURE.
AND THAT CRAP IS MAKING YOU LOSE WHAT GRIP YOU HAD LEFT.
CAMERON... HOW... HOW DARE YOU, WHELP!
YOU WILL BE THE FIRST SACRIFICE! ONLY THE ONE SERVANT WILL SURVIVE!
WHOA!
FIGHT IT, BILL! YOU CAN DO IT, MAN! DON'T MAKE ME--
YOU WAKE GRUNDY UP!
WHAM

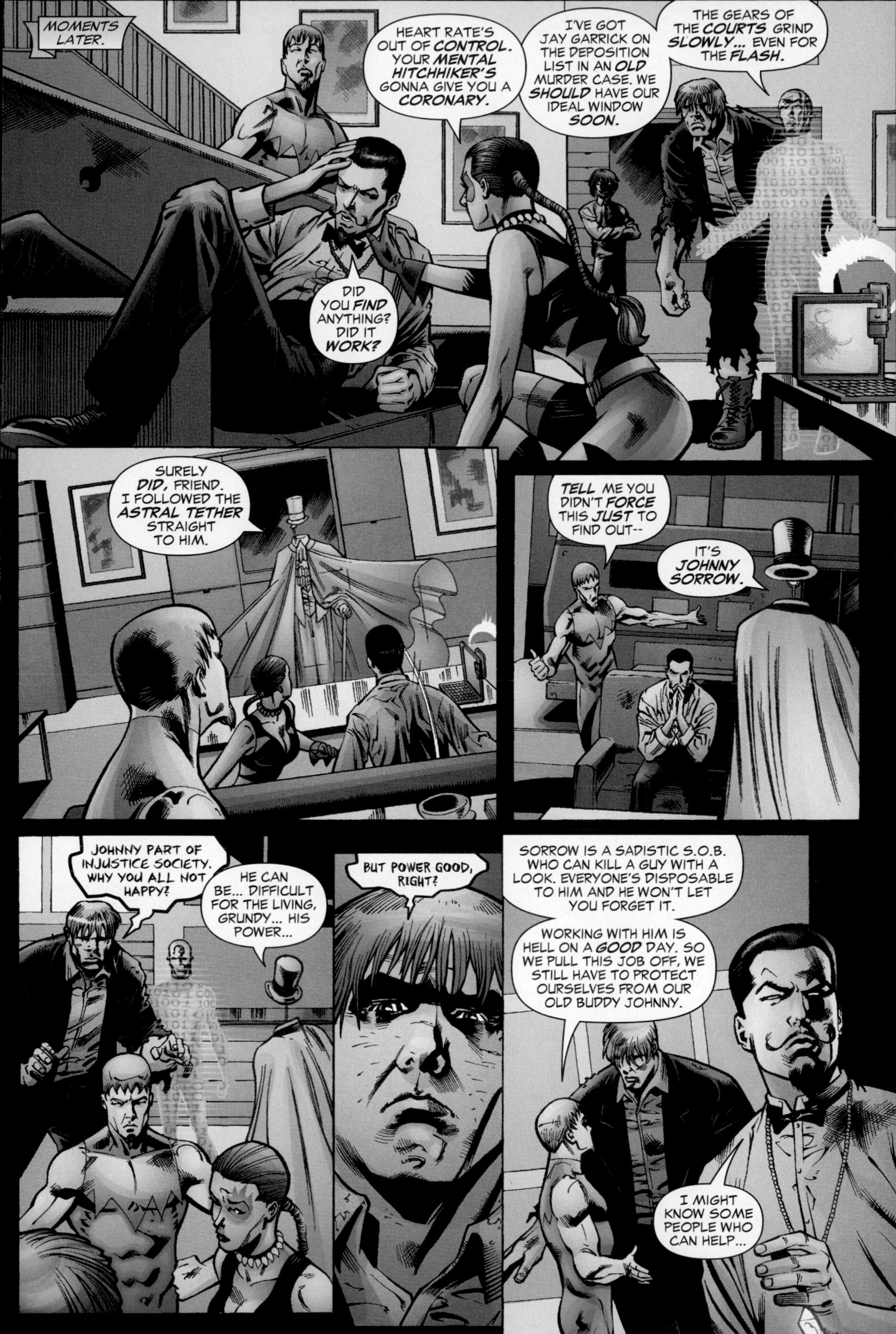
MOMENTS LATER.
HEART RATE'S OUT OF CONTROL. YOUR MENTAL HITCHHIKER'S GONNA GIVE YOU A CORONARY.
I'VE GOT JAY GARRICK ON THE DEPOSITION LIST IN AN OLD MURDER CASE. WE SHOULD HAVE OUR IDEAL WINDOW SOON.
THE GEARS OF THE COURTS GRIND SLOWLY... EVEN FOR THE FLASH.
DID YOU FIND ANYTHING? DID IT WORK?
SURELY DID, FRIEND. I FOLLOWED THE ASTRAL TETHER STRAIGHT TO HIM.
TELL ME YOU DIDN'T FORCE THIS JUST TO FIND OUT--
IT'S JOHNNY SORROW.
JOHNNY PART OF INJUSTICE SOCIETY. WHY YOU ALL NOT HAPPY?
HE CAN BE... DIFFICULT FOR THE LIVING, GRUNDY... HIS POWER...
BUT POWER GOOD, RIGHT?
SORROW IS A SADISTIC S.O.B. WHO CAN KILL A GUY WITH A LOOK. EVERYONE'S DISPOSABLE TO HIM AND HE WON'T LET YOU FORGET IT.
WORKING WITH HIM IS HELL ON A GOOD DAY. SO WE PULL THIS JOB OFF, WE STILL HAVE TO PROTECT OURSELVES FROM OUR OLD BUDDY JOHNNY.
I MIGHT KNOW SOME PEOPLE WHO CAN HELP...

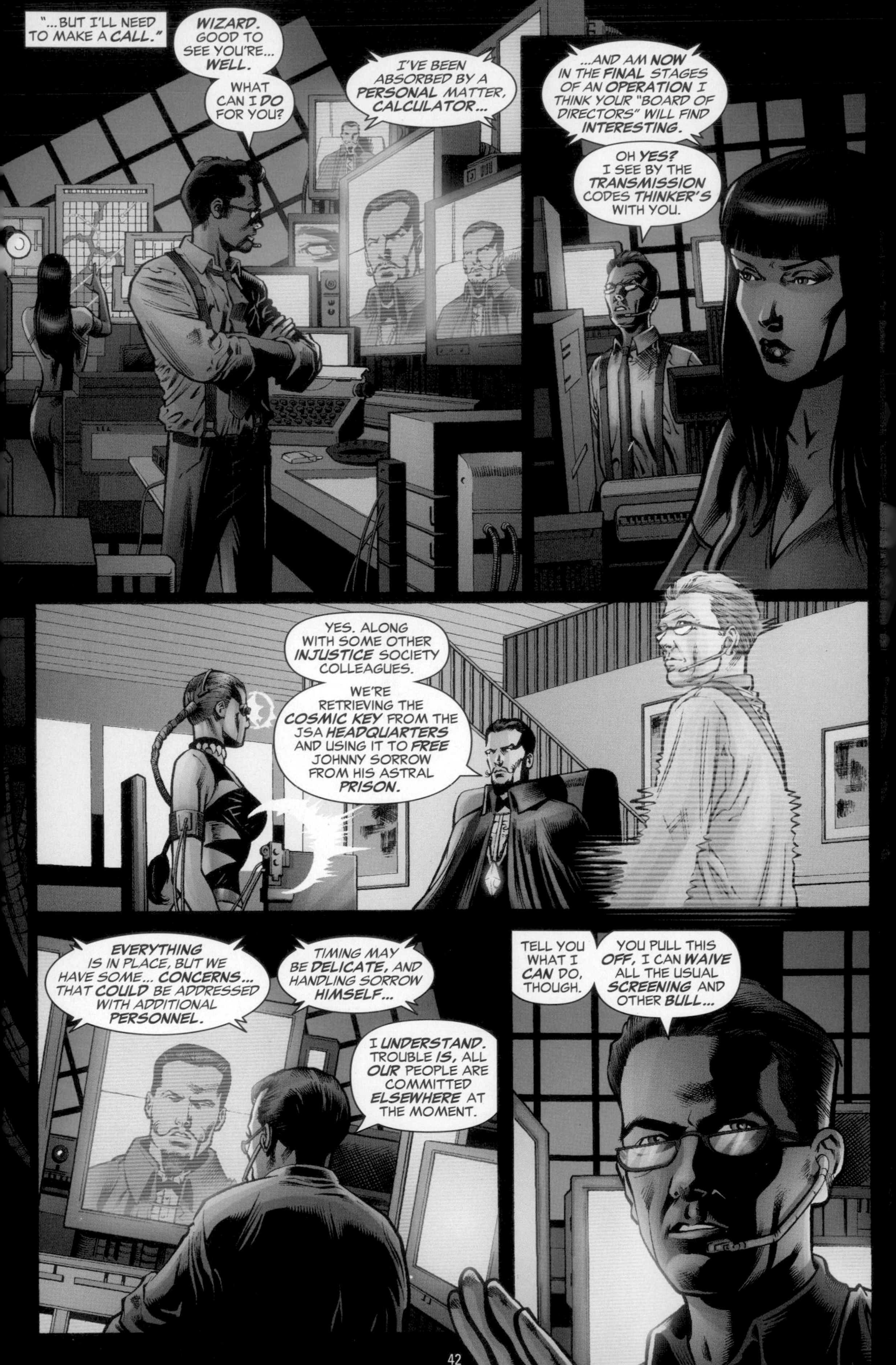
"...BUT I'LL NEED TO MAKE A CALL."
WIZARD. GOOD TO SEE YOU'RE... WELL.
WHAT CAN I DO FOR YOU?
I'VE BEEN ABSORBED BY A PERSONAL MATTER, CALCULATOR...
...AND AM NOW IN THE FINAL STAGES OF AN OPERATION I THINK YOUR "BOARD OF DIRECTORS" WILL FIND INTERESTING.
OH YES? I SEE BY THE TRANSMISSION CODES THINKER'S WITH YOU.
YES. ALONG WITH SOME OTHER INJUSTICE SOCIETY COLLEAGUES.
WE'RE RETRIEVING THE COSMIC KEY FROM THE JSA HEADQUARTERS AND USING IT TO FREE JOHNNY SORROW FROM HIS ASTRAL PRISON.
EVERYTHING IS IN PLACE, BUT WE HAVE SOME... CONCERNS... THAT COULD BE ADDRESSED WITH ADDITIONAL PERSONNEL.
TIMING MAY BE DELICATE, AND HANDLING SORROW HIMSELF...
I UNDERSTAND. TROUBLE IS, ALL OUR PEOPLE ARE COMMITTED ELSEWHERE AT THE MOMENT.
TELL YOU WHAT I CAN DO, THOUGH.
YOU PULL THIS OFF, I CAN WAIVE ALL THE USUAL SCREENING AND OTHER BULL...

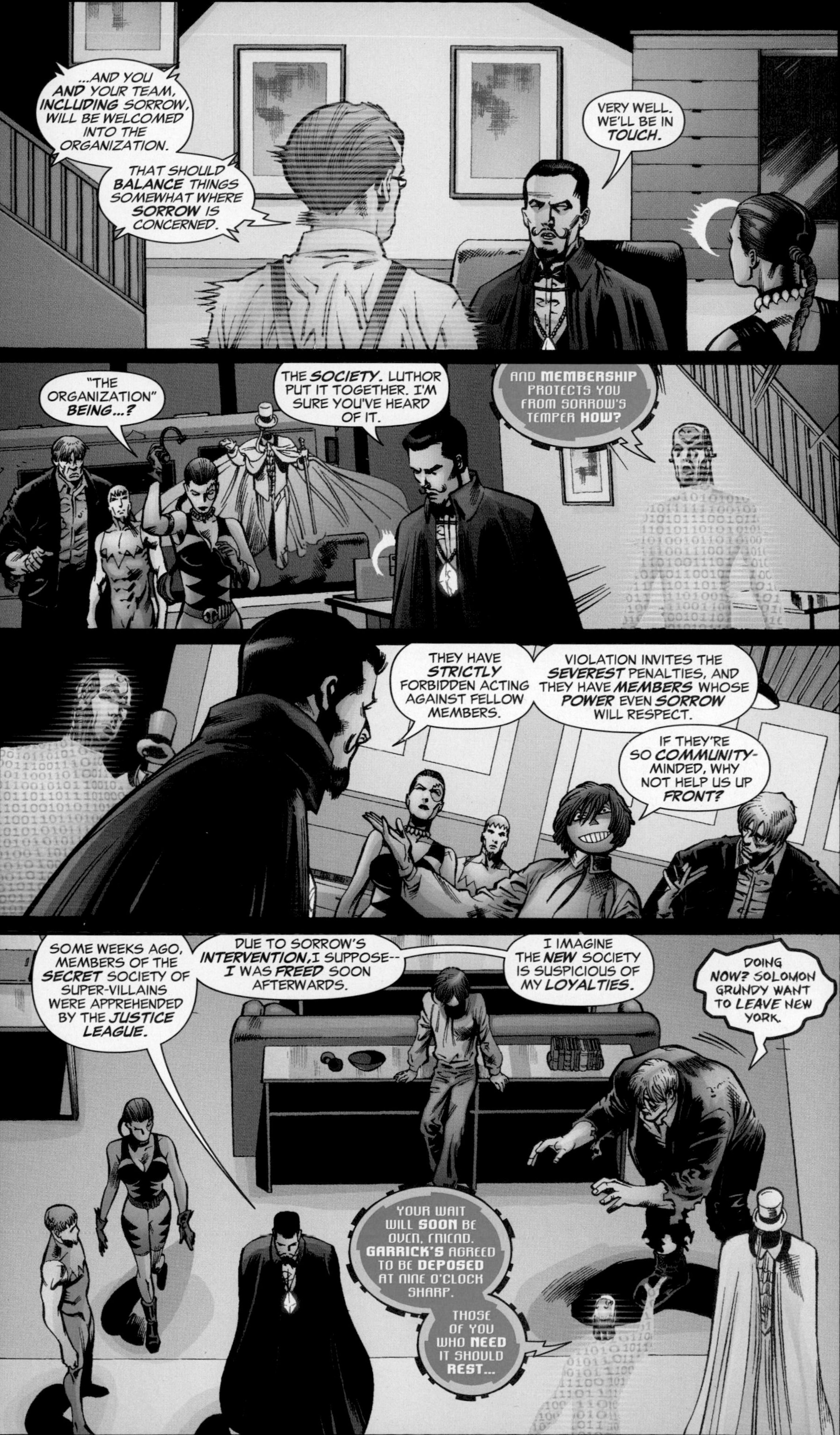
...AND YOU AND YOUR TEAM, INCLUDING SORROW, WILL BE WELCOMED INTO THE ORGANIZATION.
THAT SHOULD BALANCE THINGS SOMEWHAT WHERE SORROW IS CONCERNED.
VERY WELL. WE'LL BE IN TOUCH.
"THE ORGANIZATION" BEING...?
THE SOCIETY. LUTHOR PUT IT TOGETHER. I'M SURE YOU'VE HEARD OF IT.
AND MEMBERSHIP PROTECTS YOU FROM SORROW'S TEMPER HOW?
THEY HAVE STRICTLY FORBIDDEN ACTING AGAINST FELLOW MEMBERS.
VIOLATION INVITES THE SEVEREST PENALTIES, AND THEY HAVE MEMBERS WHOSE POWER EVEN SORROW WILL RESPECT.
IF THEY'RE SO COMMUNITY-MINDED, WHY NOT HELP US UP FRONT?
SOME WEEKS AGO, MEMBERS OF THE SECRET SOCIETY OF SUPER-VILLAINS WERE APPREHENDED BY THE JUSTICE LEAGUE.
DUE TO SORROW'S INTERVENTION, I SUPPOSE-- I WAS FREED SOON AFTERWARDS.
I IMAGINE THE NEW SOCIETY IS SUSPICIOUS OF MY LOYALTIES.
DOING NOW? SOLOMON GRUNDY WANT TO LEAVE NEW YORK.
YOUR WAIT WILL SOON BE OVER, FRIEND. GARRICK'S AGREED TO BE DEPOSED AT NINE O'CLOCK SHARP.
THOSE OF YOU WHO NEED IT SHOULD REST...

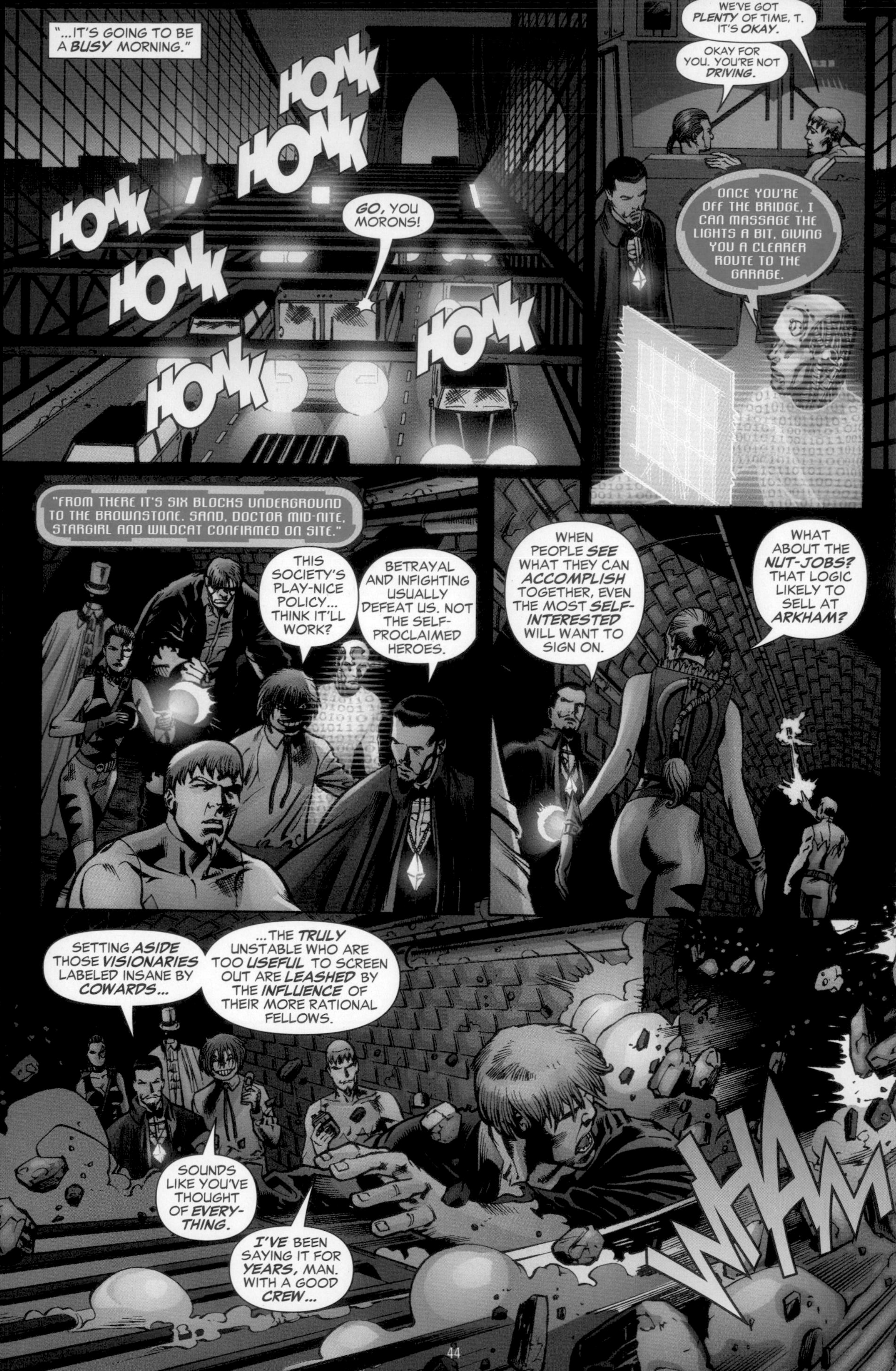
"...IT'S GOING TO BE A BUSY MORNING."
HONK HONK
HONK
HONK
HONK
HONK
GO, YOU MORONS!
WE'VE GOT PLENTY OF TIME, T. IT'S OKAY.
OKAY FOR YOU. YOU'RE NOT DRIVING.
ONCE YOU'RE OFF THE BRIDGE, I CAN MASSAGE THE LIGHTS A BIT, GIVING YOU A CLEARER ROUTE TO THE GARAGE.
"FROM THERE IT'S SIX BLOCKS UNDERGROUND TO THE BROWNSTONE. SAND, DOCTOR MID-NITE, STARGIRL AND WILDCAT CONFIRMED ON SITE."
THIS SOCIETY'S PLAY-NICE POLICY... THINK IT'LL WORK?
BETRAYAL AND INFIGHTING USUALLY DEFEAT US. NOT THE SELF-PROCLAIMED HEROES.
WHEN PEOPLE SEE WHAT THEY CAN ACCOMPLISH TOGETHER, EVEN THE MOST SELF-INTERESTED WILL WANT TO SIGN ON.
WHAT ABOUT THE NUT-JOBS? THAT LOGIC LIKELY TO SELL AT ARKHAM?
SETTING ASIDE THOSE VISIONARIES LABELED INSANE BY COWARDS...
...THE TRULY UNSTABLE WHO ARE TOO USEFUL TO SCREEN OUT ARE LEASHED BY THE INFLUENCE OF THEIR MORE RATIONAL FELLOWS.
SOUNDS LIKE YOU'VE THOUGHT OF EVERY-THING.
I'VE BEEN SAYING IT FOR YEARS, MAN. WITH A GOOD CREW...
WHAM

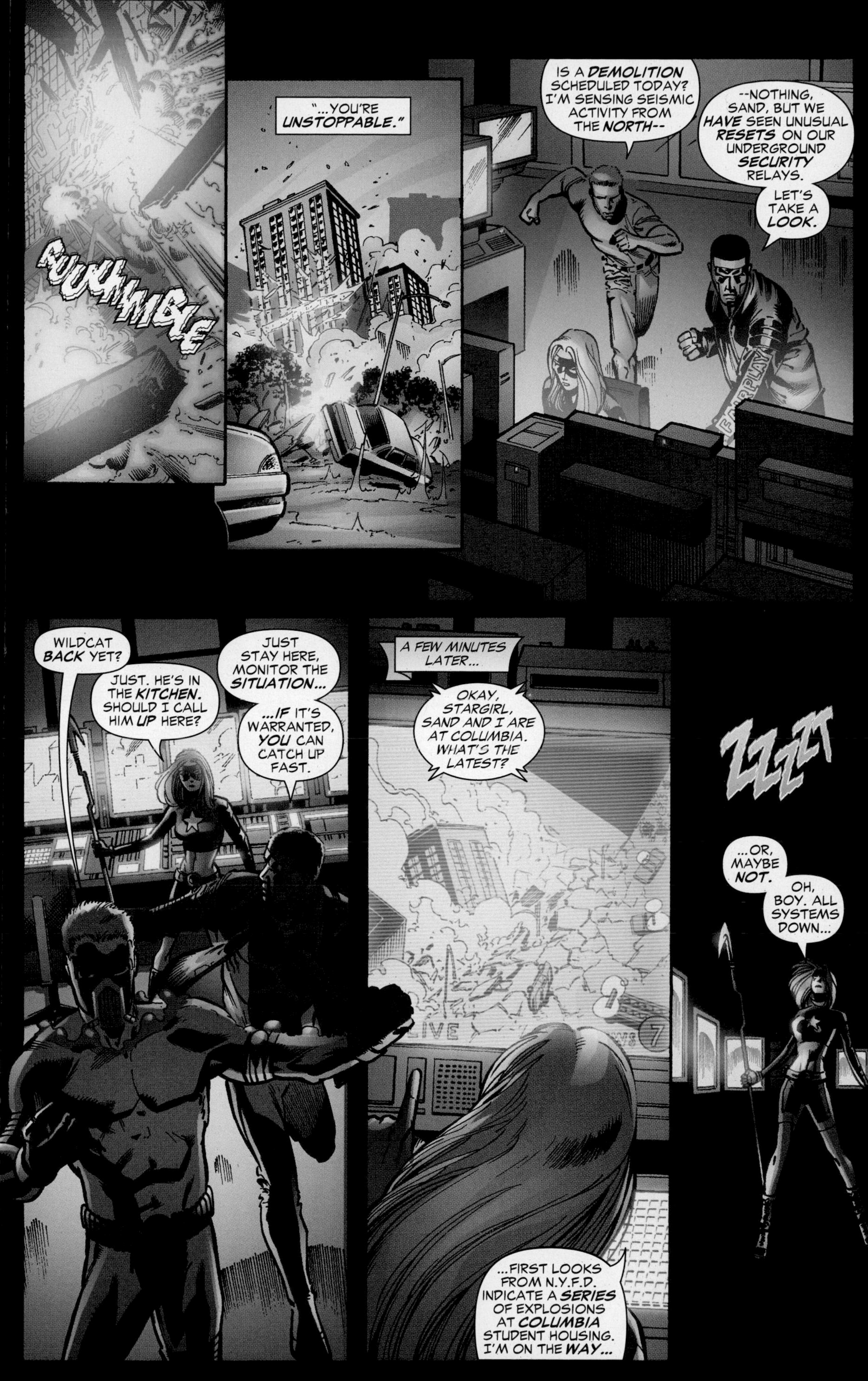
RUUUMMBLE
"...YOU'RE UNSTOPPABLE."
IS A DEMOLITION SCHEDULED TODAY? I'M SENSING SEISMIC ACTIVITY FROM THE NORTH--
--NOTHING, SAND, BUT WE HAVE SEEN UNUSUAL RESETS ON OUR UNDERGROUND SECURITY RELAYS.
LET'S TAKE A LOOK.
WILDCAT BACK YET?
JUST. HE'S IN THE KITCHEN. SHOULD I CALL HIM UP HERE?
JUST STAY HERE, MONITOR THE SITUATION...
...IF IT'S WARRANTED, YOU CAN CATCH UP FAST.
A FEW MINUTES LATER...
OKAY, STARGIRL, SAND AND I ARE AT COLUMBIA. WHAT'S THE LATEST?
LIVE
...FIRST LOOKS FROM N.Y.F.D. INDICATE A SERIES OF EXPLOSIONS AT COLUMBIA STUDENT HOUSING. I'M ON THE WAY...
ZZZZT
...OR, MAYBE NOT.
OH, BOY. ALL SYSTEMS DOWN...

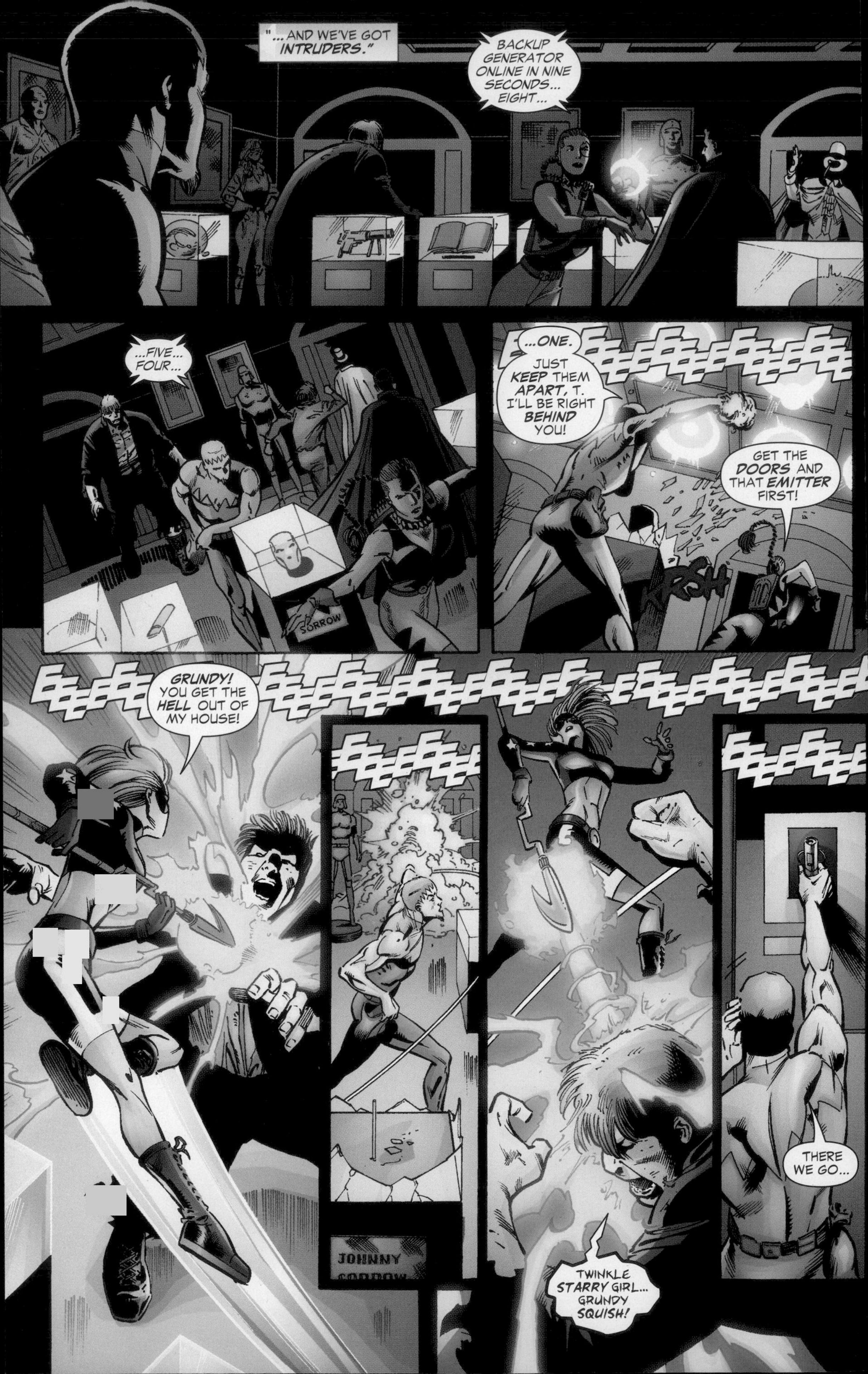
"...AND WE'VE GOT INTRUDERS."
BACKUP GENERATOR ONLINE IN NINE SECONDS... EIGHT...
...FIVE... FOUR...
SORROW
...ONE.
JUST KEEP THEM APART, T. I'LL BE RIGHT BEHIND YOU!
GET THE DOORS AND THAT EMITTER FIRST!
KRSH
GRUNDY! YOU GET THE HELL OUT OF MY HOUSE!
JOHNNY
TWINKLE STARRY GIRL... GRUNDY SQUISH!
THERE WE GO...

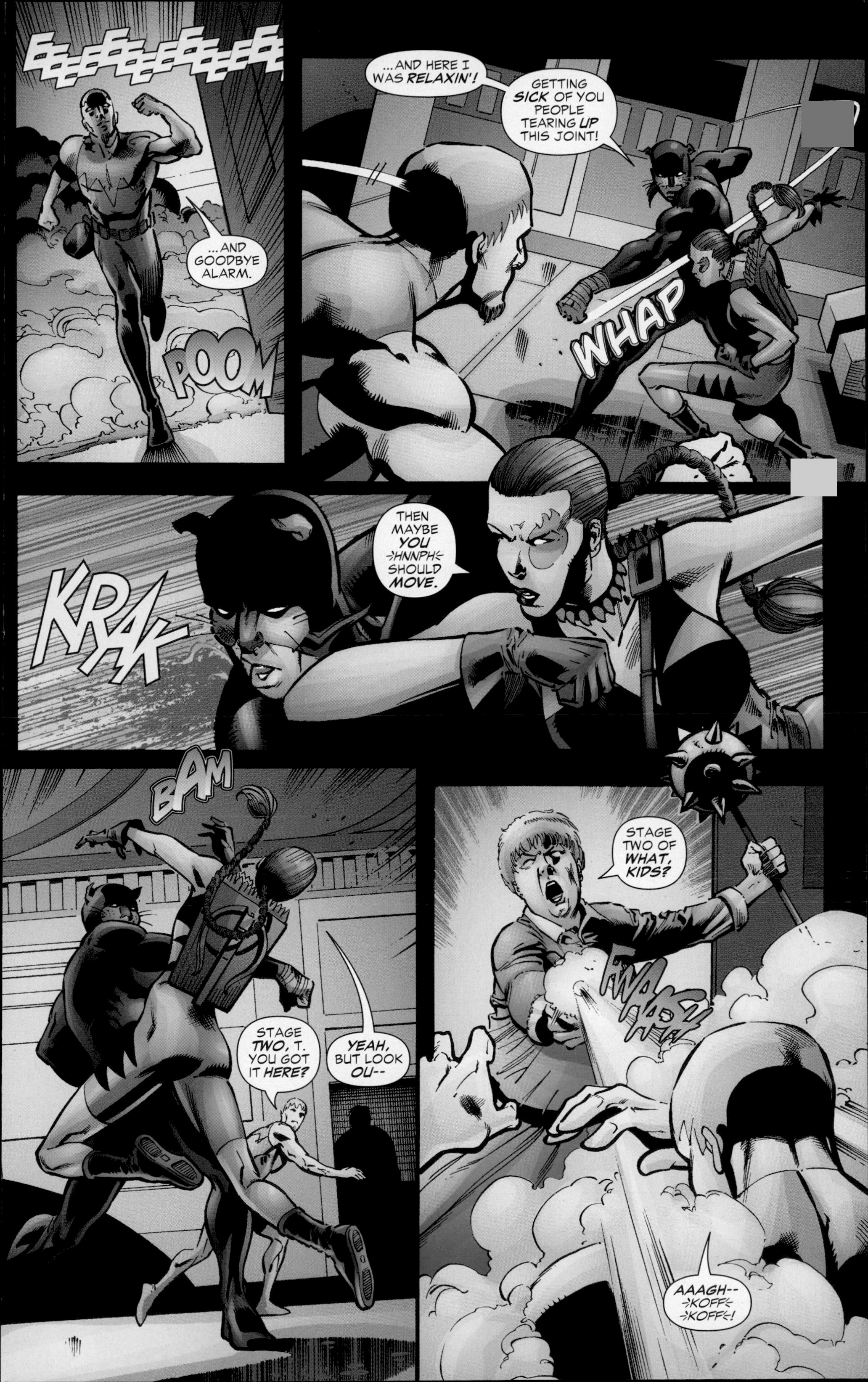
EEEEEEEEEEEEEEEEE
...AND GOODBYE ALARM.
POOM
...AND HERE I WAS RELAXIN'!
GETTING SICK OF YOU PEOPLE TEARING UP THIS JOINT!
WHAP
KRAK
THEN MAYBE YOU -HNNPH- SHOULD MOVE.
BAM
STAGE TWO, T. YOU GOT IT HERE?
YEAH, BUT LOOK OU--
STAGE TWO OF WHAT, KIDS?
FWASH
AAAGH-- -KOFF- -KOFF-!

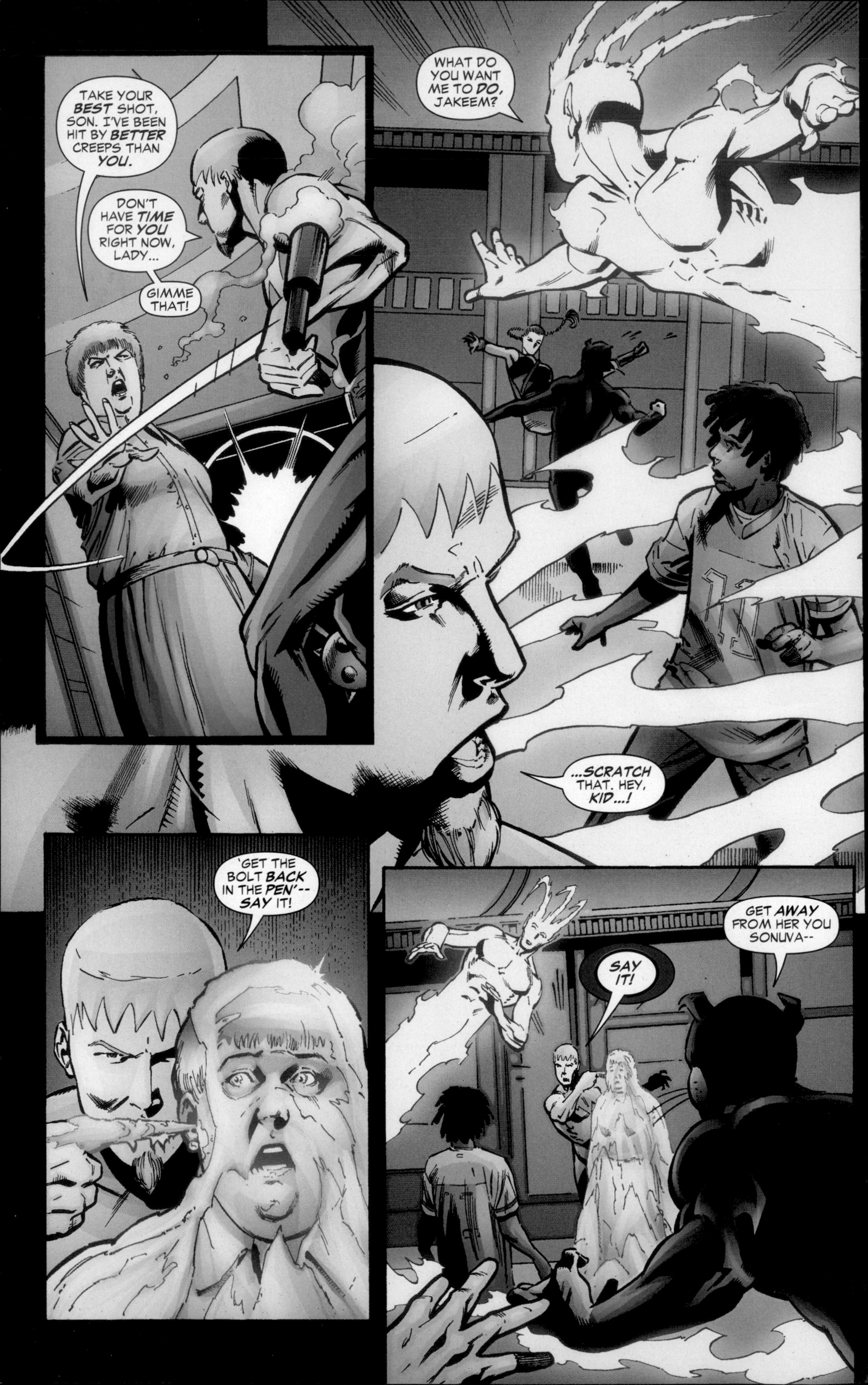
TAKE YOUR BEST SHOT, SON. I'VE BEEN HIT BY BETTER CREEPS THAN YOU.
DON'T HAVE TIME FOR YOU RIGHT NOW, LADY...
GIMME THAT!
WHAT DO YOU WANT ME TO DO, JAKEEM?
...SCRATCH THAT. HEY, KID...!
'GET THE BOLT BACK IN THE PEN'-- SAY IT!
GET AWAY FROM HER YOU SONUVA--
SAY IT!

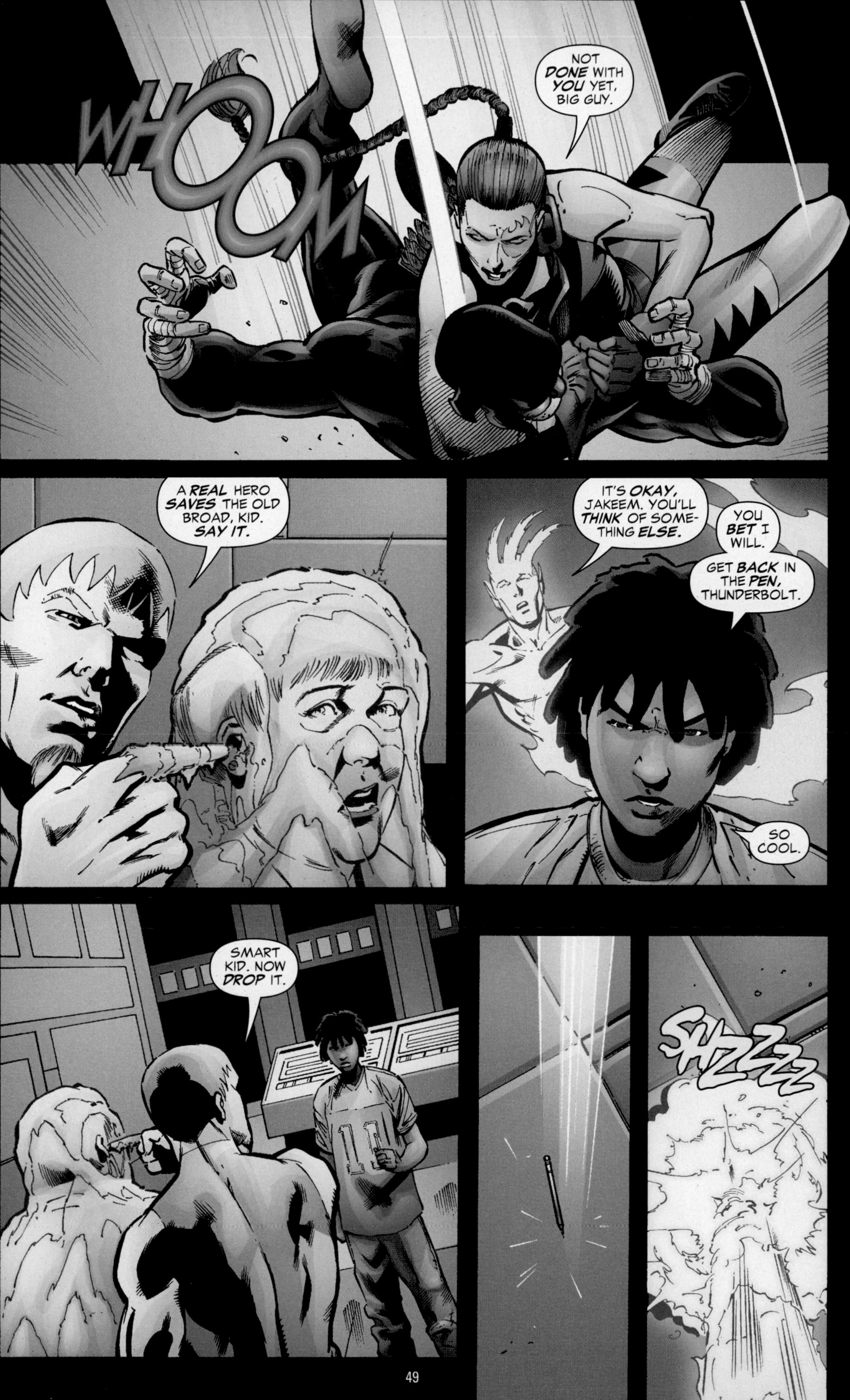
WHOOOM
NOT DONE WITH YOU YET, BIG GUY.
A REAL HERO SAVES THE OLD BROAD, KID. SAY IT.
IT'S OKAY, JAKEEM. YOU'LL THINK OF SOMETHING ELSE.
YOU BET I WILL.
GET BACK IN THE PEN, THUNDERBOLT.
SO COOL.
SMART KID. NOW DROP IT.
SHZZZZ

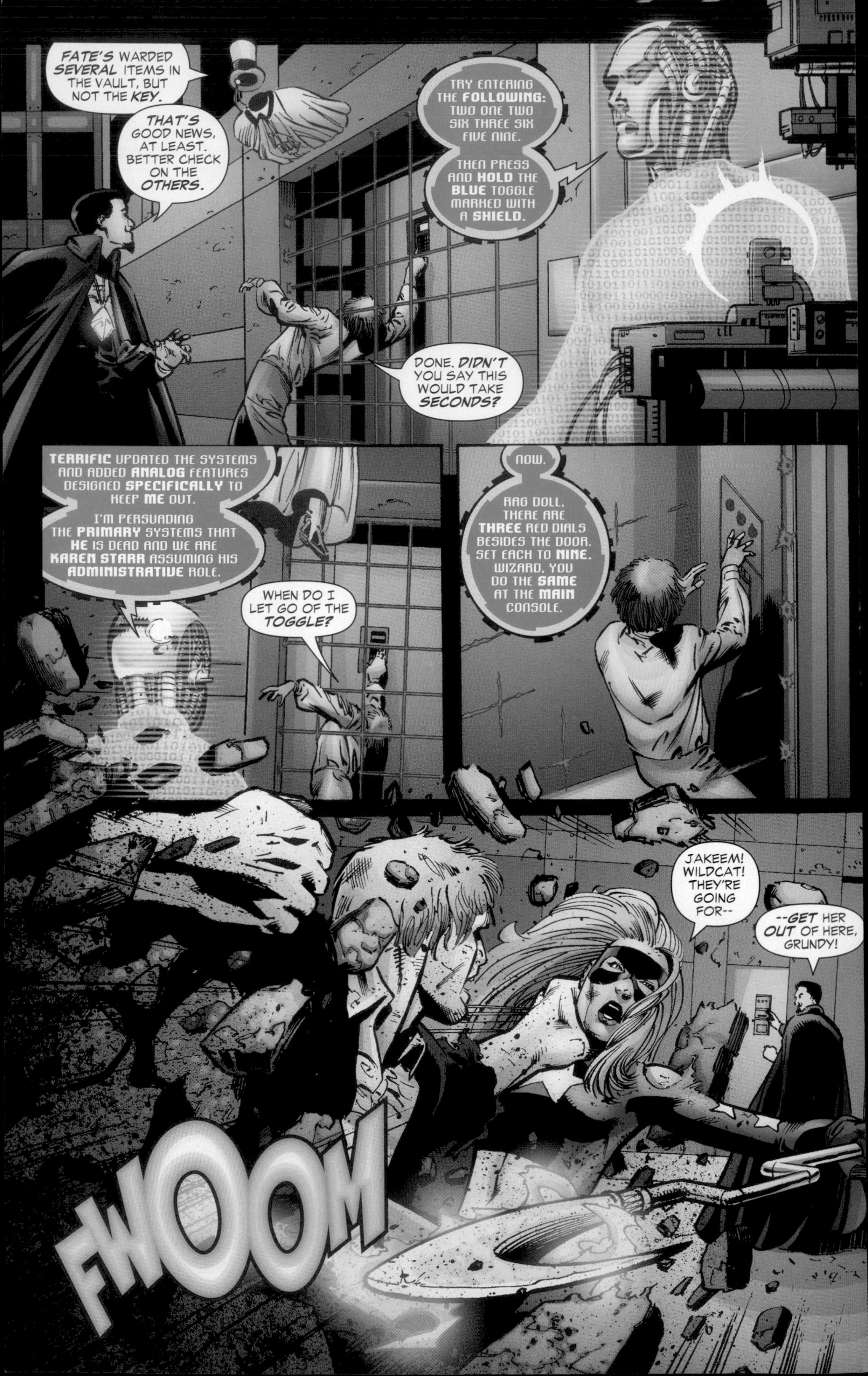
FATE'S WARDED SEVERAL ITEMS IN THE VAULT, BUT NOT THE KEY.
THAT'S GOOD NEWS, AT LEAST. BETTER CHECK ON THE OTHERS.
TRY ENTERING THE FOLLOWING: TWO ONE TWO SIX THREE SIX FIVE NINE.
THEN PRESS AND HOLD THE BLUE TOGGLE MARKED WITH A SHIELD.
DONE. DIDN'T YOU SAY THIS WOULD TAKE SECONDS?
TERRIFIC UPDATED THE SYSTEMS AND ADDED ANALOG FEATURES DESIGNED SPECIFICALLY TO KEEP ME OUT.
I'M PERSUADING THE PRIMARY SYSTEMS THAT HE IS DEAD AND WE ARE KAREN STARR ASSUMING HIS ADMINISTRATIVE ROLE.
WHEN DO I LET GO OF THE TOGGLE?
NOW.
RAG DOLL, THERE ARE THREE RED DIALS BESIDES THE DOOR. SET EACH TO NINE. WIZARD, YOU DO THE SAME AT THE MAIN CONSOLE.
JAKEEM! WILDCAT! THEY'RE GOING FOR--
--GET HER OUT OF HERE, GRUNDY!
FWOOM

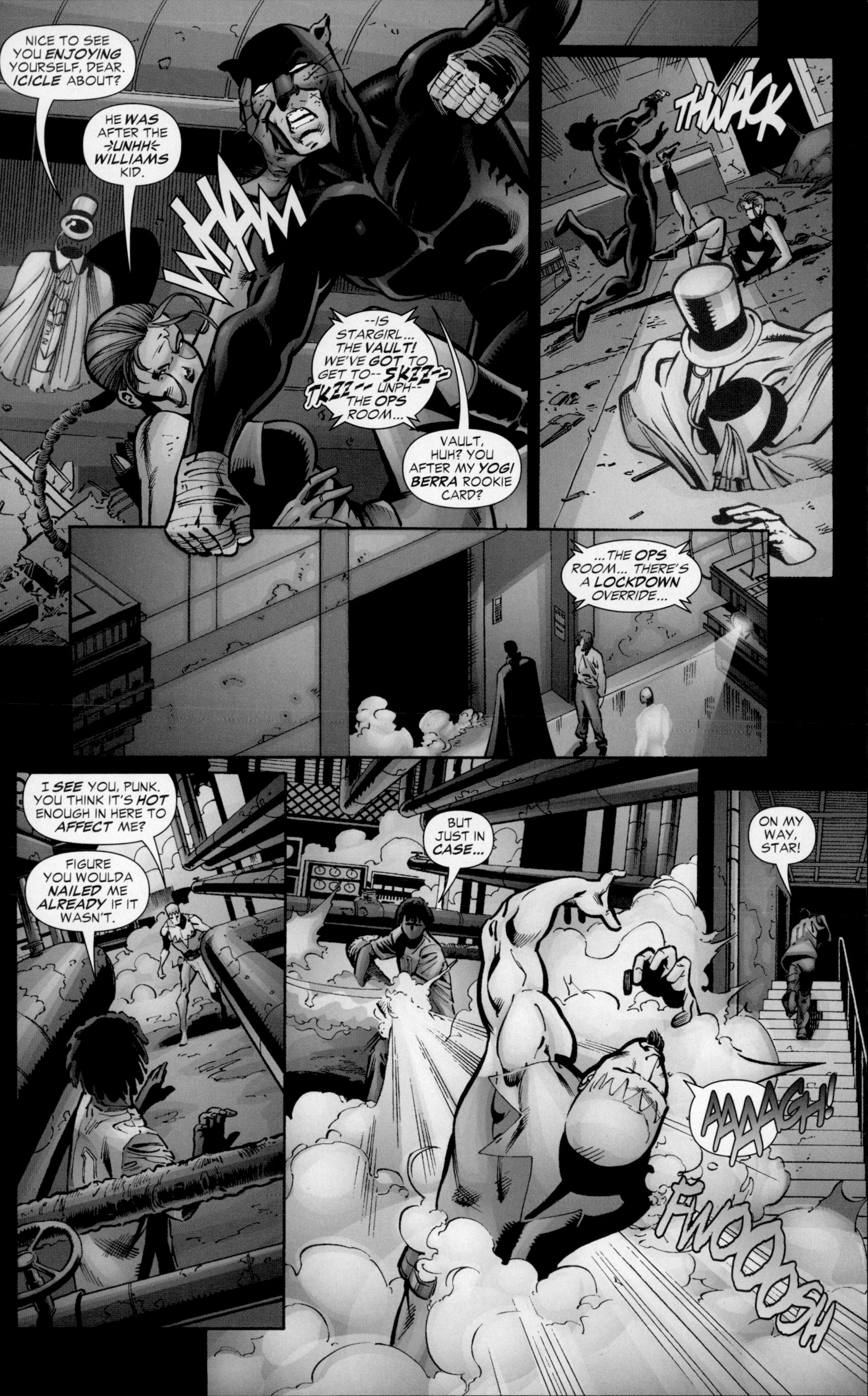
NICE TO SEE YOU ENJOYING YOURSELF, DEAR. ICICLE ABOUT?
HE WAS AFTER THE --UNHH-- WILLIAMS KID.
WHAM
--IS STARGIRL... THE VAULT! WE'VE GOT TO GET TO-- SKIZZ-- TKZZ-- UNPH-- THE OPS ROOM...
VAULT, HUH? YOU AFTER MY YOGI BERRA ROOKIE CARD?
THWACK
...THE OPS ROOM... THERE'S A LOCKDOWN OVERRIDE...
I SEE YOU, PUNK. YOU THINK IT'S HOT ENOUGH IN HERE TO AFFECT ME?
FIGURE YOU WOULDA NAILED ME ALREADY IF IT WASN'T.
BUT JUST IN CASE...
ON MY WAY, STAR!
AAAAGH!
FWOOOOSH

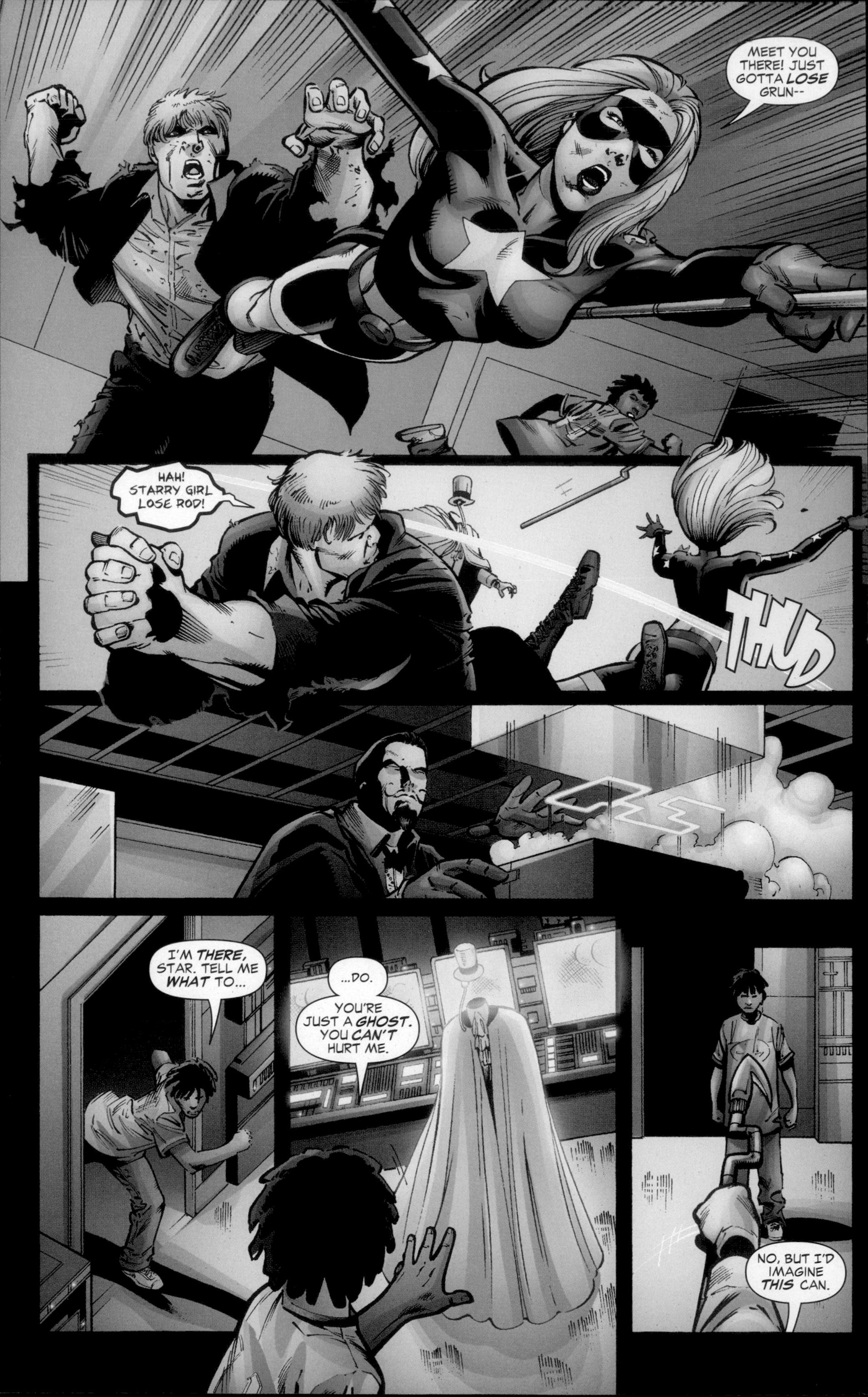
MEET YOU THERE! JUST GOTTA LOSE GRUN--
HAH! STARRY GIRL LOSE ROD!
THUD
I'M THERE, STAR. TELL ME WHAT TO...
...DO.
YOU'RE JUST A GHOST. YOU CAN'T HURT ME.
NO, BUT I'D IMAGINE THIS CAN.

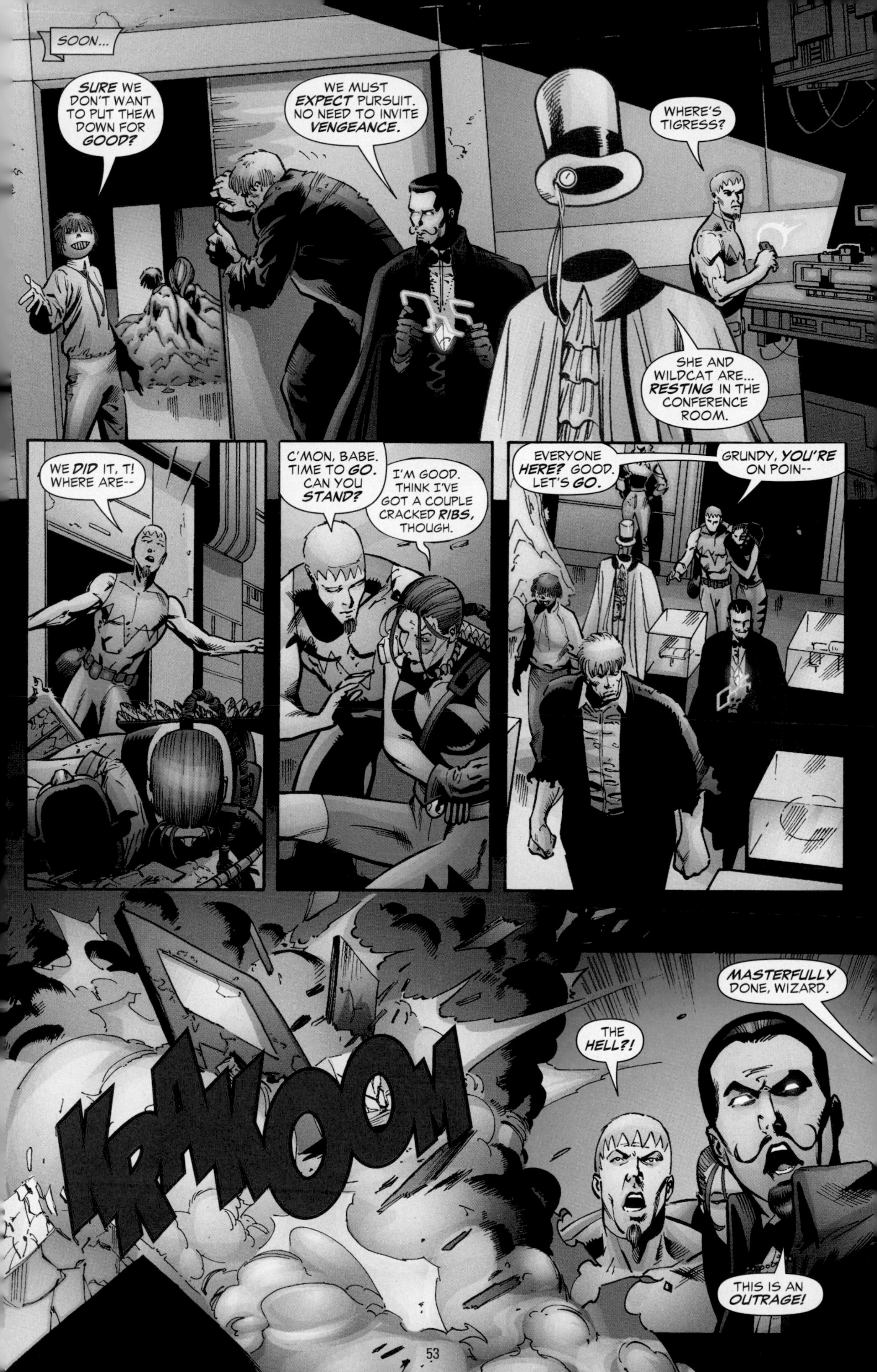
SOON...
SURE WE DON'T WANT TO PUT THEM DOWN FOR GOOD?
WE MUST EXPECT PURSUIT. NO NEED TO INVITE VENGEANCE.
WHERE'S TIGRESS?
SHE AND WILDCAT ARE... RESTING IN THE CONFERENCE ROOM.
WE DID IT, T! WHERE ARE--
C'MON, BABE. TIME TO GO. CAN YOU STAND?
I'M GOOD. THINK I'VE GOT A COUPLE CRACKED RIBS, THOUGH.
EVERYONE HERE? GOOD. LET'S GO.
GRUNDY, YOU'RE ON POIN--
KRAKOOM
MASTERFULLY DONE, WIZARD.
THE HELL?!
THIS IS AN OUTRAGE!

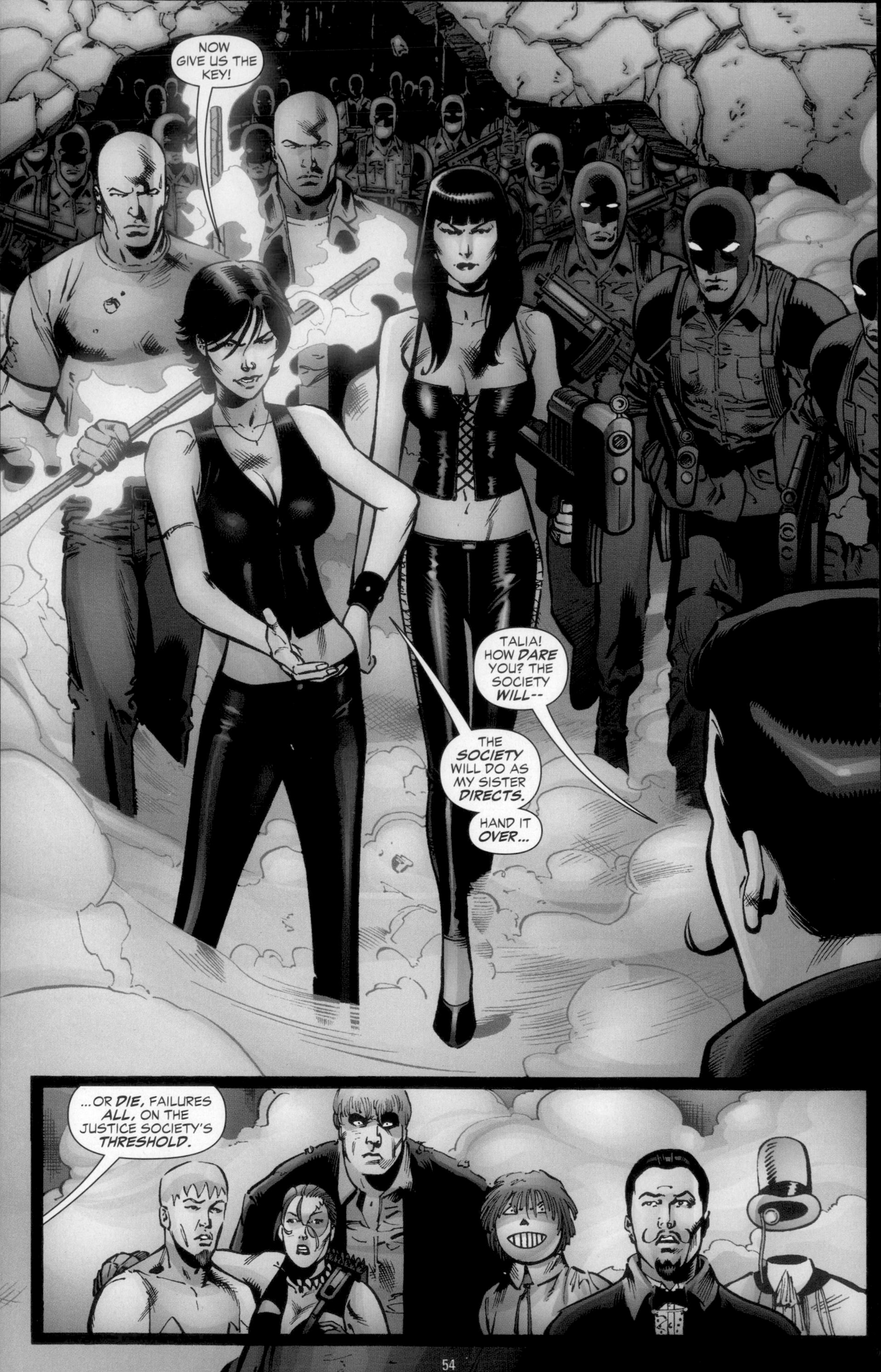
NOW GIVE US THE KEY!
TALIA! HOW DARE YOU? THE SOCIETY WILL--
THE SOCIETY WILL DO AS MY SISTER DIRECTS.
HAND IT OVER...
...OR DIE, FAILURES ALL, ON THE JUSTICE SOCIETY'S THRESHOLD.

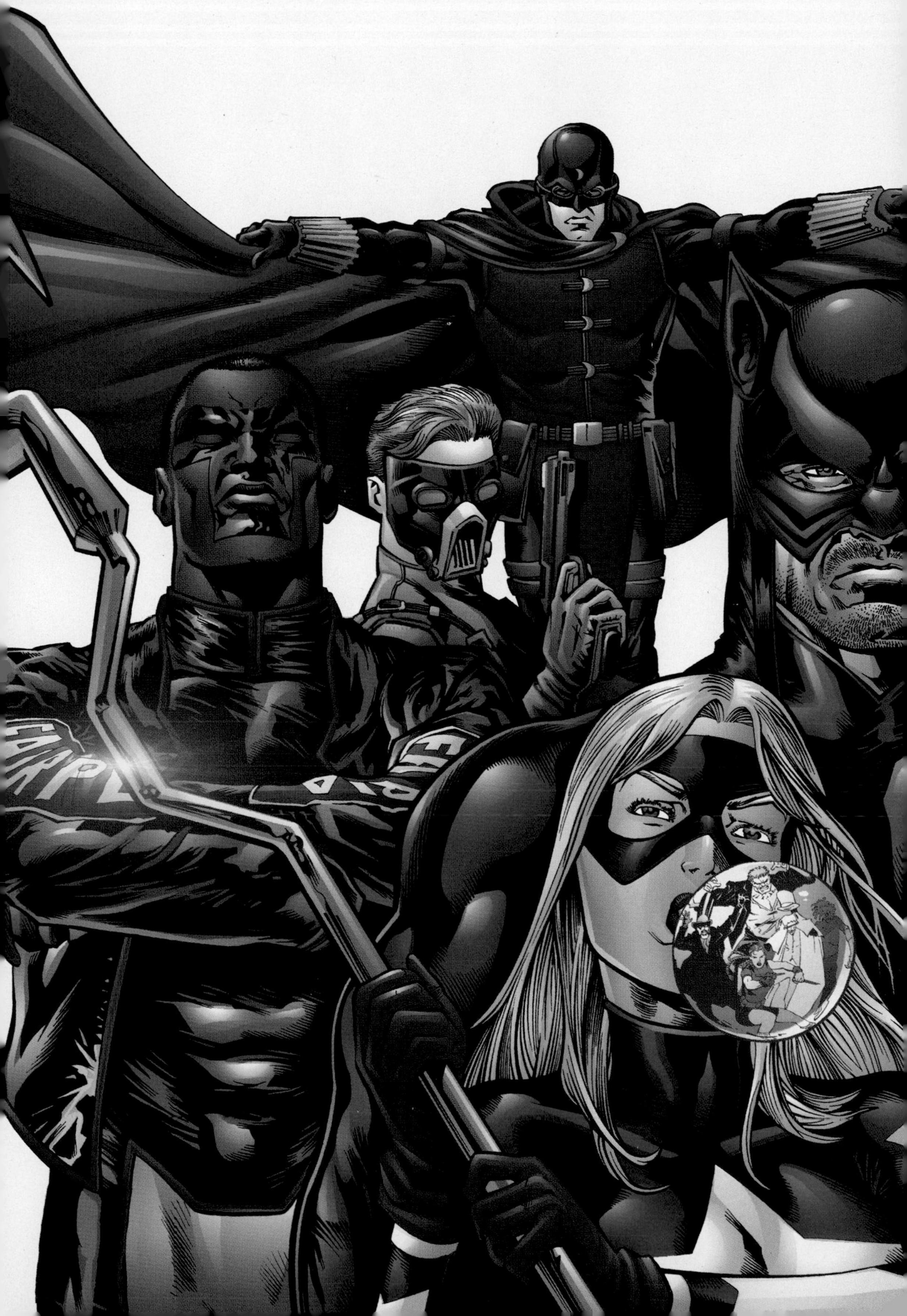

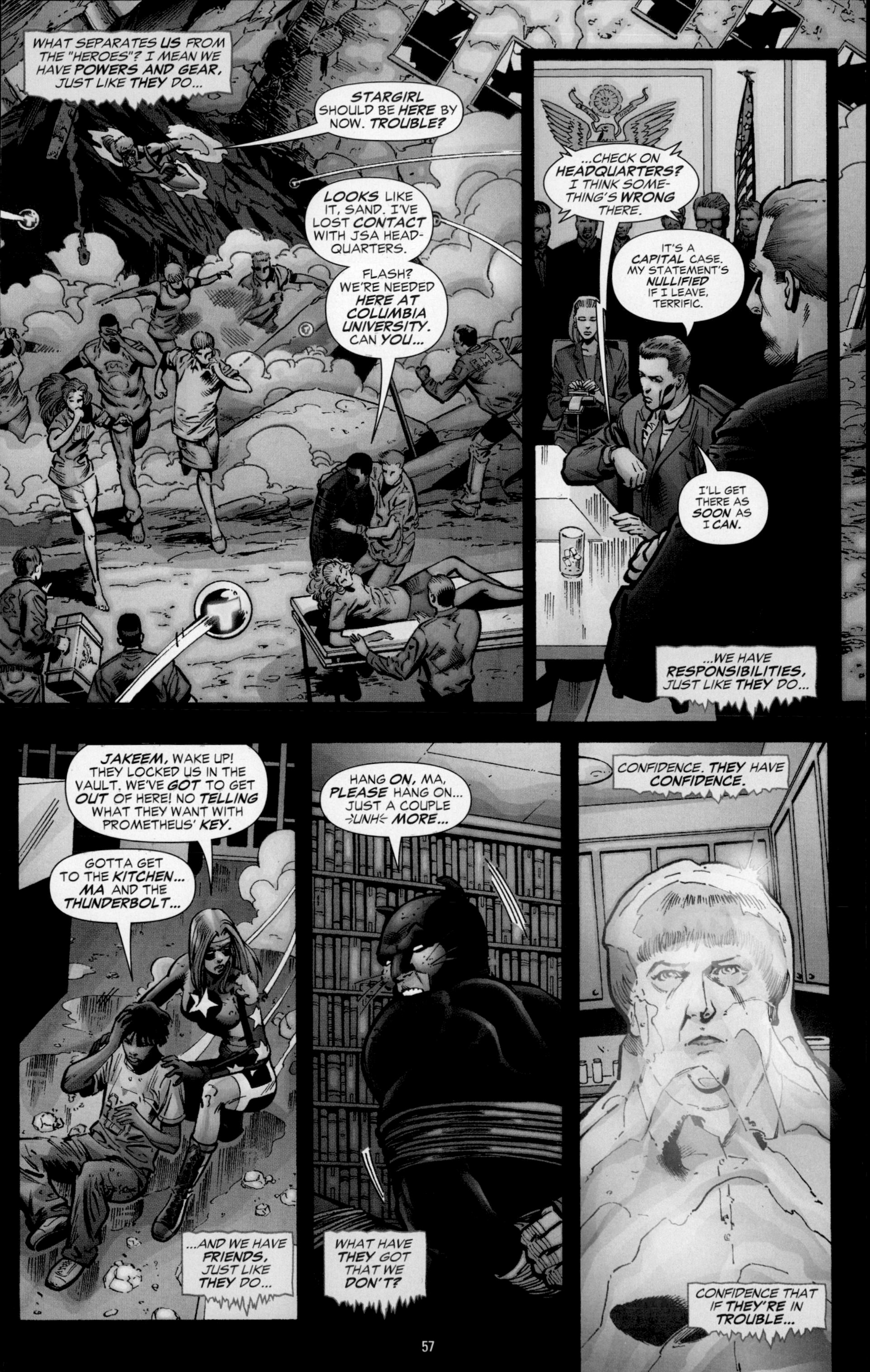
WHAT SEPARATES US FROM THE "HEROES"? I MEAN WE HAVE POWERS AND GEAR, JUST LIKE THEY DO...
STARGIRL SHOULD BE HERE BY NOW. TROUBLE?
LOOKS LIKE IT, SAND. I'VE LOST CONTACT WITH JSA HEADQUARTERS.
FLASH? WE'RE NEEDED HERE AT COLUMBIA UNIVERSITY. CAN YOU...
...CHECK ON HEADQUARTERS? I THINK SOMETHING'S WRONG THERE.
IT'S A CAPITAL CASE. MY STATEMENT'S NULLIFIED IF I LEAVE, TERRIFIC.
I'LL GET THERE AS SOON AS I CAN.
...WE HAVE RESPONSIBILITIES, JUST LIKE THEY DO...
JAKEEM, WAKE UP! THEY LOCKED US IN THE VAULT. WE'VE GOT TO GET OUT OF HERE! NO TELLING WHAT THEY WANT WITH PROMETHEUS' KEY.
GOTTA GET TO THE KITCHEN... MA AND THE THUNDERBOLT...
...AND WE HAVE FRIENDS, JUST LIKE THEY DO...
HANG ON, MA, PLEASE HANG ON... JUST A COUPLE →UNH← MORE...
WHAT HAVE THEY GOT THAT WE DON'T?
CONFIDENCE. THEY HAVE CONFIDENCE.
CONFIDENCE THAT IF THEY'RE IN TROUBLE...

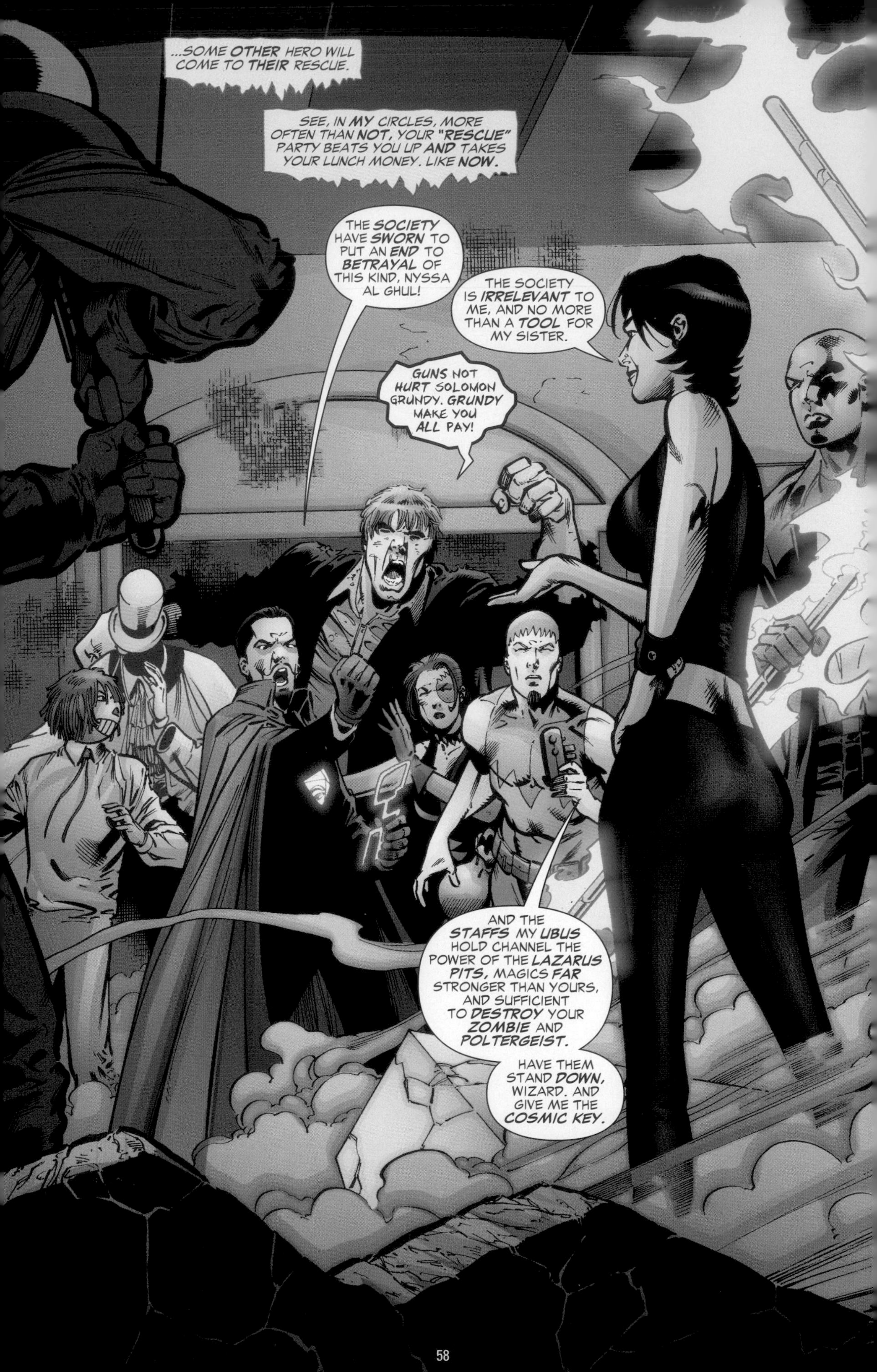
...SOME OTHER HERO WILL COME TO THEIR RESCUE.
SEE, IN MY CIRCLES, MORE OFTEN THAN NOT, YOUR "RESCUE" PARTY BEATS YOU UP AND TAKES YOUR LUNCH MONEY. LIKE NOW.
THE SOCIETY HAVE SWORN TO PUT AN END TO BETRAYAL OF THIS KIND, NYSSA AL GHUL!
THE SOCIETY IS IRRELEVANT TO ME, AND NO MORE THAN A TOOL FOR MY SISTER.
GUNS NOT HURT SOLOMON GRUNDY. GRUNDY MAKE YOU ALL PAY!
AND THE STAFFS MY UBUS HOLD CHANNEL THE POWER OF THE LAZARUS PITS, MAGICS FAR STRONGER THAN YOURS, AND SUFFICIENT TO DESTROY YOUR ZOMBIE AND POLTERGEIST.
HAVE THEM STAND DOWN, WIZARD. AND GIVE ME THE COSMIC KEY.

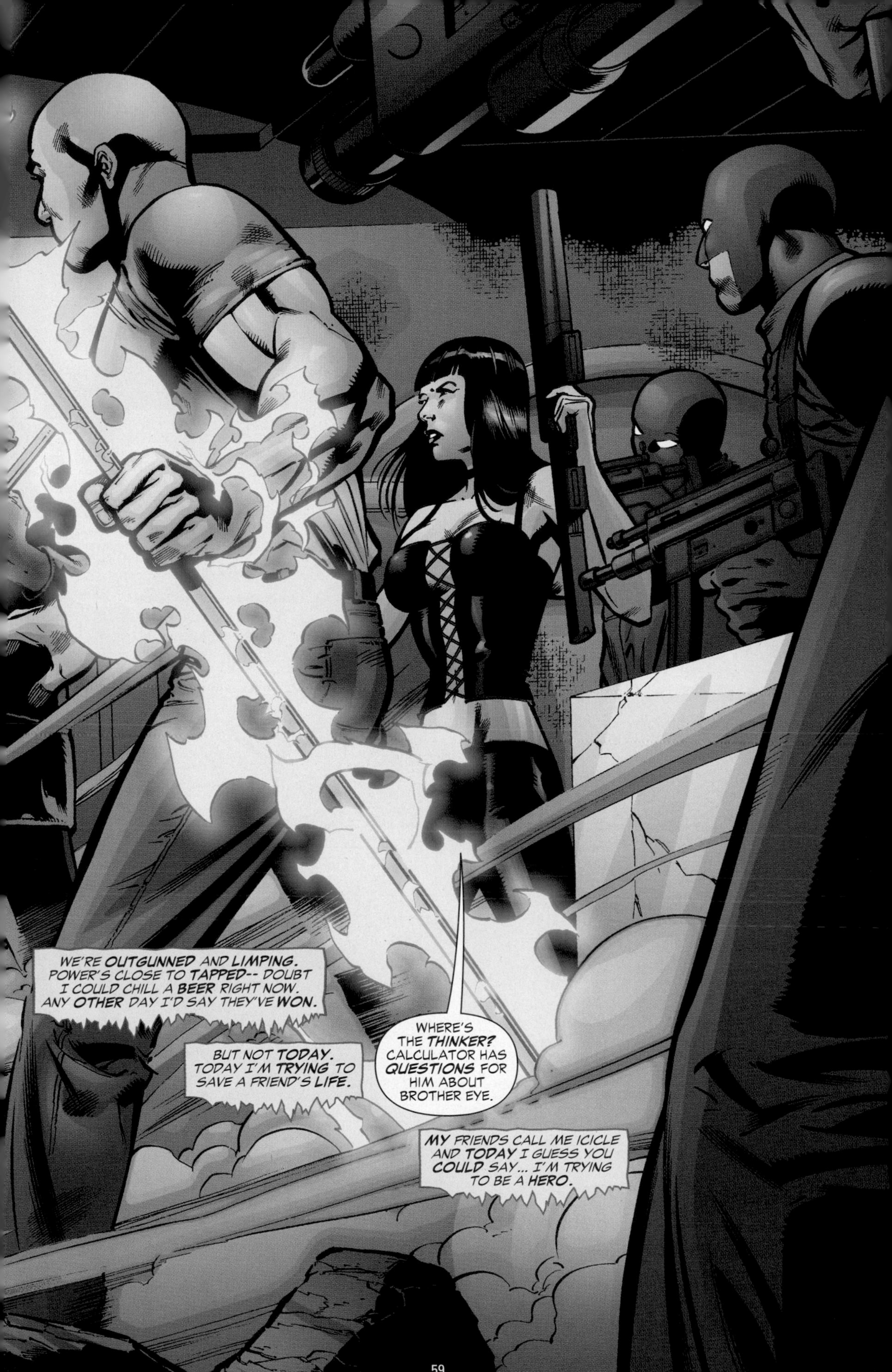

WE'RE OUTGUNNED AND LIMPING. POWER'S CLOSE TO TAPPED-- DOUBT I COULD CHILL A BEER RIGHT NOW. ANY OTHER DAY I'D SAY THEY'VE WON.
BUT NOT TODAY. TODAY I'M TRYING TO SAVE A FRIEND'S LIFE.
WHERE'S THE THINKER? CALCULATOR HAS QUESTIONS FOR HIM ABOUT BROTHER EYE.
MY FRIENDS CALL ME ICICLE AND TODAY I GUESS YOU COULD SAY... I'M TRYING TO BE A HERO.

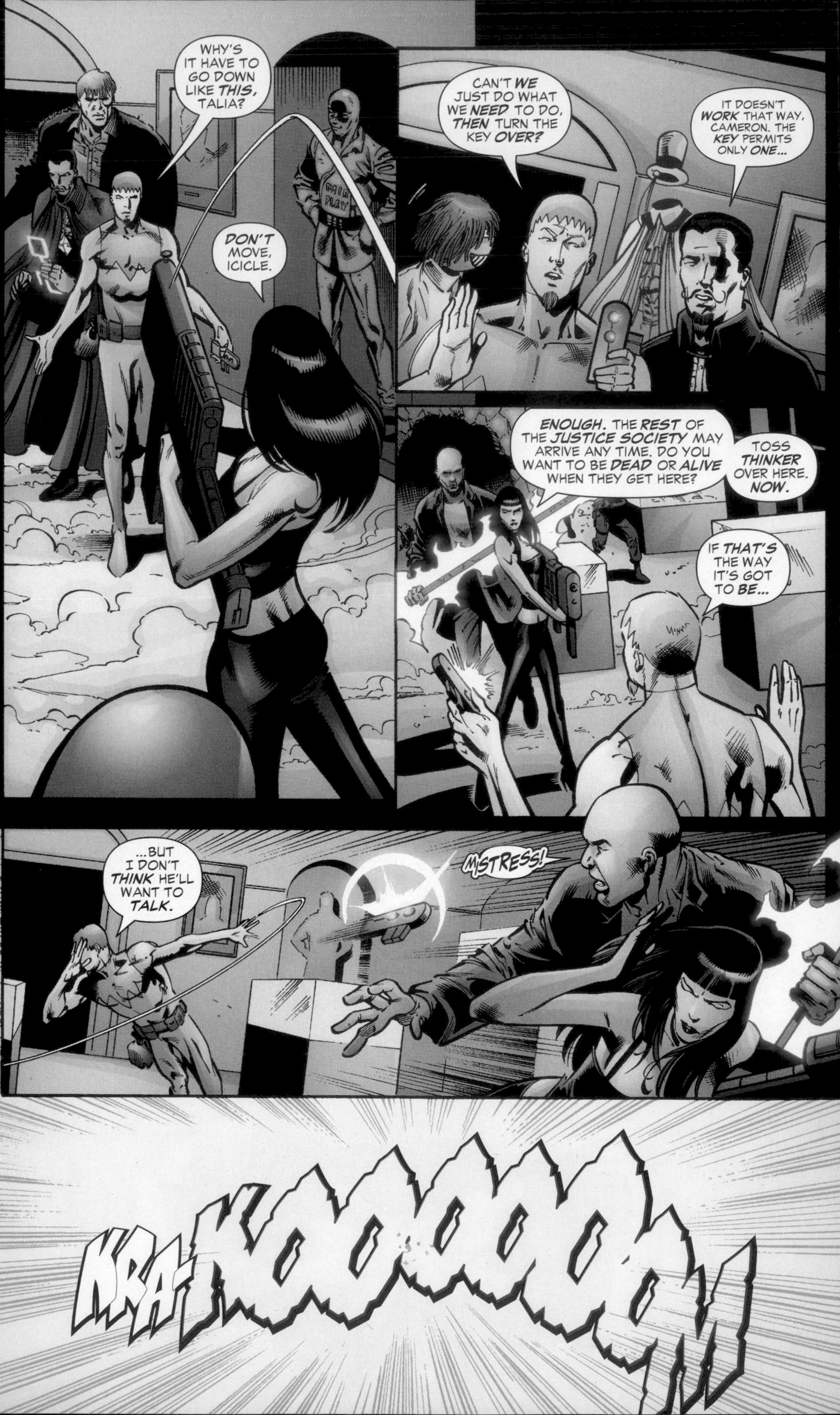
WHY'S IT HAVE TO GO DOWN LIKE THIS, TALIA?
DON'T MOVE, ICICLE.
CAN'T WE JUST DO WHAT WE NEED TO DO, THEN TURN THE KEY OVER?
IT DOESN'T WORK THAT WAY, CAMERON. THE KEY PERMITS ONLY ONE...
ENOUGH. THE REST OF THE JUSTICE SOCIETY MAY ARRIVE ANY TIME. DO YOU WANT TO BE DEAD OR ALIVE WHEN THEY GET HERE?
TOSS THINKER OVER HERE. NOW.
IF THAT'S THE WAY IT'S GOT TO BE...
...BUT I DON'T THINK HE'LL WANT TO TALK.
MISTRESS!
KRA-KOOOOOOOM

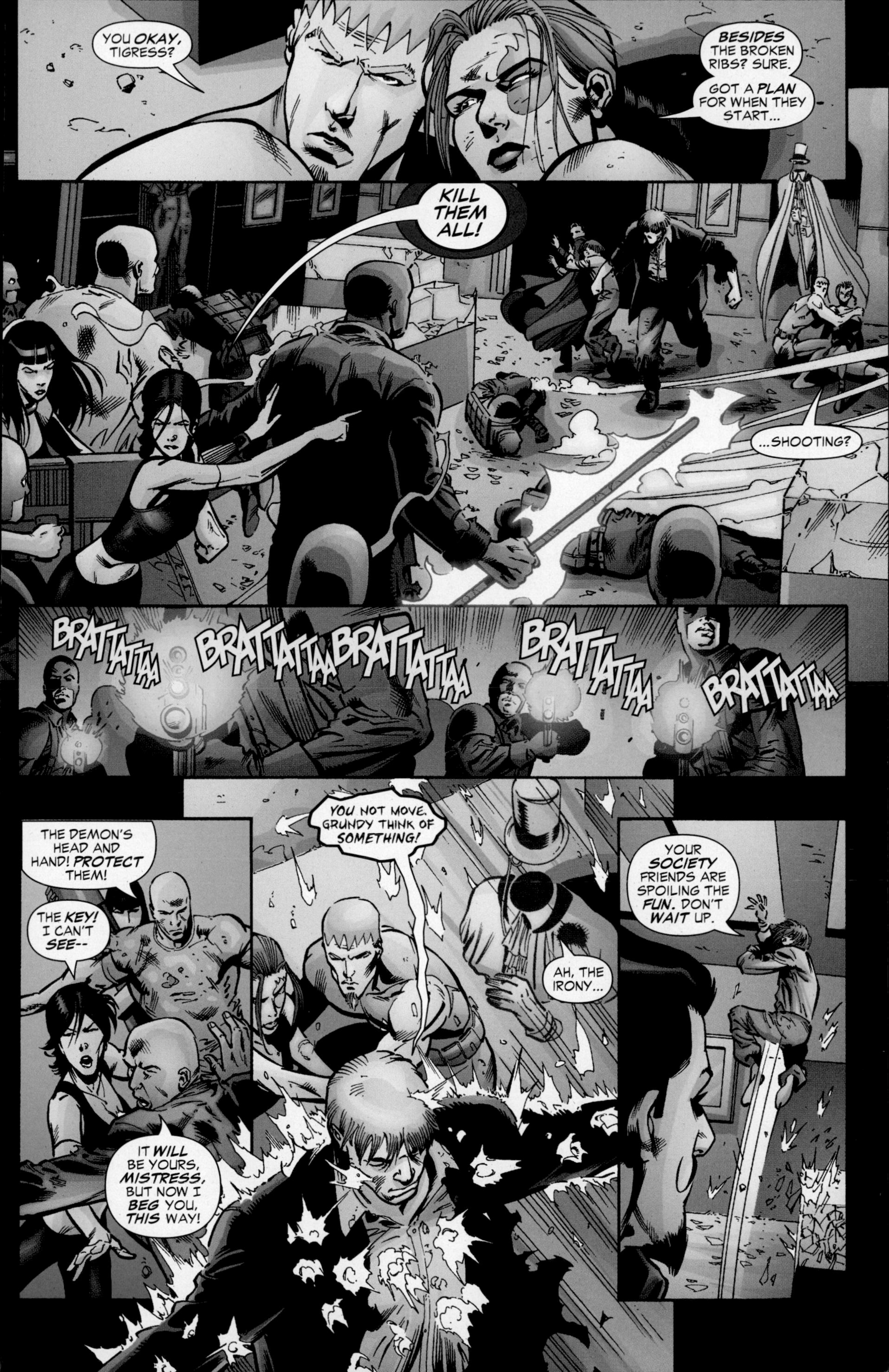

YOU OKAY, TIGRESS?
BESIDES THE BROKEN RIBS? SURE.
GOT A PLAN FOR WHEN THEY START...
KILL THEM ALL!
...SHOOTING?
BRATTATTAA
BRATTATTAA
BRATTATTAA
BRATTATTAA
BRATTATTAA
THE DEMON'S HEAD AND HAND! PROTECT THEM!
THE KEY! I CAN'T SEE--
IT WILL BE YOURS, MISTRESS, BUT NOW I BEG YOU, THIS WAY!
YOU NOT MOVE. GRUNDY THINK OF SOMETHING!
AH, THE IRONY...
YOUR SOCIETY FRIENDS ARE SPOILING THE FUN. DON'T WAIT UP.

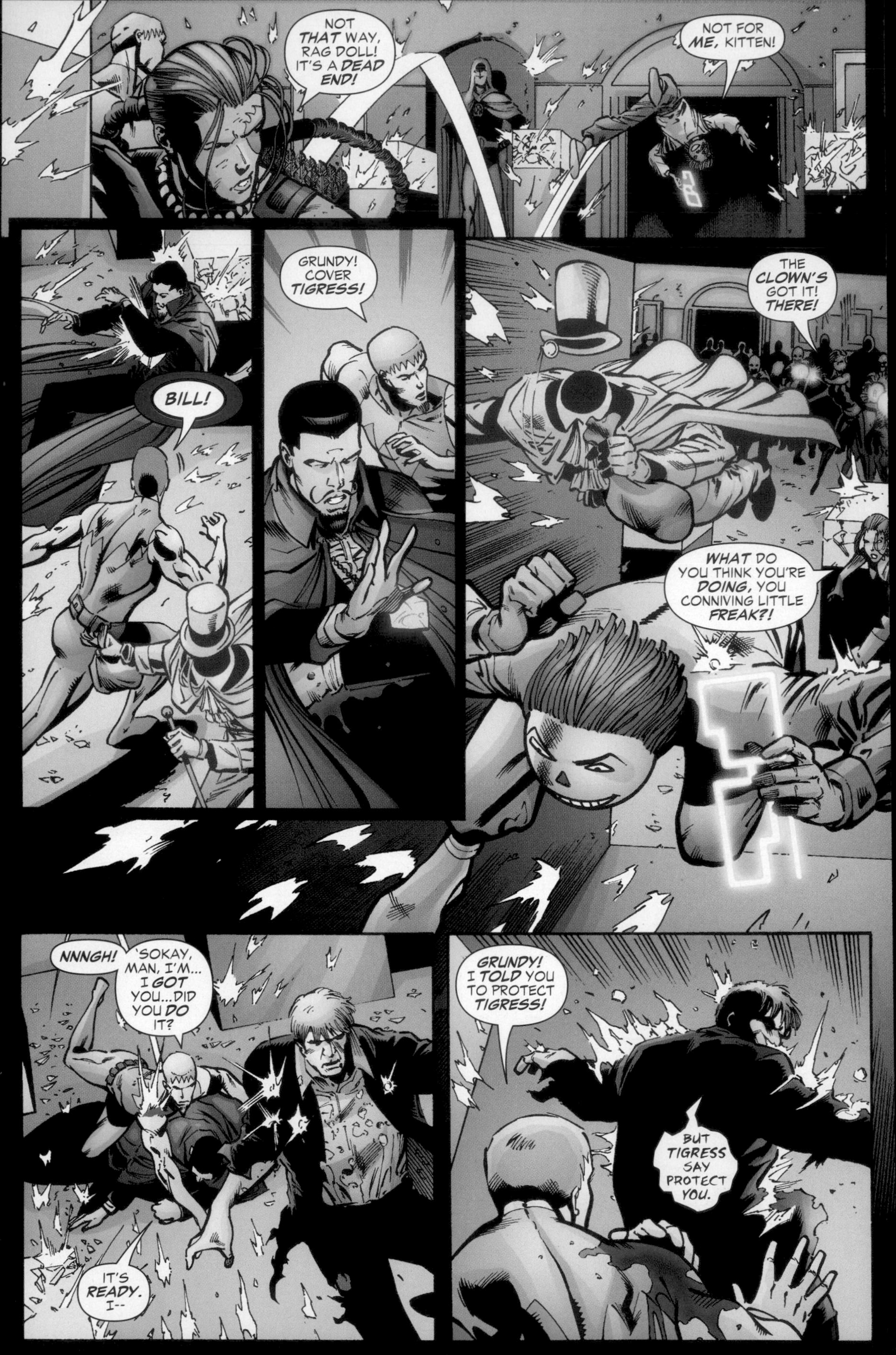
NOT *THAT* WAY, RAG DOLL! IT'S A *DEAD END!*
NOT FOR *ME,* KITTEN!
GRUNDY! COVER *TIGRESS!*
BILL!
THE *CLOWN'S* GOT IT! *THERE!*
WHAT DO YOU THINK YOU'RE *DOING,* YOU CONNIVING LITTLE *FREAK?!*
NNNGH!
'SOKAY, MAN, I'M... I *GOT* YOU...DID YOU *DO* IT?
IT'S *READY.* I--
GRUNDY! I *TOLD* YOU TO PROTECT *TIGRESS!*
BUT *TIGRESS* SAY PROTECT *YOU.*

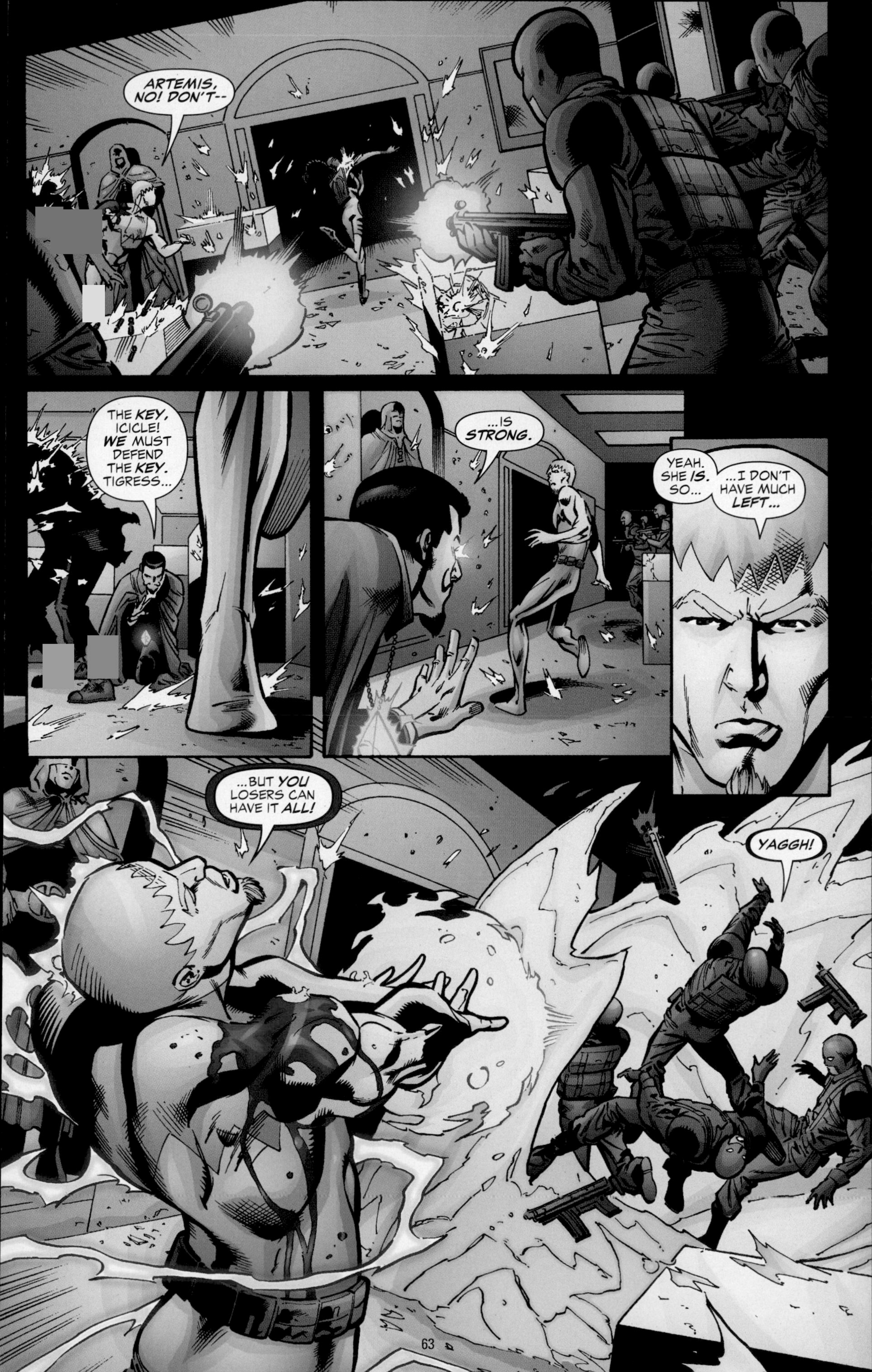
ARTEMIS, NO! DON'T--
THE KEY, ICICLE! WE MUST DEFEND THE KEY. TIGRESS...
...IS STRONG.
YEAH. SHE IS. SO...
...I DON'T HAVE MUCH LEFT...
...BUT YOU LOSERS CAN HAVE IT ALL!
YAGGH!

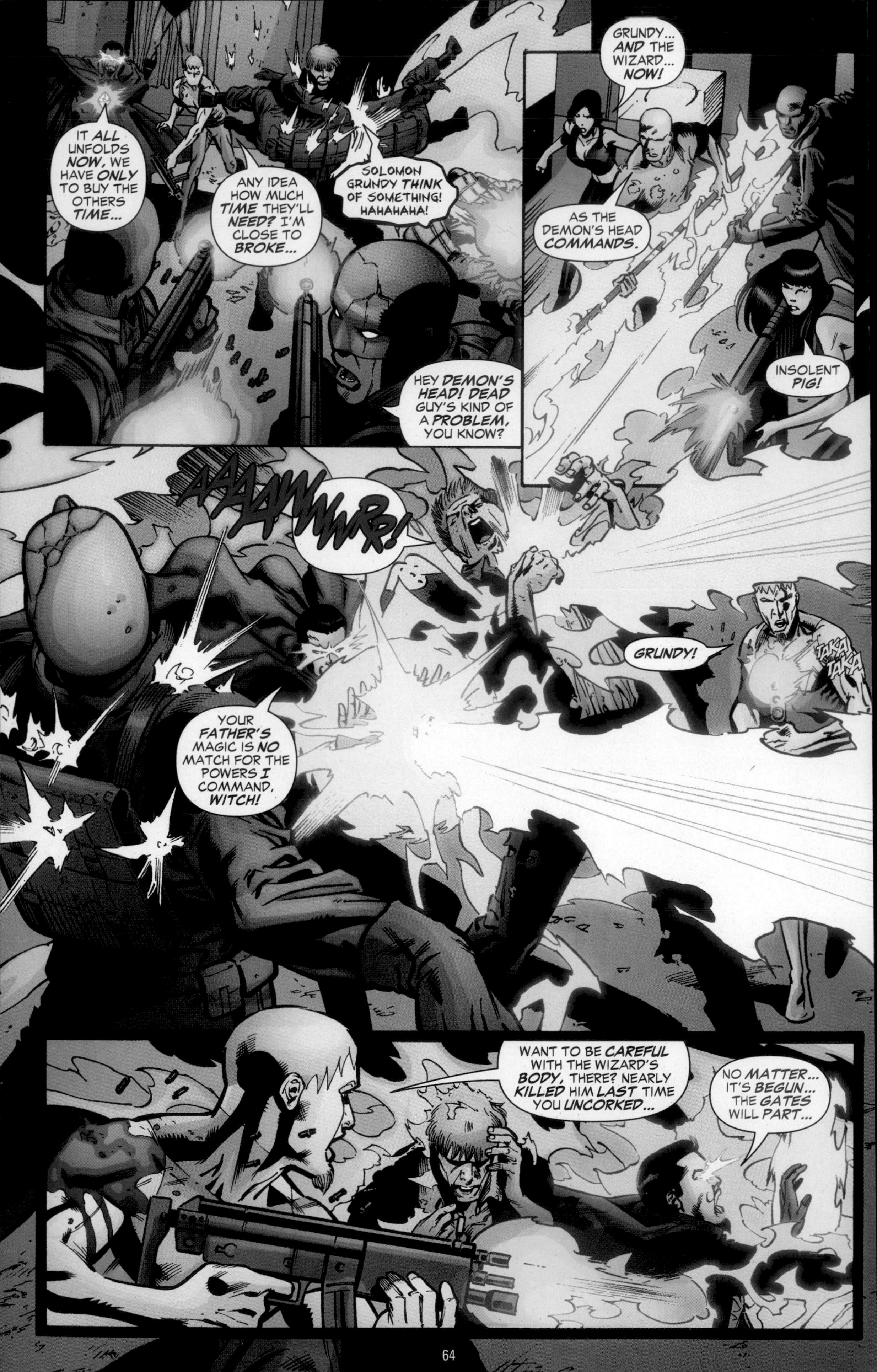
IT ALL UNFOLDS NOW, WE HAVE ONLY TO BUY THE OTHERS TIME...
ANY IDEA HOW MUCH TIME THEY'LL NEED? I'M CLOSE TO BROKE...
SOLOMON GRUNDY THINK OF SOMETHING! HAHAHAHA!
HEY DEMON'S HEAD! DEAD GUY'S KIND OF A PROBLEM, YOU KNOW?
GRUNDY... AND THE WIZARD... NOW!
AS THE DEMON'S HEAD COMMANDS.
INSOLENT PIG!
AAAAWWRR!
GRUNDY!
TAKA TAKA
YOUR FATHER'S MAGIC IS NO MATCH FOR THE POWERS I COMMAND, WITCH!
WANT TO BE CAREFUL WITH THE WIZARD'S BODY, THERE? NEARLY KILLED HIM LAST TIME YOU UNCORKED...
NO MATTER... IT'S BEGUN... THE GATES WILL PART...

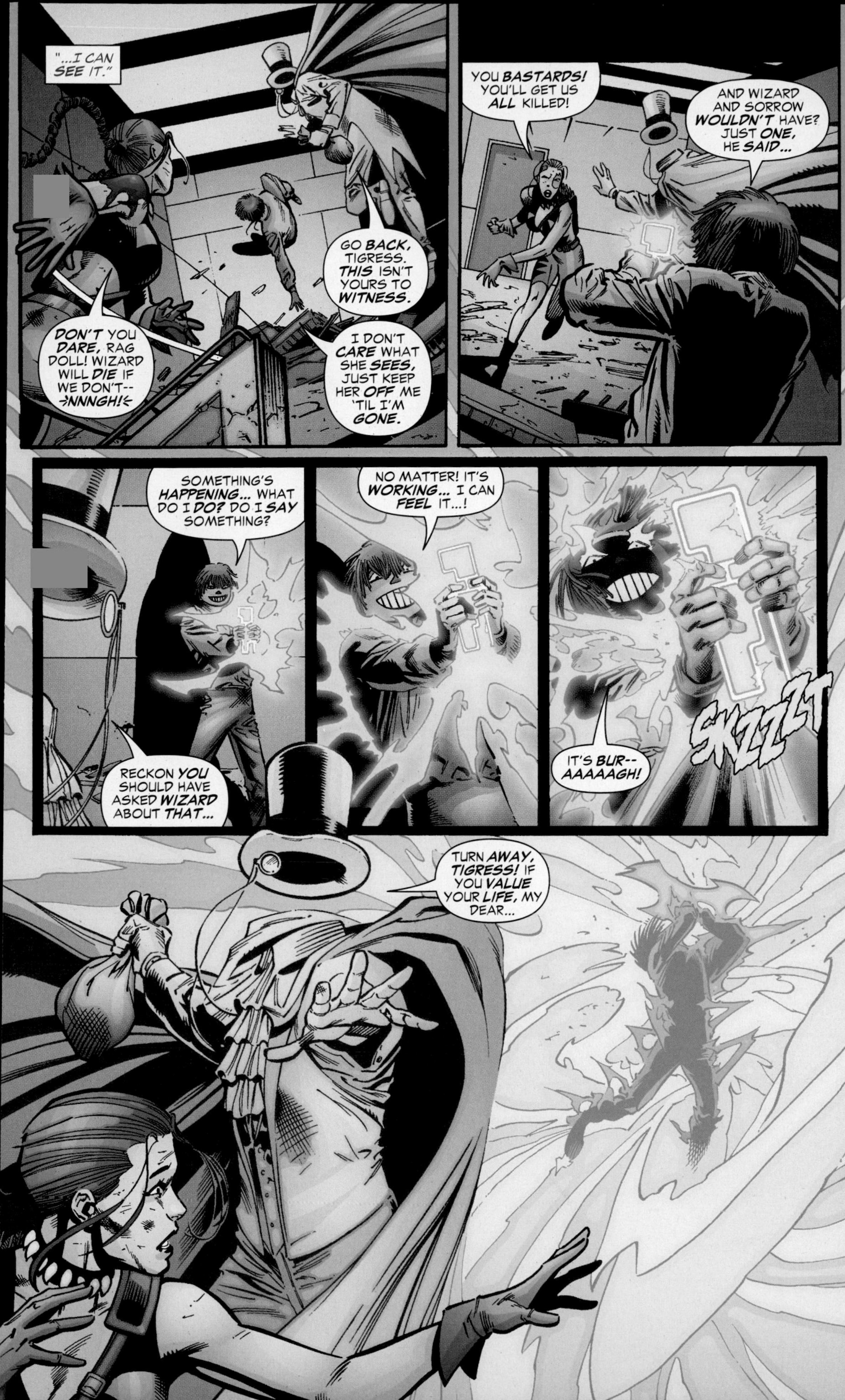
"...I CAN SEE IT."
DON'T YOU DARE, RAG DOLL! WIZARD WILL DIE IF WE DON'T-- NNNGH!
GO BACK, TIGRESS. THIS ISN'T YOURS TO WITNESS.
I DON'T CARE WHAT SHE SEES, JUST KEEP HER OFF ME 'TIL I'M GONE.
YOU BASTARDS! YOU'LL GET US ALL KILLED!
AND WIZARD AND SORROW WOULDN'T HAVE? JUST ONE, HE SAID...
SOMETHING'S HAPPENING... WHAT DO I DO? DO I SAY SOMETHING?
RECKON YOU SHOULD HAVE ASKED WIZARD ABOUT THAT...
NO MATTER! IT'S WORKING... I CAN FEEL IT...!
IT'S BUR-- AAAAAGH!
SKZZZT
TURN AWAY, TIGRESS! IF YOU VALUE YOUR LIFE, MY DEAR...

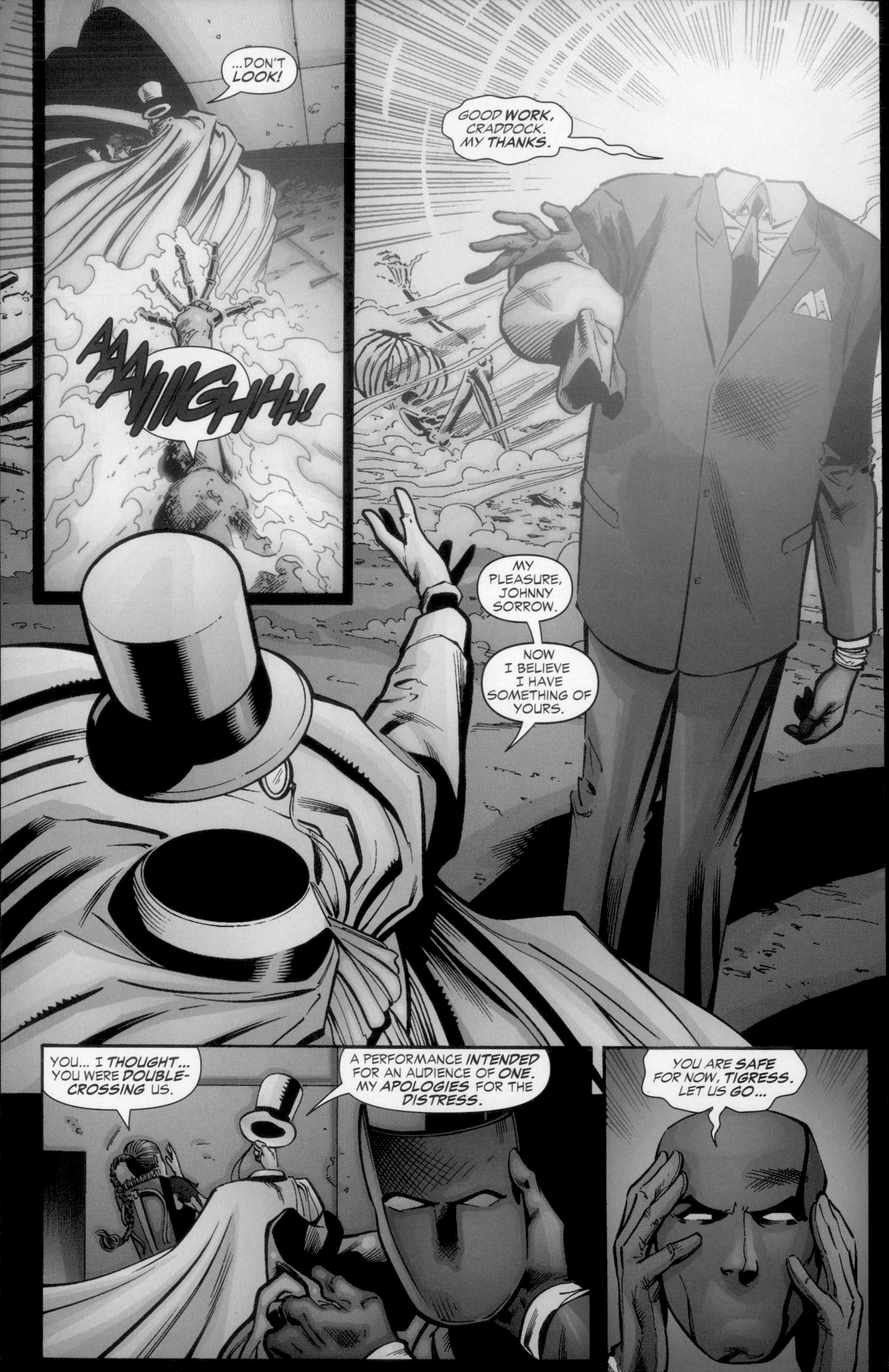
...DON'T LOOK!
AAAIIIGHHH!
GOOD WORK, CRADDOCK. MY THANKS.
MY PLEASURE, JOHNNY SORROW.
NOW I BELIEVE I HAVE SOMETHING OF YOURS.
YOU... I THOUGHT... YOU WERE DOUBLE-CROSSING US.
A PERFORMANCE INTENDED FOR AN AUDIENCE OF ONE. MY APOLOGIES FOR THE DISTRESS.
YOU ARE SAFE FOR NOW, TIGRESS. LET US GO...

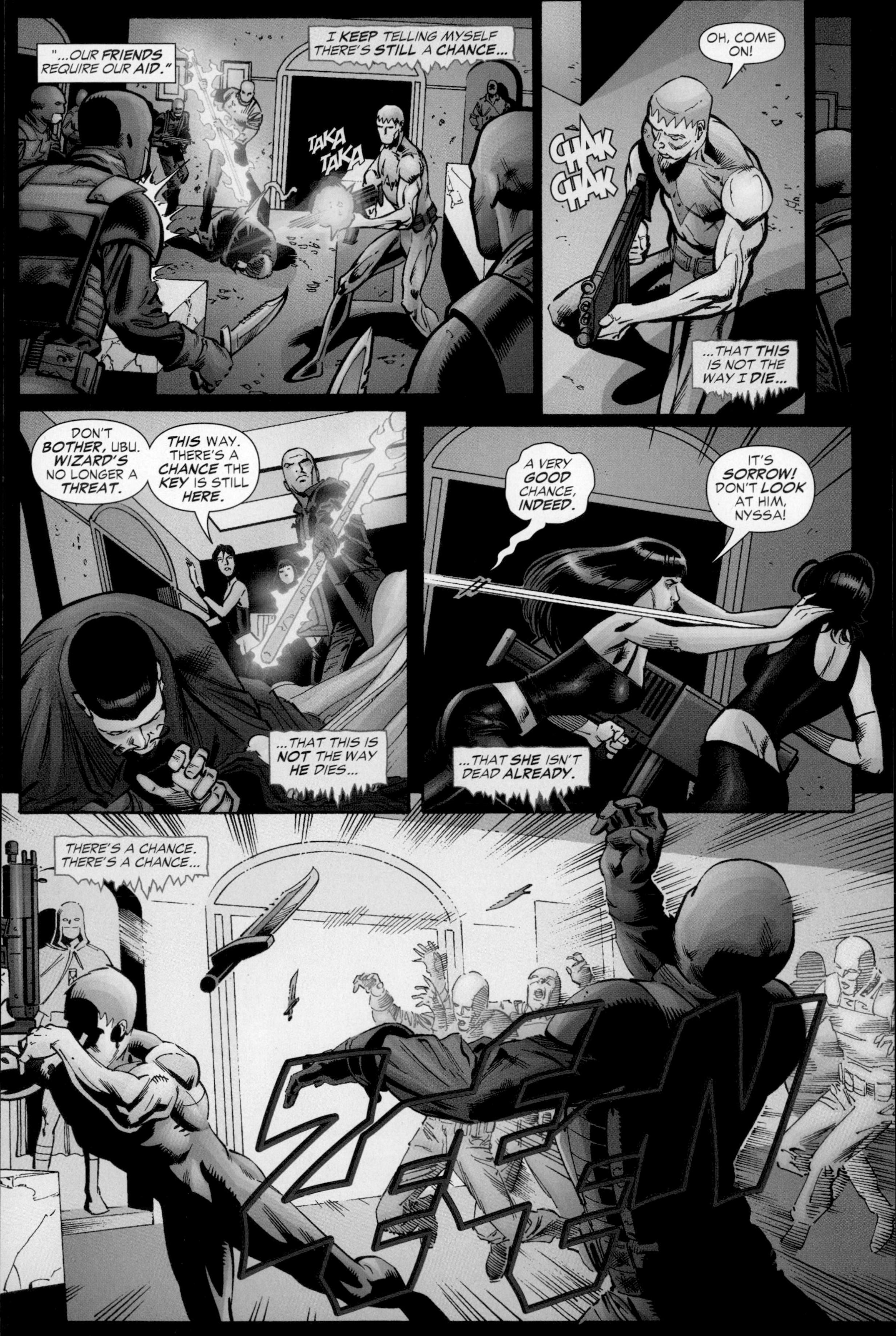
"...OUR FRIENDS REQUIRE OUR AID."
I KEEP TELLING MYSELF THERE'S STILL A CHANCE...
TAKA TAKA
OH, COME ON!
CHAK CHAK
...THAT THIS IS NOT THE WAY I DIE...
DON'T BOTHER, UBU. WIZARD'S NO LONGER A THREAT.
THIS WAY. THERE'S A CHANCE THE KEY IS STILL HERE.
...THAT THIS IS NOT THE WAY HE DIES...
A VERY GOOD CHANCE, INDEED.
IT'S SORROW! DON'T LOOK AT HIM, NYSSA!
...THAT SHE ISN'T DEAD ALREADY.
THERE'S A CHANCE. THERE'S A CHANCE...
ZZZM

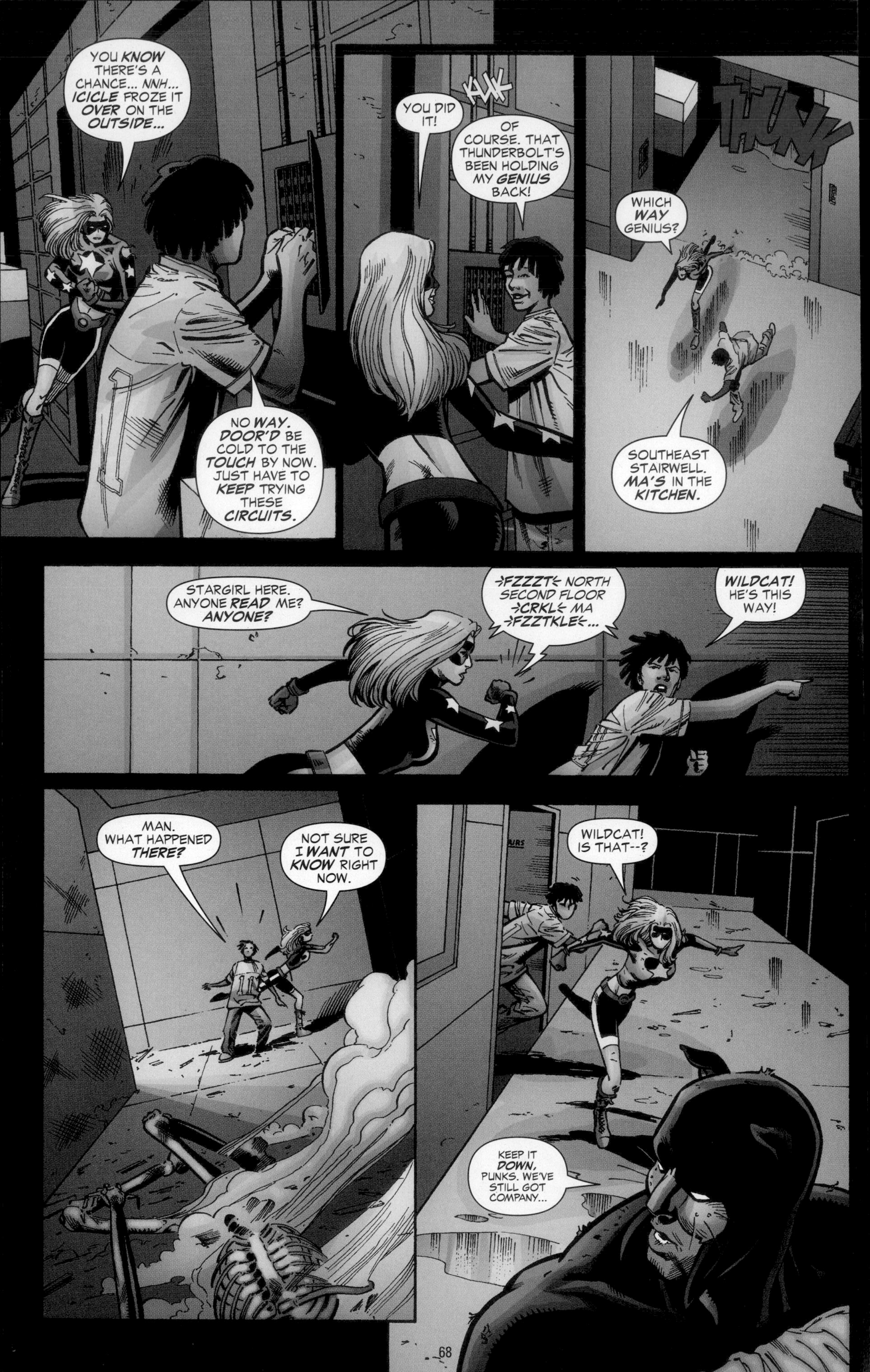
YOU KNOW THERE'S A CHANCE... NNH... ICICLE FROZE IT OVER ON THE OUTSIDE...
NO WAY. DOOR'D BE COLD TO THE TOUCH BY NOW. JUST HAVE TO KEEP TRYING THESE CIRCUITS.
KLIK
YOU DID IT!
OF COURSE. THAT THUNDERBOLT'S BEEN HOLDING MY GENIUS BACK!
THUNK
WHICH WAY GENIUS?
SOUTHEAST STAIRWELL. MA'S IN THE KITCHEN.
STARGIRL HERE. ANYONE READ ME? ANYONE?
FZZZT NORTH SECOND FLOOR CRKL MA FZZTKLE...
WILDCAT! HE'S THIS WAY!
MAN. WHAT HAPPENED THERE?
NOT SURE I WANT TO KNOW RIGHT NOW.
WILDCAT! IS THAT--?
KEEP IT DOWN, PUNKS. WE'VE STILL GOT COMPANY...

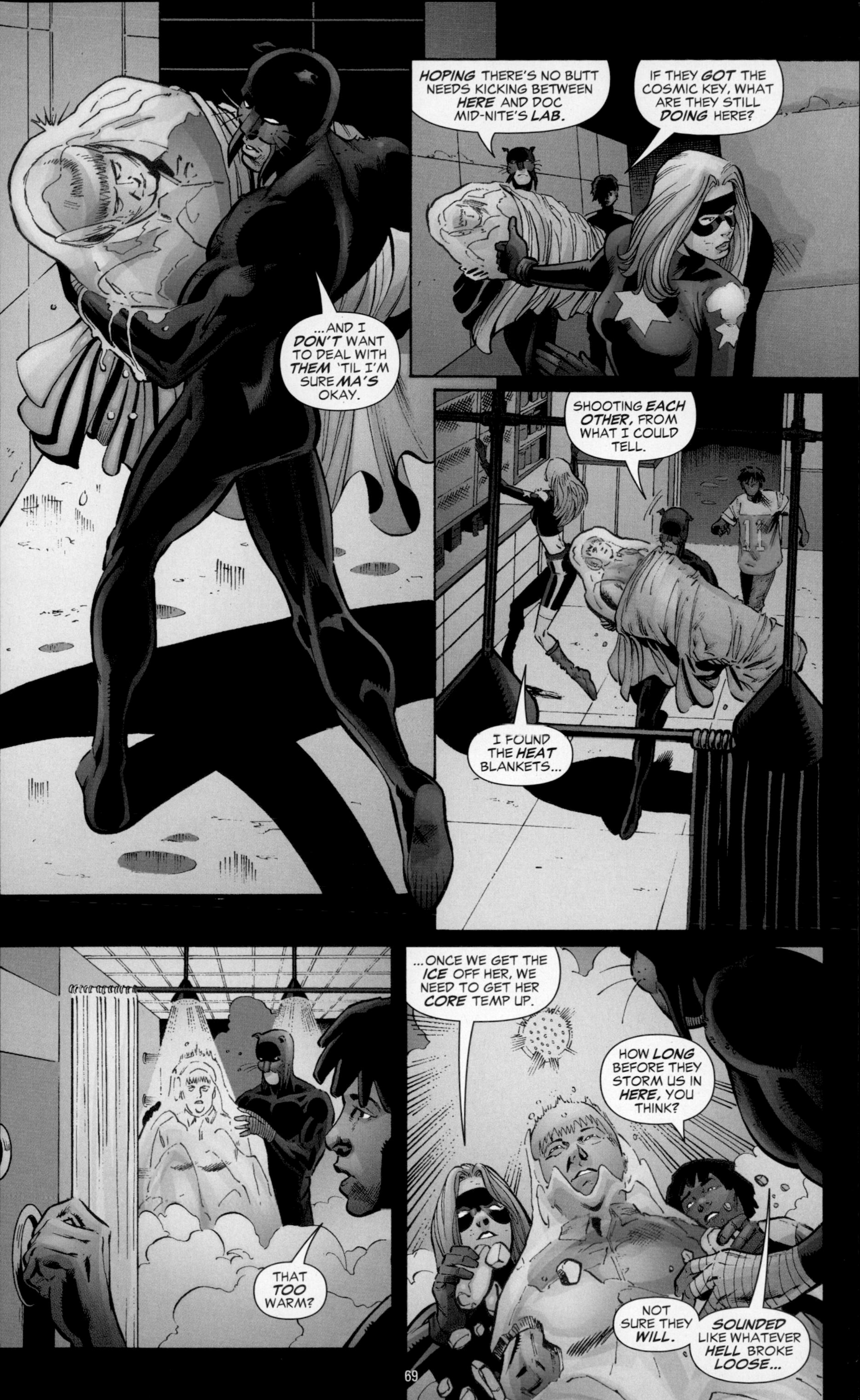
...AND I DON'T WANT TO DEAL WITH THEM 'TIL I'M SURE MA'S OKAY.
HOPING THERE'S NO BUTT NEEDS KICKING BETWEEN HERE AND DOC MID-NITE'S LAB.
IF THEY GOT THE COSMIC KEY, WHAT ARE THEY STILL DOING HERE?
SHOOTING EACH OTHER, FROM WHAT I COULD TELL.
I FOUND THE HEAT BLANKETS...
THAT TOO WARM?
...ONCE WE GET THE ICE OFF HER, WE NEED TO GET HER CORE TEMP UP.
HOW LONG BEFORE THEY STORM US IN HERE, YOU THINK?
NOT SURE THEY WILL.
SOUNDED LIKE WHATEVER HELL BROKE LOOSE...

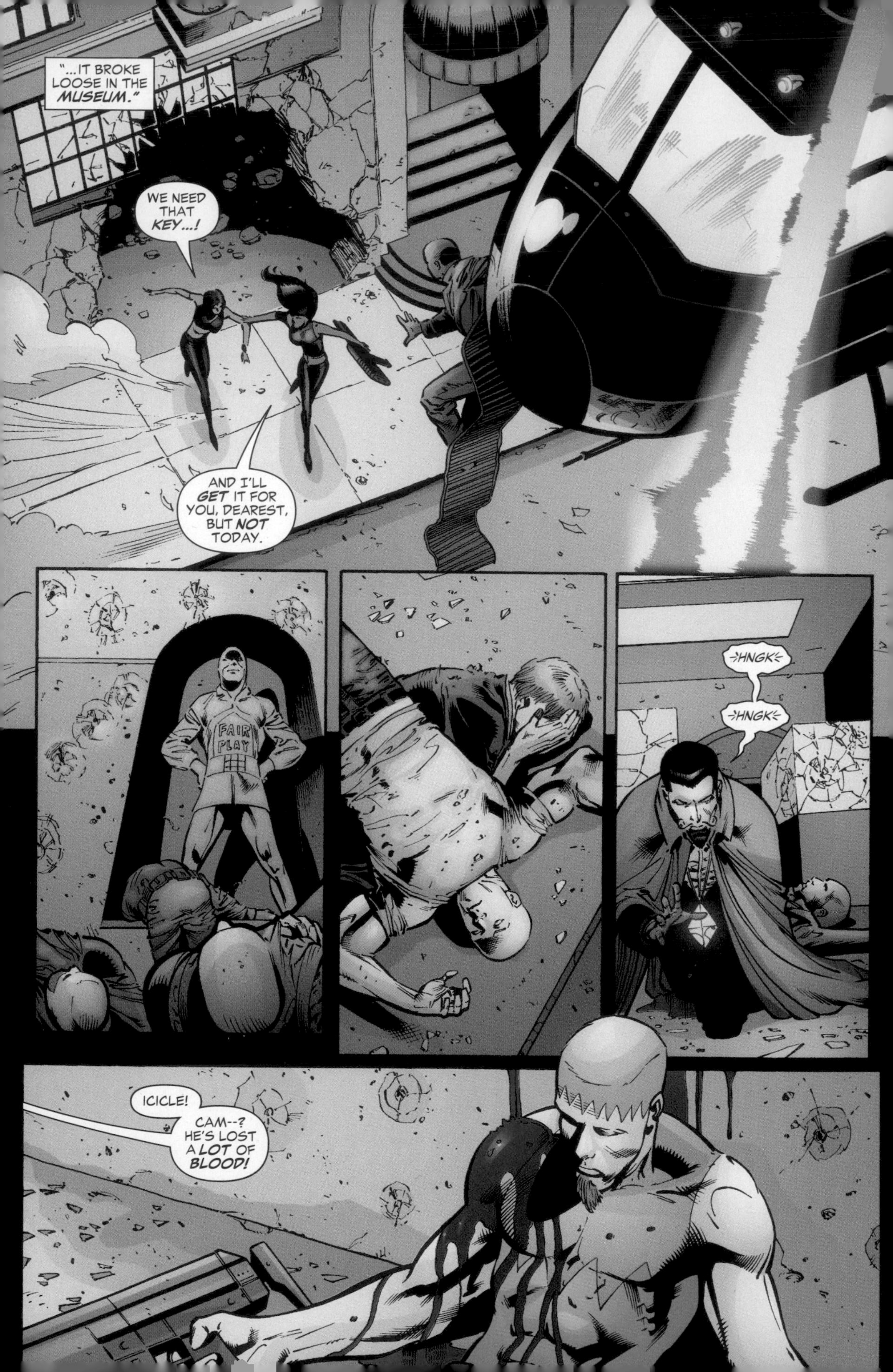
"...IT BROKE LOOSE IN THE MUSEUM."
WE NEED THAT KEY...!
AND I'LL GET IT FOR YOU, DEAREST, BUT NOT TODAY.
FAIR PLAY
HNGK
HNGK
ICICLE!
CAM--? HE'S LOST A LOT OF BLOOD!

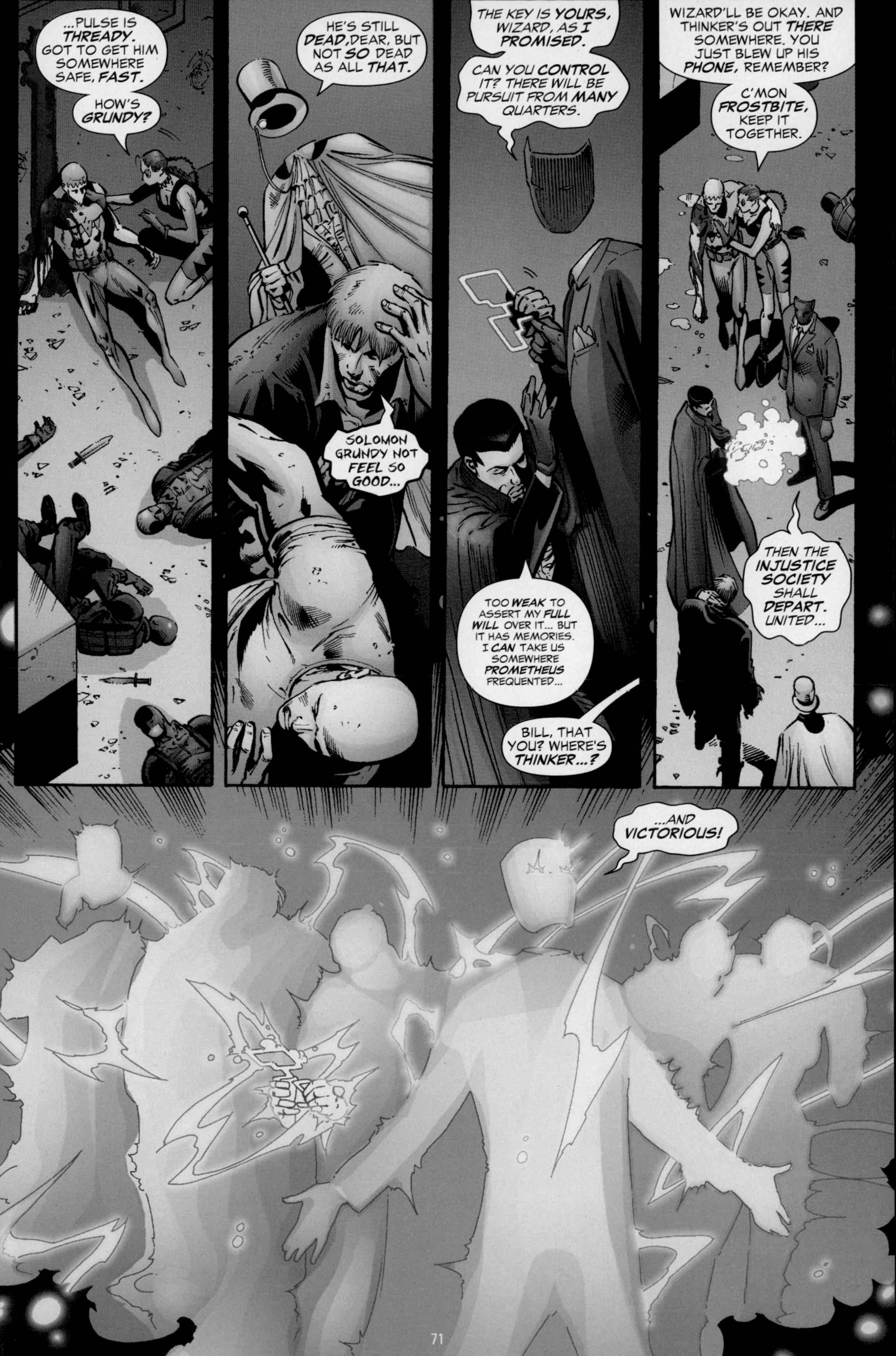

...PULSE IS THREADY. GOT TO GET HIM SOMEWHERE SAFE, FAST.
HOW'S GRUNDY?
HE'S STILL DEAD, DEAR, BUT NOT SO DEAD AS ALL THAT.
SOLOMON GRUNDY NOT FEEL SO GOOD...
THE KEY IS YOURS, WIZARD, AS I PROMISED.
CAN YOU CONTROL IT? THERE WILL BE PURSUIT FROM MANY QUARTERS.
TOO WEAK TO ASSERT MY FULL WILL OVER IT... BUT IT HAS MEMORIES. I CAN TAKE US SOMEWHERE PROMETHEUS FREQUENTED...
BILL, THAT YOU? WHERE'S THINKER...?
WIZARD'LL BE OKAY. AND THINKER'S OUT THERE SOMEWHERE. YOU JUST BLEW UP HIS PHONE, REMEMBER?
C'MON FROSTBITE, KEEP IT TOGETHER.
THEN THE INJUSTICE SOCIETY SHALL DEPART. UNITED...
...AND VICTORIOUS!

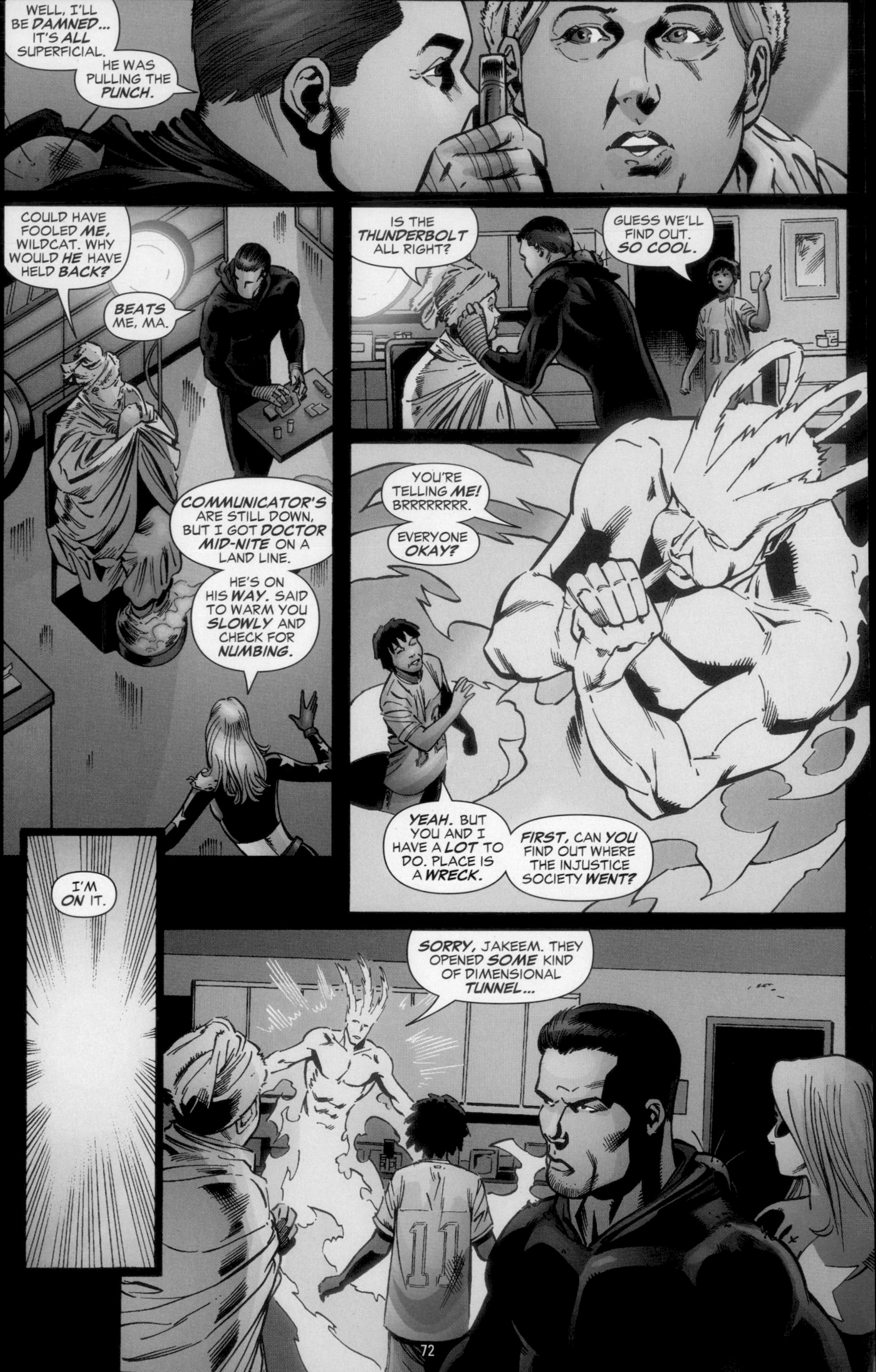

WELL, I'LL BE DAMNED... IT'S ALL SUPERFICIAL.
HE WAS PULLING THE PUNCH.
COULD HAVE FOOLED ME, WILDCAT. WHY WOULD HE HAVE HELD BACK?
BEATS ME, MA.
COMMUNICATOR'S ARE STILL DOWN, BUT I GOT DOCTOR MID-NITE ON A LAND LINE.
HE'S ON HIS WAY. SAID TO WARM YOU SLOWLY AND CHECK FOR NUMBING.
IS THE THUNDERBOLT ALL RIGHT?
GUESS WE'LL FIND OUT. SO COOL.
YOU'RE TELLING ME! BRRRRRRRR.
EVERYONE OKAY?
YEAH. BUT YOU AND I HAVE A LOT TO DO. PLACE IS A WRECK.
FIRST, CAN YOU FIND OUT WHERE THE INJUSTICE SOCIETY WENT?
I'M ON IT.
SORRY, JAKEEM. THEY OPENED SOME KIND OF DIMENSIONAL TUNNEL...

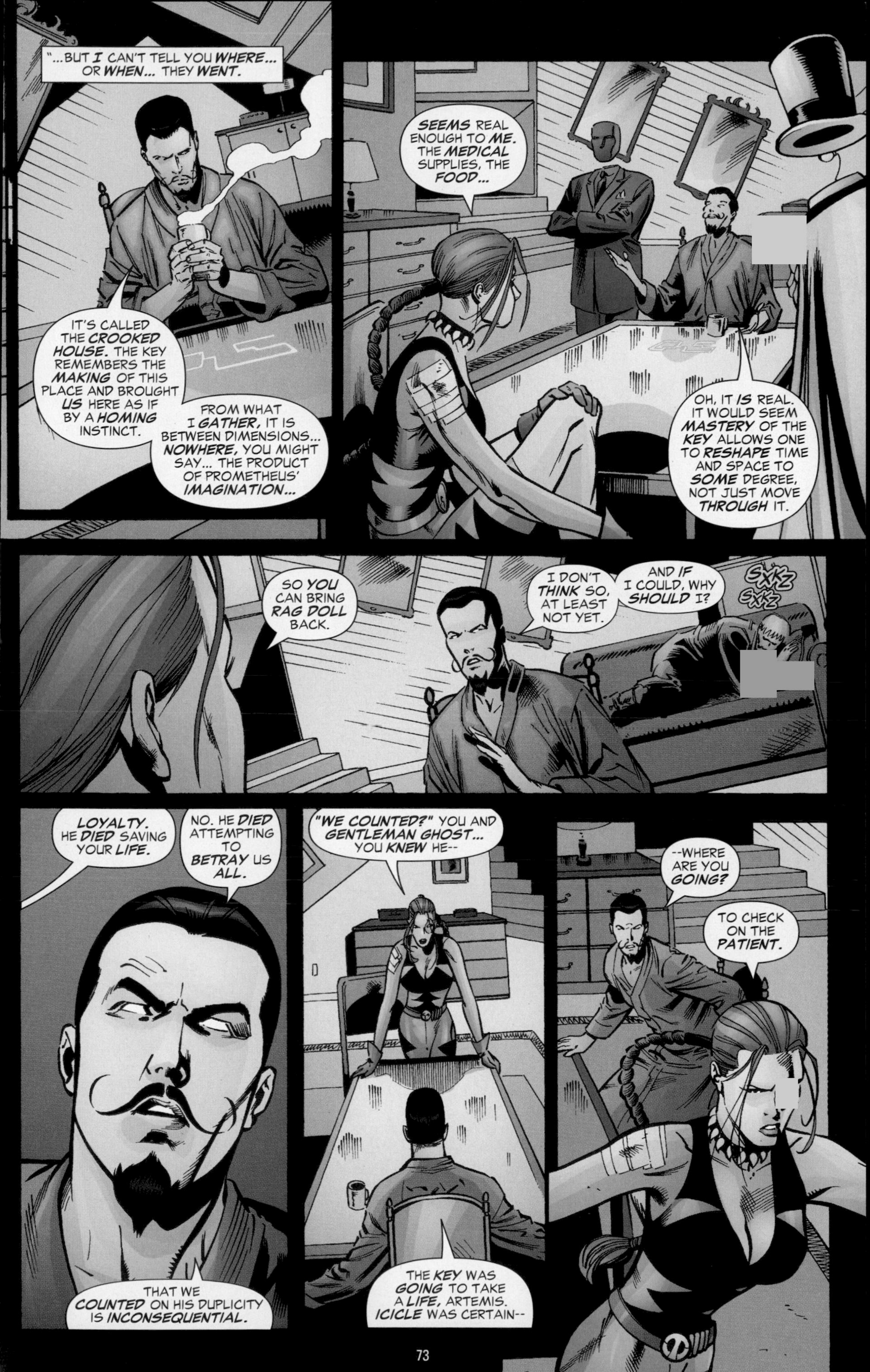
"...BUT I CAN'T TELL YOU WHERE... OR WHEN... THEY WENT.
IT'S CALLED THE CROOKED HOUSE. THE KEY REMEMBERS THE MAKING OF THIS PLACE AND BROUGHT US HERE AS IF BY A HOMING INSTINCT.
FROM WHAT I GATHER, IT IS BETWEEN DIMENSIONS... NOWHERE, YOU MIGHT SAY... THE PRODUCT OF PROMETHEUS' IMAGINATION...
SEEMS REAL ENOUGH TO ME. THE MEDICAL SUPPLIES, THE FOOD...
OH, IT IS REAL. IT WOULD SEEM MASTERY OF THE KEY ALLOWS ONE TO RESHAPE TIME AND SPACE TO SOME DEGREE, NOT JUST MOVE THROUGH IT.
SO YOU CAN BRING RAG DOLL BACK.
I DON'T THINK SO, AT LEAST NOT YET.
AND IF I COULD, WHY SHOULD I?
SXKZ SXKZ
LOYALTY. HE DIED SAVING YOUR LIFE.
NO. HE DIED ATTEMPTING TO BETRAY US ALL.
THAT WE COUNTED ON HIS DUPLICITY IS INCONSEQUENTIAL.
"WE COUNTED?" YOU AND GENTLEMAN GHOST... YOU KNEW HE--
THE KEY WAS GOING TO TAKE A LIFE, ARTEMIS. ICICLE WAS CERTAIN--
--WHERE ARE YOU GOING?
TO CHECK ON THE PATIENT.

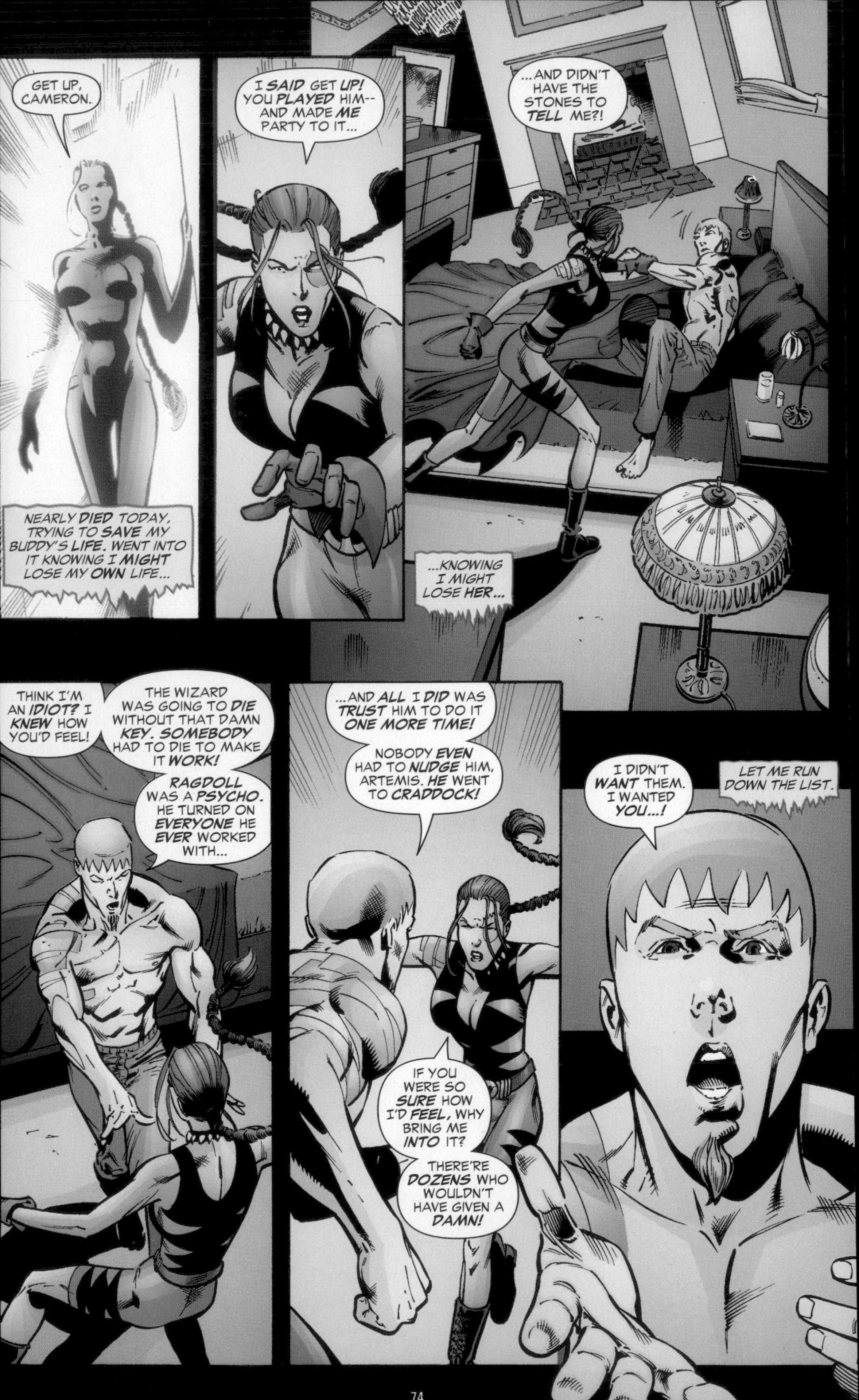

GET UP, CAMERON.
NEARLY DIED TODAY, TRYING TO SAVE MY BUDDY'S LIFE. WENT INTO IT KNOWING I MIGHT LOSE MY OWN LIFE...
I SAID GET UP! YOU PLAYED HIM-- AND MADE ME PARTY TO IT...
...AND DIDN'T HAVE THE STONES TO TELL ME?!
...KNOWING I MIGHT LOSE HER...
THINK I'M AN IDIOT? I KNEW HOW YOU'D FEEL!
THE WIZARD WAS GOING TO DIE WITHOUT THAT DAMN KEY. SOMEBODY HAD TO DIE TO MAKE IT WORK!
RAGDOLL WAS A PSYCHO. HE TURNED ON EVERYONE HE EVER WORKED WITH...
...AND ALL I DID WAS TRUST HIM TO DO IT ONE MORE TIME!
NOBODY EVEN HAD TO NUDGE HIM, ARTEMIS. HE WENT TO CRADDOCK!
IF YOU WERE SO SURE HOW I'D FEEL, WHY BRING ME INTO IT?
THERE'RE DOZENS WHO WOULDN'T HAVE GIVEN A DAMN!
I DIDN'T WANT THEM. I WANTED YOU...!
LET ME RUN DOWN THE LIST.

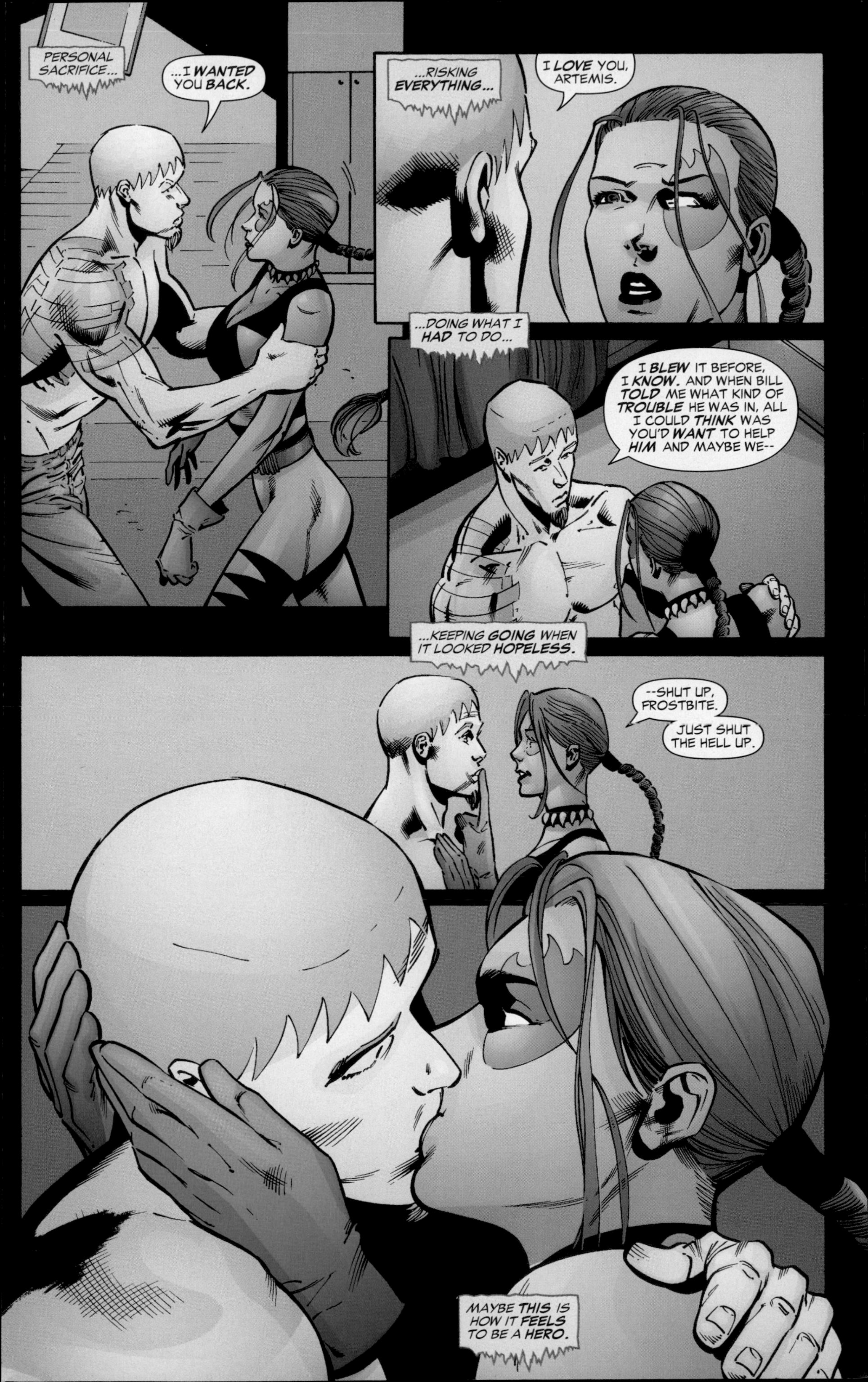
PERSONAL SACRIFICE...
...I WANTED YOU BACK.
...RISKING EVERYTHING...
I LOVE YOU, ARTEMIS.
...DOING WHAT I HAD TO DO...
I BLEW IT BEFORE, I KNOW. AND WHEN BILL TOLD ME WHAT KIND OF TROUBLE HE WAS IN, ALL I COULD THINK WAS YOU'D WANT TO HELP HIM AND MAYBE WE--
...KEEPING GOING WHEN IT LOOKED HOPELESS.
--SHUT UP, FROSTBITE.
JUST SHUT THE HELL UP.
MAYBE THIS IS HOW IT FEELS TO BE A HERO.

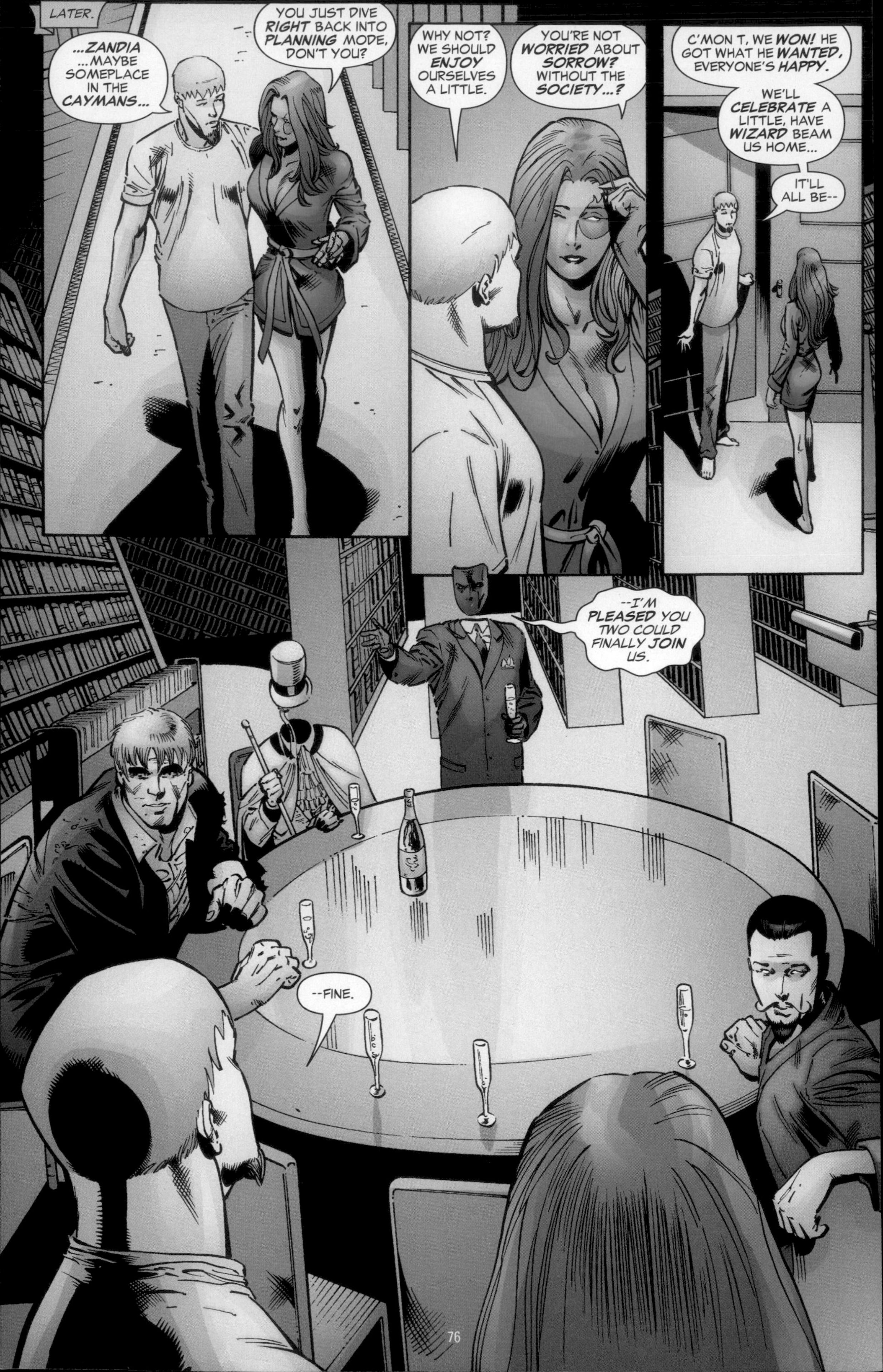
LATER.
...ZANDIA ...MAYBE SOMEPLACE IN THE CAYMANS...
YOU JUST DIVE RIGHT BACK INTO PLANNING MODE, DON'T YOU?
WHY NOT? WE SHOULD ENJOY OURSELVES A LITTLE.
YOU'RE NOT WORRIED ABOUT SORROW? WITHOUT THE SOCIETY...?
C'MON T, WE WON! HE GOT WHAT HE WANTED, EVERYONE'S HAPPY.
WE'LL CELEBRATE A LITTLE, HAVE WIZARD BEAM US HOME...
IT'LL ALL BE--
--I'M PLEASED YOU TWO COULD FINALLY JOIN US.
--FINE.

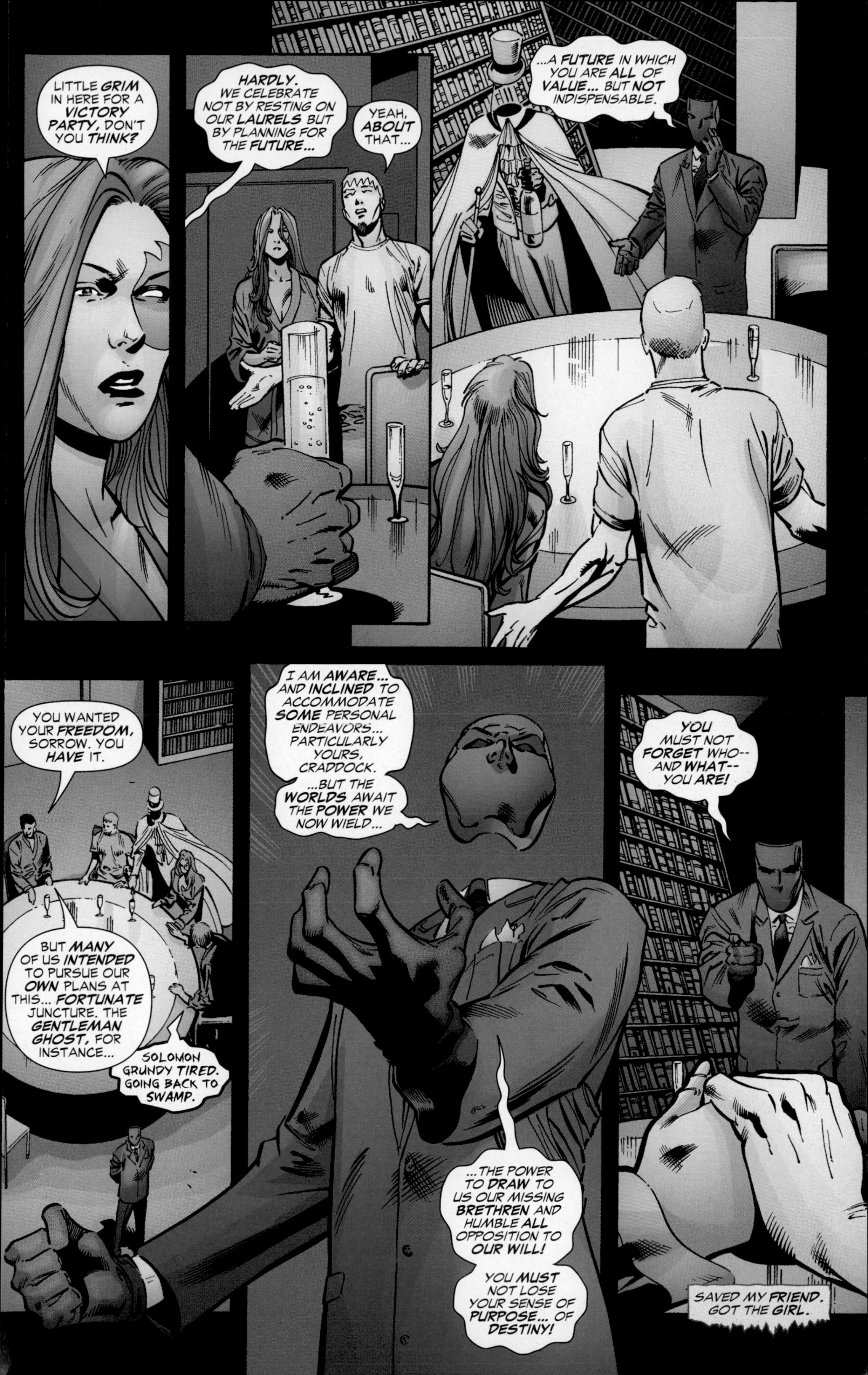
LITTLE GRIM IN HERE FOR A VICTORY PARTY, DON'T YOU THINK?
HARDLY. WE CELEBRATE NOT BY RESTING ON OUR LAURELS BUT BY PLANNING FOR THE FUTURE...
YEAH, ABOUT THAT...
...A FUTURE IN WHICH YOU ARE ALL OF VALUE... BUT NOT INDISPENSABLE.
YOU WANTED YOUR FREEDOM, SORROW. YOU HAVE IT.
BUT MANY OF US INTENDED TO PURSUE OUR OWN PLANS AT THIS... FORTUNATE JUNCTURE. THE GENTLEMAN GHOST, FOR INSTANCE...
SOLOMON GRUNDY TIRED. GOING BACK TO SWAMP.
I AM AWARE... AND INCLINED TO ACCOMMODATE SOME PERSONAL ENDEAVORS... PARTICULARLY YOURS, CRADDOCK.
...BUT THE WORLDS AWAIT THE POWER WE NOW WIELD...
...THE POWER TO DRAW TO US OUR MISSING BRETHREN AND HUMBLE ALL OPPOSITION TO OUR WILL!
YOU MUST NOT LOSE YOUR SENSE OF PURPOSE... OF DESTINY!
YOU MUST NOT FORGET WHO-- AND WHAT-- YOU ARE!
SAVED MY FRIEND. GOT THE GIRL.

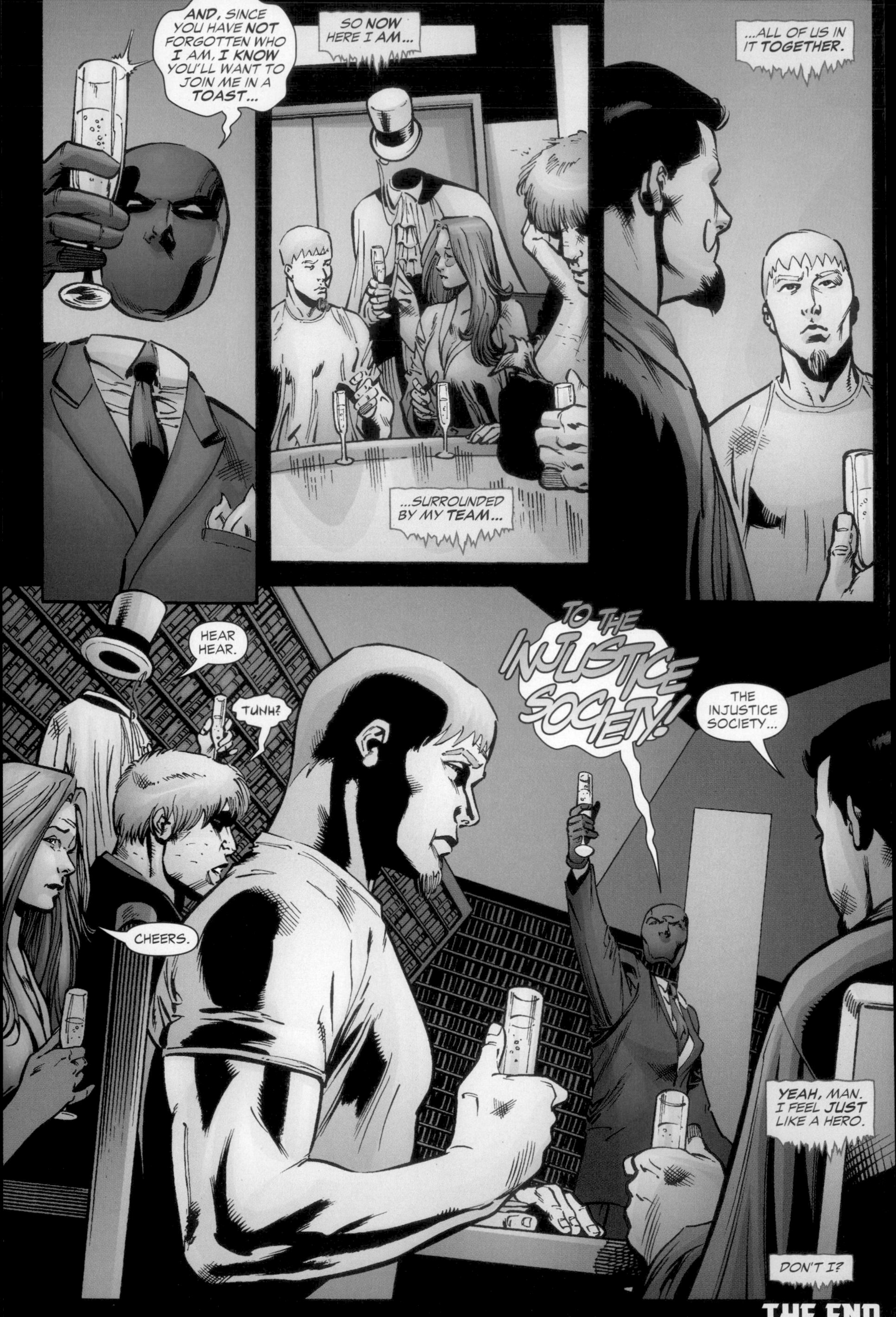
AND, SINCE YOU HAVE NOT FORGOTTEN WHO I AM, I KNOW YOU'LL WANT TO JOIN ME IN A TOAST...
SO NOW HERE I AM...
...SURROUNDED BY MY TEAM...
...ALL OF US IN IT TOGETHER.
HEAR HEAR.
TUNH?
TO THE INJUSTICE SOCIETY!
THE INJUSTICE SOCIETY...
CHEERS.
YEAH, MAN. I FEEL JUST LIKE A HERO.
DON'T I?
THE END.

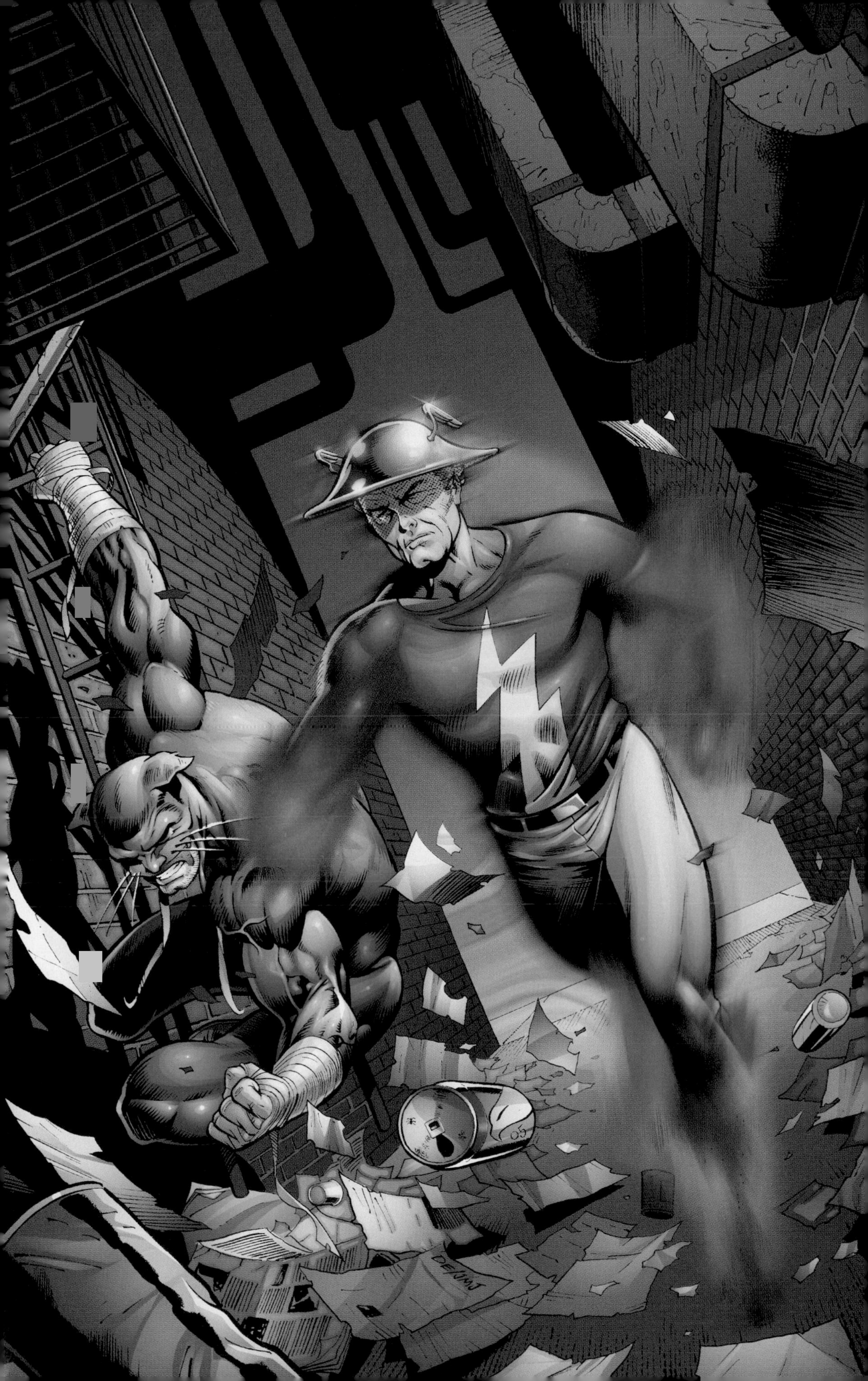

THE SPEAR AND THE DRAGON

Peter J. Tomasi Writer
Don Kramer Penciller
Keith Champagne Inkers
John Kalisz Colorist
Rob Leigh Letterer
Dale Eaglesham, Jose Marzan, Jr. & Ruy Jose Original Covers

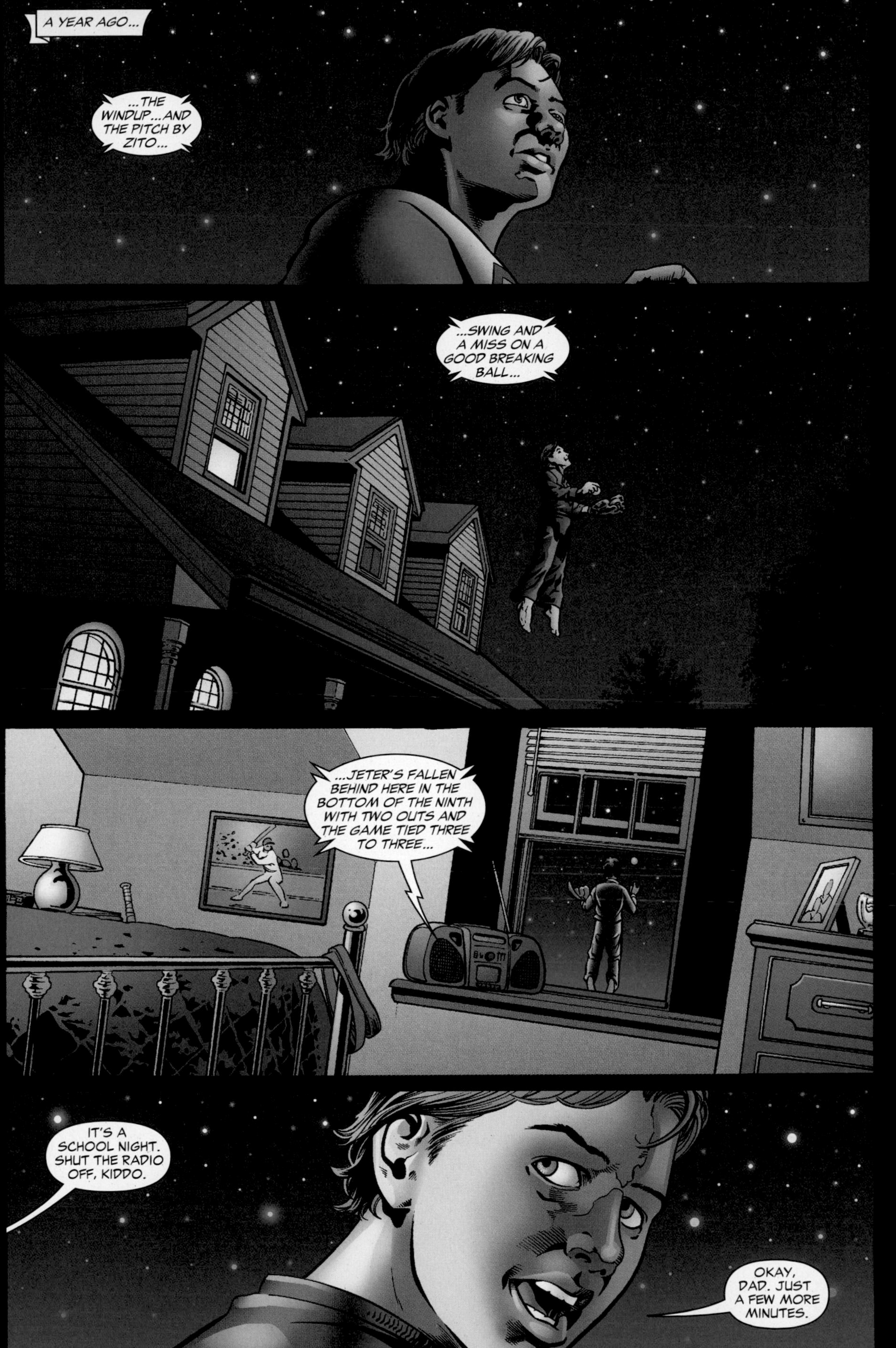
A YEAR AGO...
...THE WINDUP...AND THE PITCH BY ZITO...
...SWING AND A MISS ON A GOOD BREAKING BALL...
...JETER'S FALLEN BEHIND HERE IN THE BOTTOM OF THE NINTH WITH TWO OUTS AND THE GAME TIED THREE TO THREE...
IT'S A SCHOOL NIGHT. SHUT THE RADIO OFF, KIDDO.
OKAY, DAD. JUST A FEW MORE MINUTES.

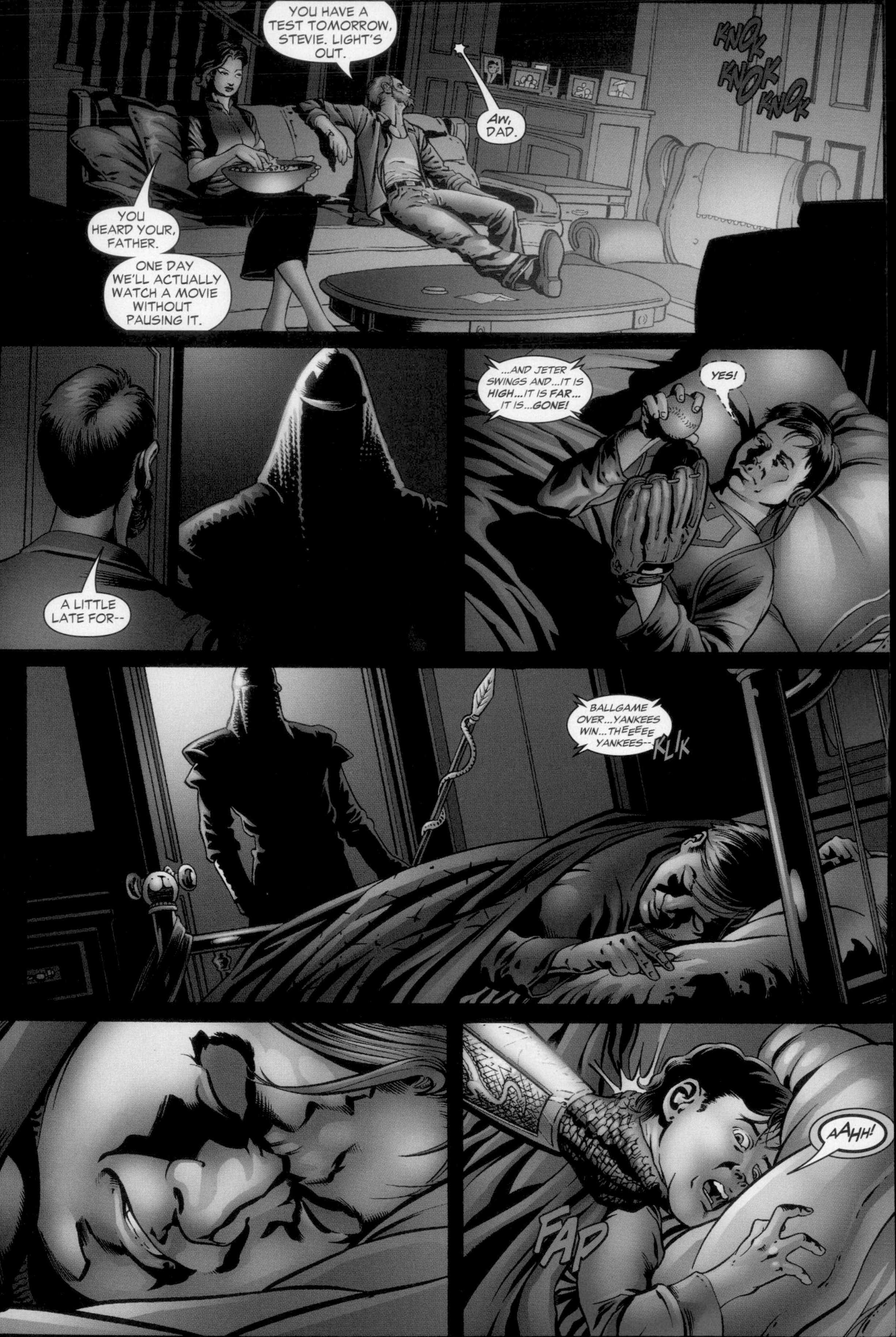
YOU HAVE A TEST TOMORROW, STEVIE. LIGHT'S OUT.
AW, DAD.
KNOK KNOK KNOK
YOU HEARD YOUR, FATHER.
ONE DAY WE'LL ACTUALLY WATCH A MOVIE WITHOUT PAUSING IT.
A LITTLE LATE FOR--
...AND JETER SWINGS AND...IT IS HIGH...IT IS FAR... IT IS...GONE!
YES!
BALLGAME OVER...YANKEES WIN...THEEEEE YANKEES--
KLIK
AAHH!
FAP

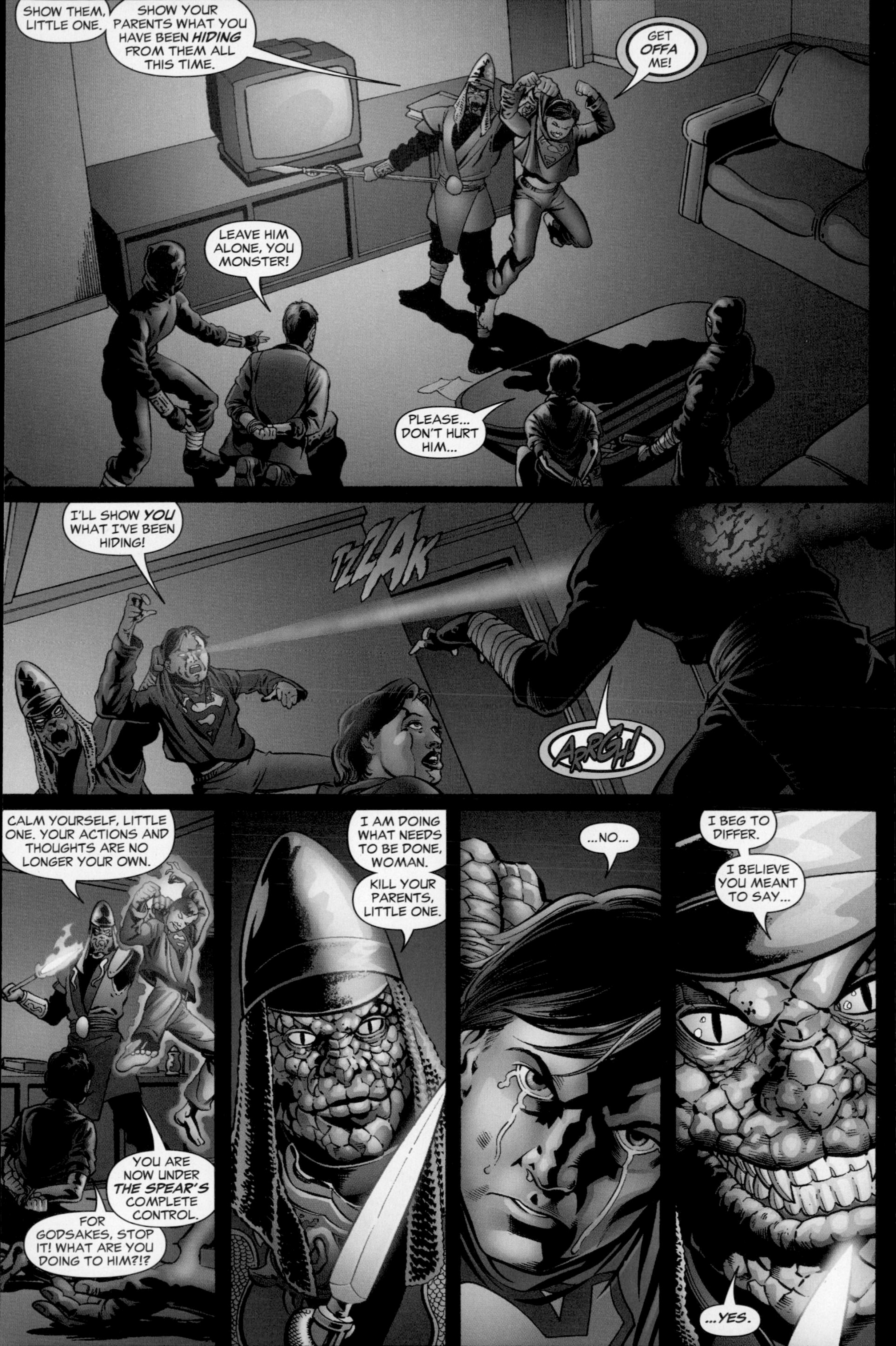
SHOW THEM, LITTLE ONE.
SHOW YOUR PARENTS WHAT YOU HAVE BEEN HIDING FROM THEM ALL THIS TIME.
GET OFFA ME!
LEAVE HIM ALONE, YOU MONSTER!
PLEASE... DON'T HURT HIM...
I'LL SHOW YOU WHAT I'VE BEEN HIDING!
TZZAK
ARRGH!
CALM YOURSELF, LITTLE ONE. YOUR ACTIONS AND THOUGHTS ARE NO LONGER YOUR OWN.
YOU ARE NOW UNDER THE SPEAR'S COMPLETE CONTROL.
FOR GODSAKES, STOP IT! WHAT ARE YOU DOING TO HIM?!?
I AM DOING WHAT NEEDS TO BE DONE, WOMAN.
KILL YOUR PARENTS, LITTLE ONE.
...NO...
I BEG TO DIFFER.
I BELIEVE YOU MEANT TO SAY...
...YES.

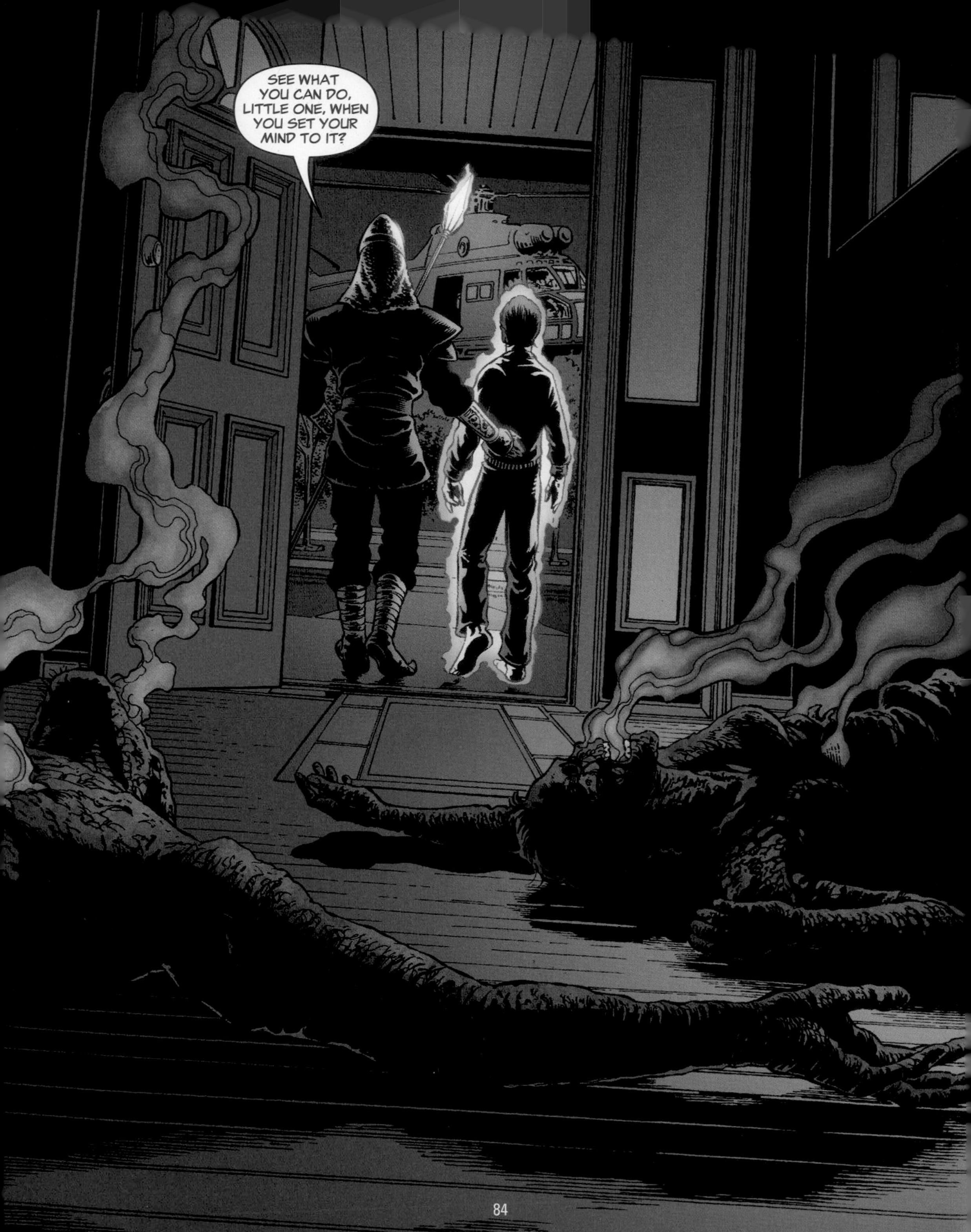
SEE WHAT YOU CAN DO, LITTLE ONE, WHEN YOU SET YOUR MIND TO IT?

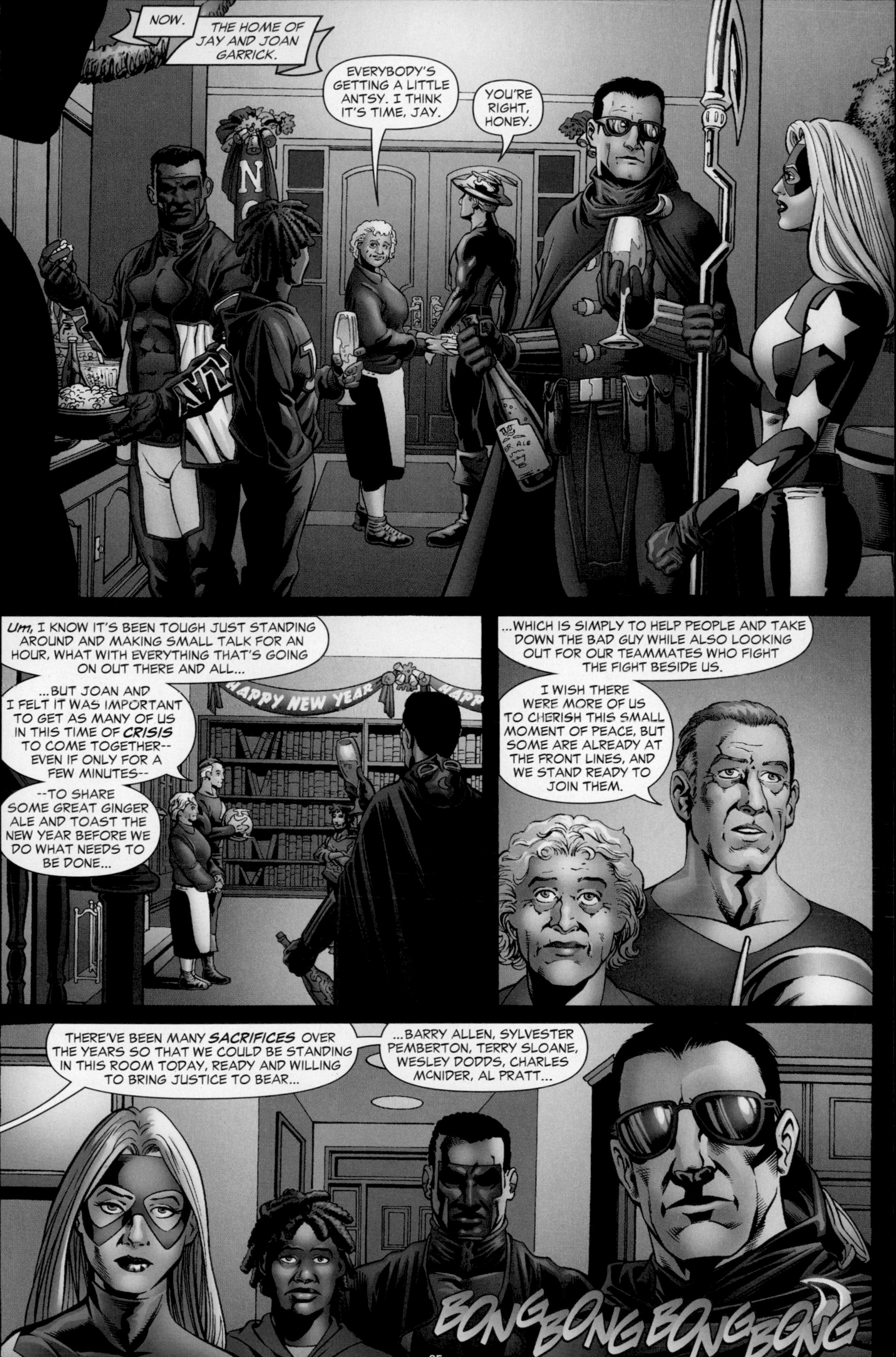
NOW.
THE HOME OF JAY AND JOAN GARRICK.
EVERYBODY'S GETTING A LITTLE ANTSY. I THINK IT'S TIME, JAY.
YOU'RE RIGHT, HONEY.
Um, I KNOW IT'S BEEN TOUGH JUST STANDING AROUND AND MAKING SMALL TALK FOR AN HOUR, WHAT WITH EVERYTHING THAT'S GOING ON OUT THERE AND ALL...
...BUT JOAN AND I FELT IT WAS IMPORTANT TO GET AS MANY OF US IN THIS TIME OF CRISIS TO COME TOGETHER-- EVEN IF ONLY FOR A FEW MINUTES--
--TO SHARE SOME GREAT GINGER ALE AND TOAST THE NEW YEAR BEFORE WE DO WHAT NEEDS TO BE DONE...
HAPPY NEW YEAR
...WHICH IS SIMPLY TO HELP PEOPLE AND TAKE DOWN THE BAD GUY WHILE ALSO LOOKING OUT FOR OUR TEAMMATES WHO FIGHT THE FIGHT BESIDE US.
I WISH THERE WERE MORE OF US TO CHERISH THIS SMALL MOMENT OF PEACE, BUT SOME ARE ALREADY AT THE FRONT LINES, AND WE STAND READY TO JOIN THEM.
THERE'VE BEEN MANY SACRIFICES OVER THE YEARS SO THAT WE COULD BE STANDING IN THIS ROOM TODAY, READY AND WILLING TO BRING JUSTICE TO BEAR...
...BARRY ALLEN, SYLVESTER PEMBERTON, TERRY SLOANE, WESLEY DODDS, CHARLES MCNIDER, AL PRATT...
BONG BONG BONG BONG

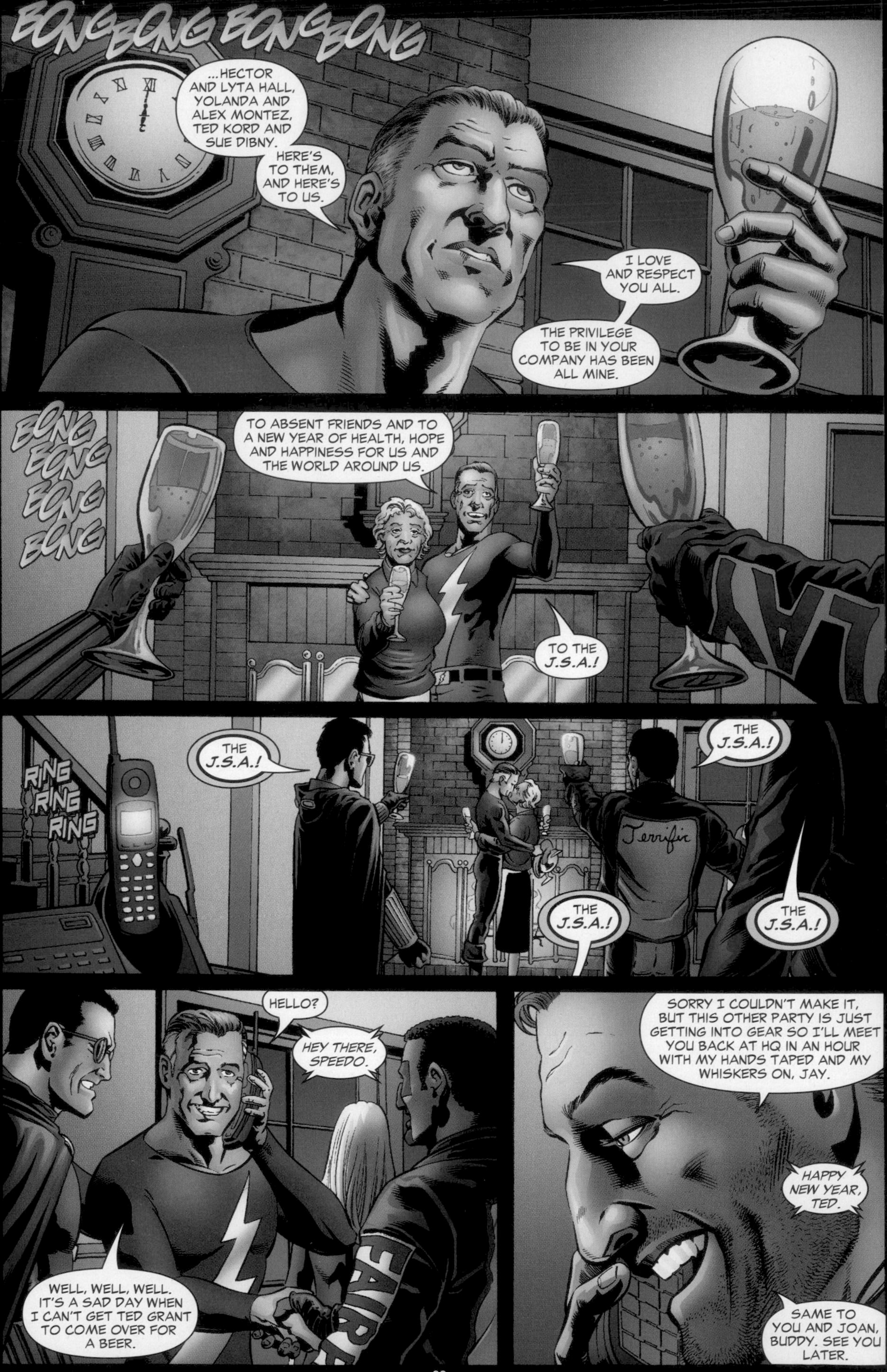
BONG BONG BONG BONG
...HECTOR AND LYTA HALL, YOLANDA AND ALEX MONTEZ, TED KORD AND SUE DIBNY.
HERE'S TO THEM, AND HERE'S TO US.
I LOVE AND RESPECT YOU ALL.
THE PRIVILEGE TO BE IN YOUR COMPANY HAS BEEN ALL MINE.
BONG BONG BONG BONG
TO ABSENT FRIENDS AND TO A NEW YEAR OF HEALTH, HOPE AND HAPPINESS FOR US AND THE WORLD AROUND US.
TO THE J.S.A.!
RING RING RING
THE J.S.A.!
THE J.S.A.!
THE J.S.A.!
THE J.S.A.!
Terrific
HELLO?
HEY THERE, SPEEDO.
WELL, WELL, WELL. IT'S A SAD DAY WHEN I CAN'T GET TED GRANT TO COME OVER FOR A BEER.
SORRY I COULDN'T MAKE IT, BUT THIS OTHER PARTY IS JUST GETTING INTO GEAR SO I'LL MEET YOU BACK AT HQ IN AN HOUR WITH MY HANDS TAPED AND MY WHISKERS ON, JAY.
HAPPY NEW YEAR, TED.
SAME TO YOU AND JOAN, BUDDY. SEE YOU LATER.

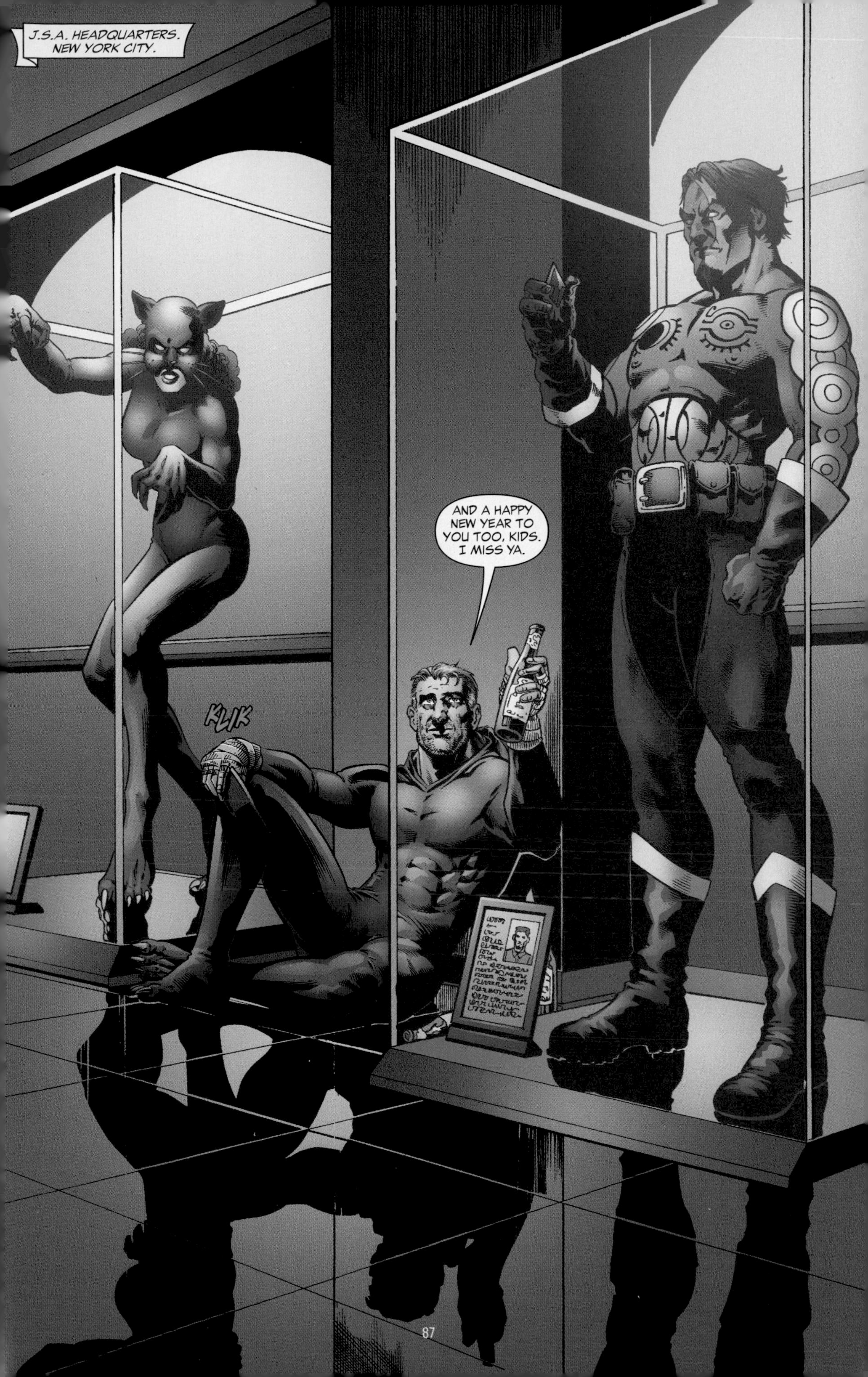
J.S.A. HEADQUARTERS. NEW YORK CITY.
AND A HAPPY NEW YEAR TO YOU TOO, KIDS. I MISS YA.
KLIK

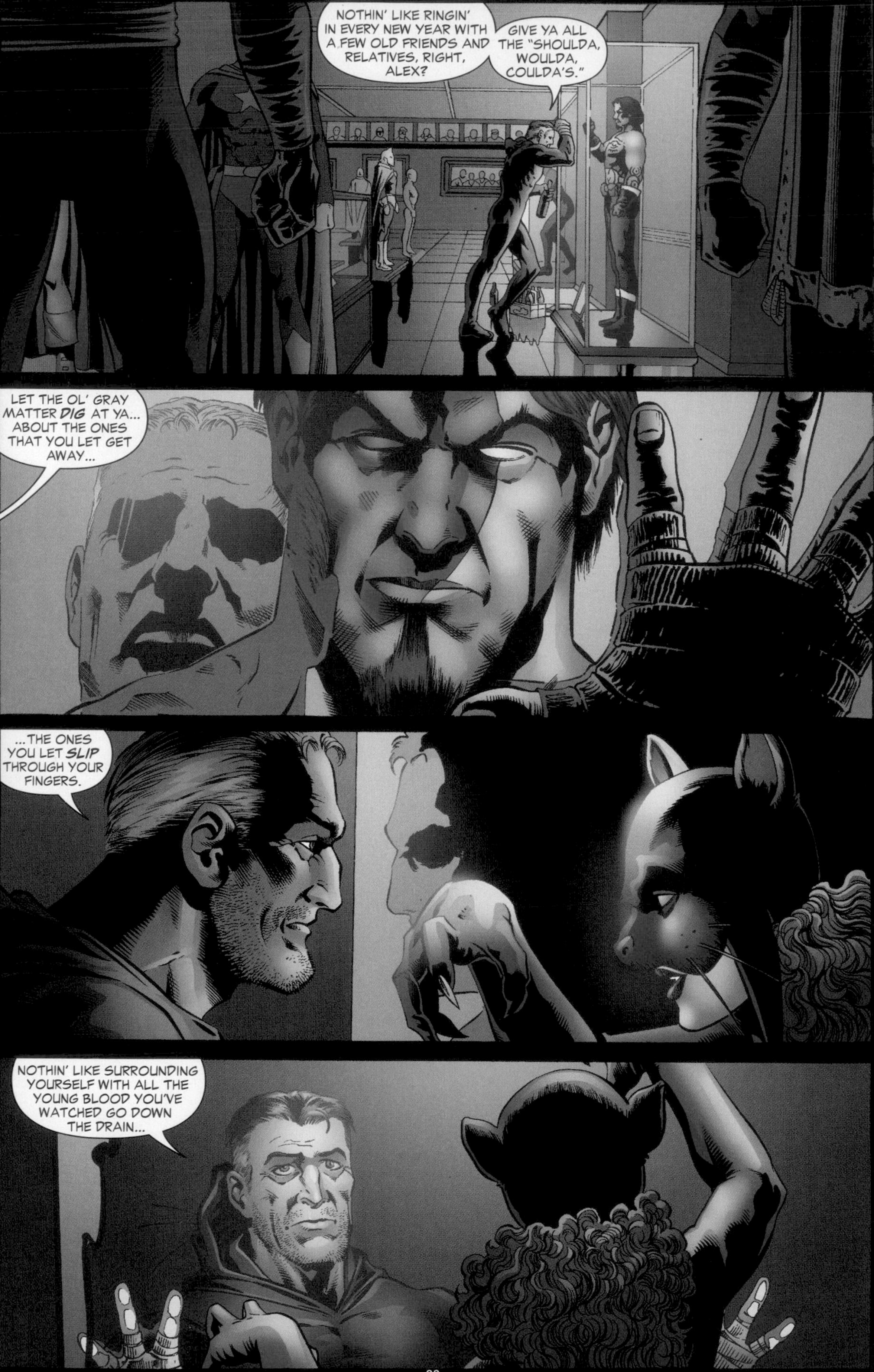
NOTHIN' LIKE RINGIN' IN EVERY NEW YEAR WITH A FEW OLD FRIENDS AND RELATIVES, RIGHT, ALEX?
GIVE YA ALL THE "SHOULDA, WOULDA, COULDA'S."
LET THE OL' GRAY MATTER DIG AT YA... ABOUT THE ONES THAT YOU LET GET AWAY...
...THE ONES YOU LET SLIP THROUGH YOUR FINGERS.
NOTHIN' LIKE SURROUNDING YOURSELF WITH ALL THE YOUNG BLOOD YOU'VE WATCHED GO DOWN THE DRAIN...

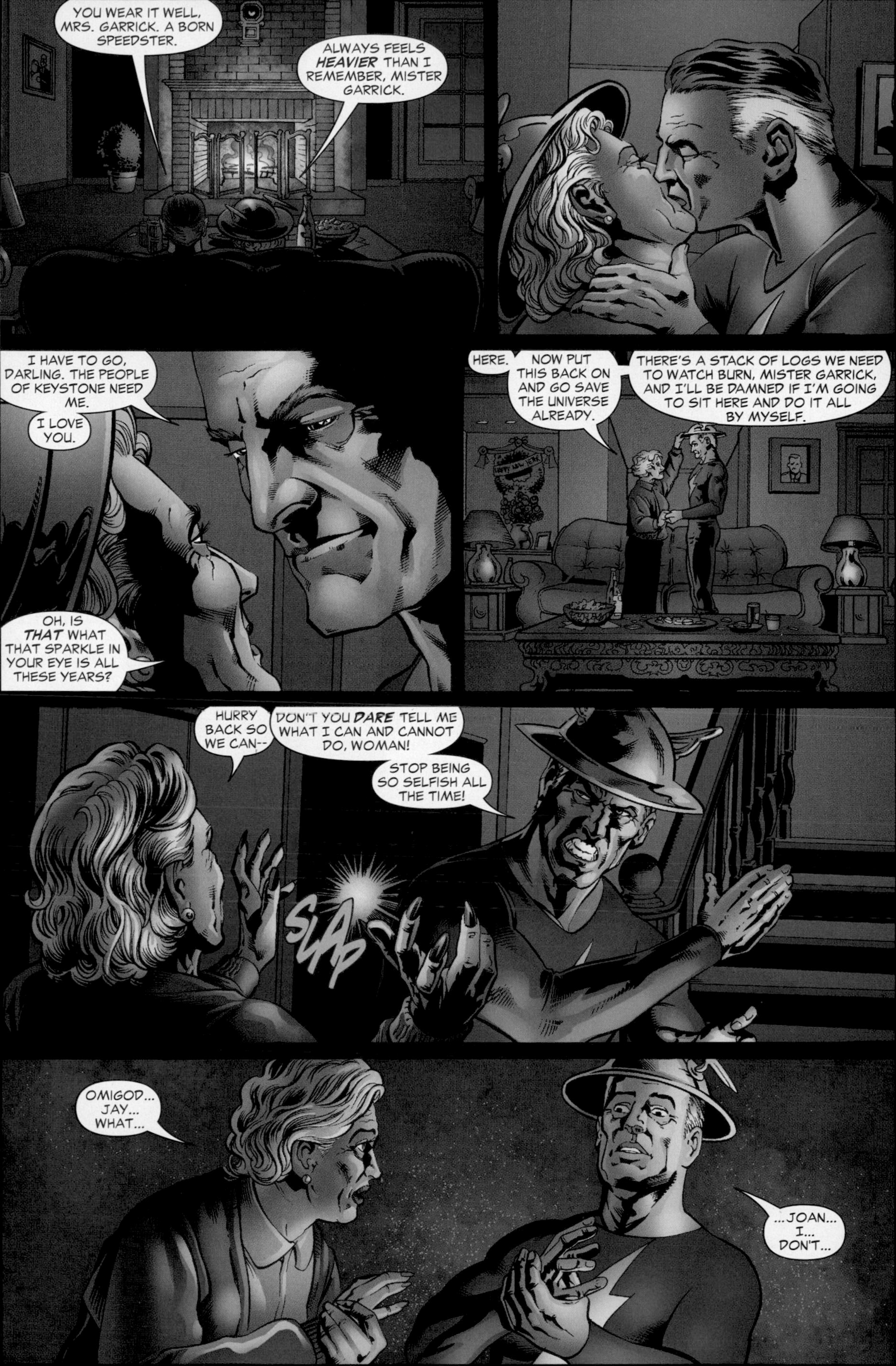

YOU WEAR IT WELL, MRS. GARRICK. A BORN SPEEDSTER.
ALWAYS FEELS HEAVIER THAN I REMEMBER, MISTER GARRICK.
I HAVE TO GO, DARLING. THE PEOPLE OF KEYSTONE NEED ME.
I LOVE YOU.
OH, IS THAT WHAT THAT SPARKLE IN YOUR EYE IS ALL THESE YEARS?
HERE.
NOW PUT THIS BACK ON AND GO SAVE THE UNIVERSE ALREADY.
THERE'S A STACK OF LOGS WE NEED TO WATCH BURN, MISTER GARRICK, AND I'LL BE DAMNED IF I'M GOING TO SIT HERE AND DO IT ALL BY MYSELF.
HURRY BACK SO WE CAN--
DON'T YOU DARE TELL ME WHAT I CAN AND CANNOT DO, WOMAN!
STOP BEING SO SELFISH ALL THE TIME!
SLAP
OMIGOD... JAY... WHAT...
...JOAN... I... DON'T...

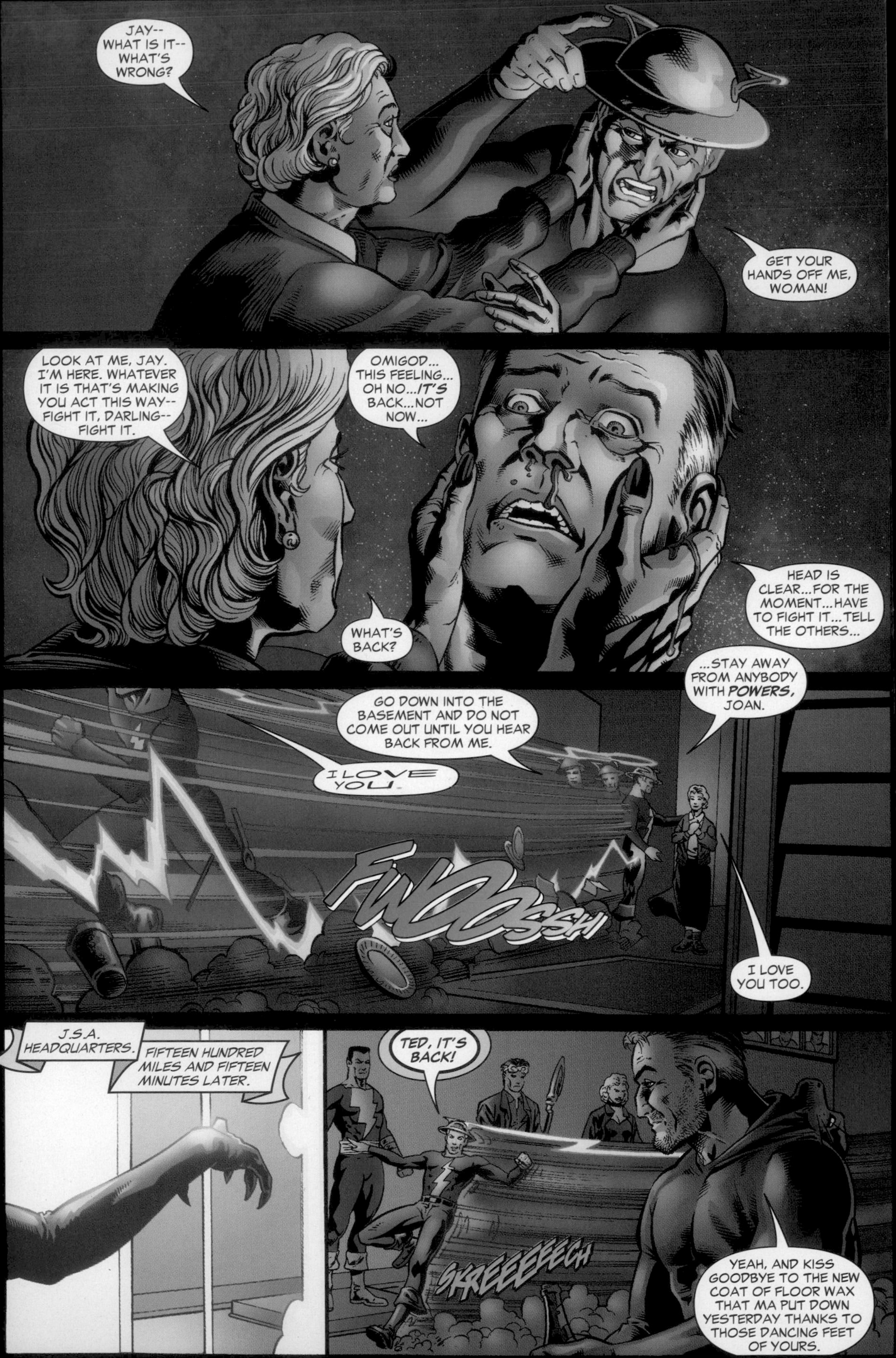
JAY-- WHAT IS IT-- WHAT'S WRONG?
GET YOUR HANDS OFF ME, WOMAN!
LOOK AT ME, JAY. I'M HERE. WHATEVER IT IS THAT'S MAKING YOU ACT THIS WAY-- FIGHT IT, DARLING-- FIGHT IT.
OMIGOD... THIS FEELING... OH NO...IT'S BACK...NOT NOW...
WHAT'S BACK?
HEAD IS CLEAR...FOR THE MOMENT...HAVE TO FIGHT IT...TELL THE OTHERS...
...STAY AWAY FROM ANYBODY WITH POWERS, JOAN.
GO DOWN INTO THE BASEMENT AND DO NOT COME OUT UNTIL YOU HEAR BACK FROM ME.
I LOVE YOU.
FWOOSSH!
I LOVE YOU TOO.
J.S.A. HEADQUARTERS.
FIFTEEN HUNDRED MILES AND FIFTEEN MINUTES LATER.
TED, IT'S BACK!
SKREEEEEECH
YEAH, AND KISS GOODBYE TO THE NEW COAT OF FLOOR WAX THAT MA PUT DOWN YESTERDAY THANKS TO THOSE DANCING FEET OF YOURS.

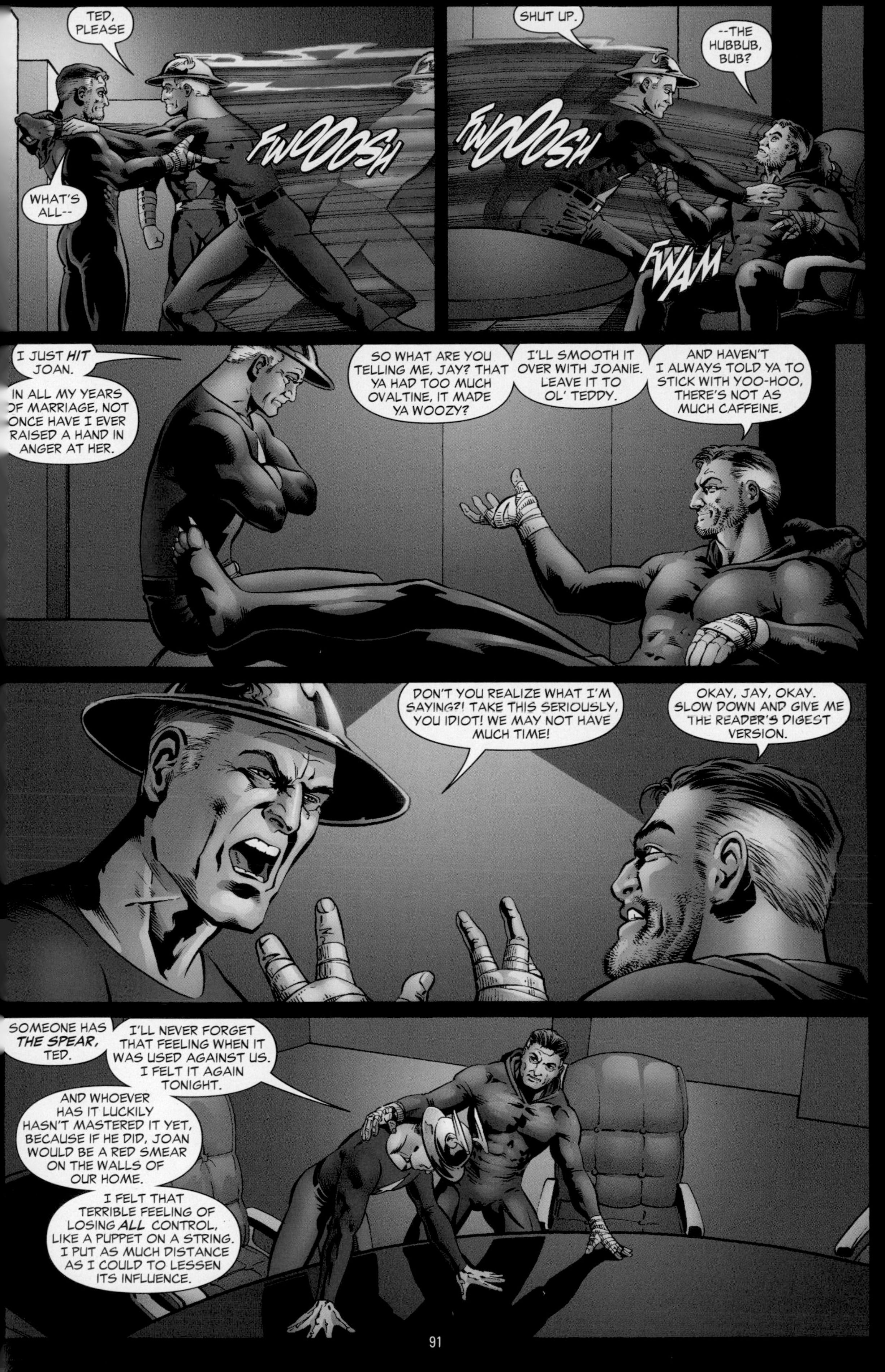
TED, PLEASE
WHAT'S ALL--
FWOOOSH
SHUT UP.
--THE HUBBUB, BUB?
FWOOOSH
FWAM
I JUST HIT JOAN.
IN ALL MY YEARS OF MARRIAGE, NOT ONCE HAVE I EVER RAISED A HAND IN ANGER AT HER.
SO WHAT ARE YOU TELLING ME, JAY? THAT YA HAD TOO MUCH OVALTINE, IT MADE YA WOOZY?
I'LL SMOOTH IT OVER WITH JOANIE. LEAVE IT TO OL' TEDDY.
AND HAVEN'T I ALWAYS TOLD YA TO STICK WITH YOO-HOO, THERE'S NOT AS MUCH CAFFEINE.
DON'T YOU REALIZE WHAT I'M SAYING?! TAKE THIS SERIOUSLY, YOU IDIOT! WE MAY NOT HAVE MUCH TIME!
OKAY, JAY, OKAY. SLOW DOWN AND GIVE ME THE READER'S DIGEST VERSION.
SOMEONE HAS THE SPEAR, TED.
I'LL NEVER FORGET THAT FEELING WHEN IT WAS USED AGAINST US. I FELT IT AGAIN TONIGHT.
AND WHOEVER HAS IT LUCKILY HASN'T MASTERED IT YET, BECAUSE IF HE DID, JOAN WOULD BE A RED SMEAR ON THE WALLS OF OUR HOME.
I FELT THAT TERRIBLE FEELING OF LOSING ALL CONTROL, LIKE A PUPPET ON A STRING. I PUT AS MUCH DISTANCE AS I COULD TO LESSEN ITS INFLUENCE.

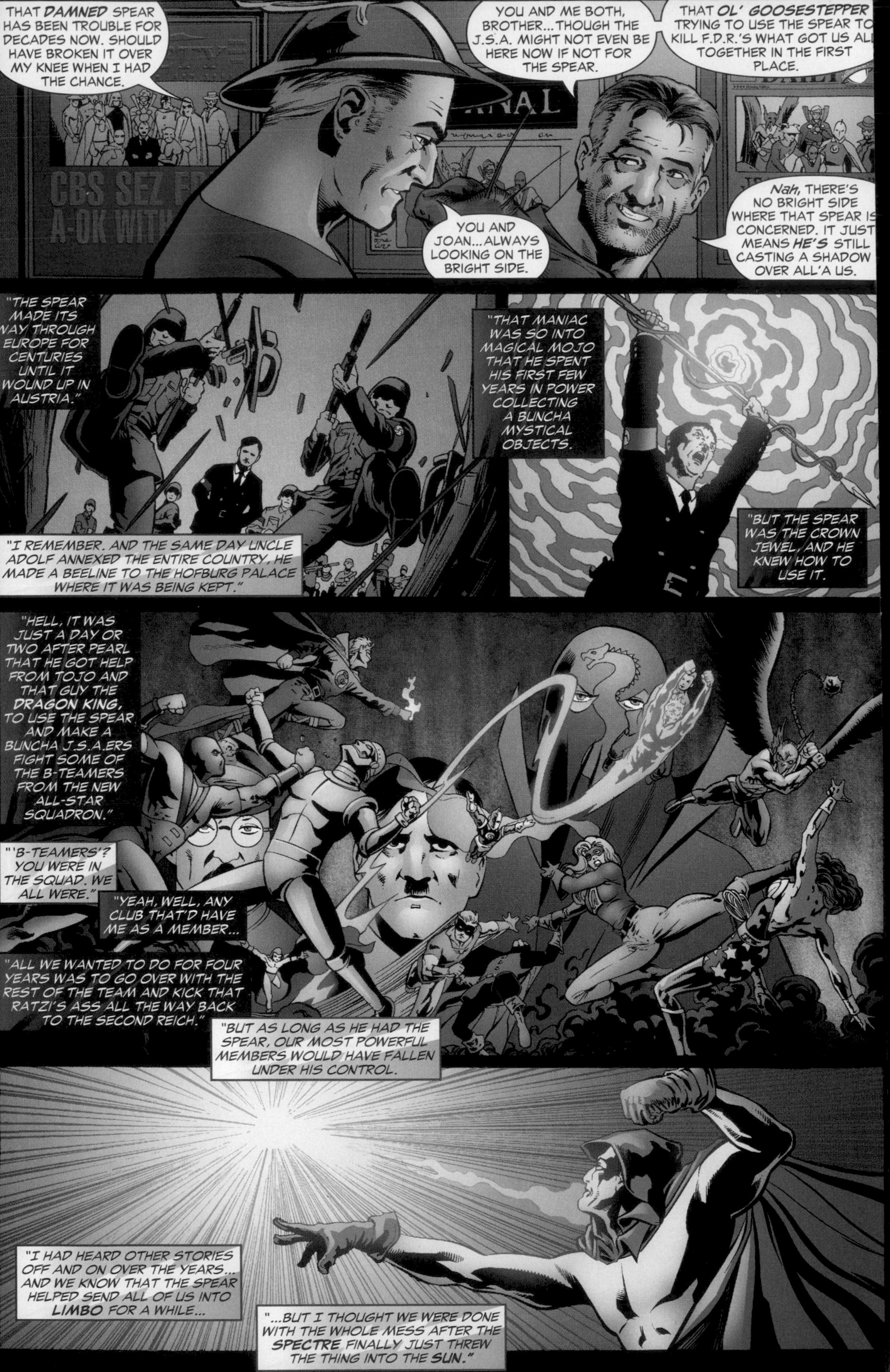
THAT DAMNED SPEAR HAS BEEN TROUBLE FOR DECADES NOW. SHOULD HAVE BROKEN IT OVER MY KNEE WHEN I HAD THE CHANCE.
YOU AND ME BOTH, BROTHER... THOUGH THE J.S.A. MIGHT NOT EVEN BE HERE NOW IF NOT FOR THE SPEAR.
THAT OL' GOOSESTEPPER TRYING TO USE THE SPEAR TO KILL F.D.R.'S WHAT GOT US ALL TOGETHER IN THE FIRST PLACE.
CBS SEZ FR
A-OK WITH
YOU AND JOAN... ALWAYS LOOKING ON THE BRIGHT SIDE.
Nah, THERE'S NO BRIGHT SIDE WHERE THAT SPEAR IS CONCERNED. IT JUST MEANS HE'S STILL CASTING A SHADOW OVER ALL'A US.
"THE SPEAR MADE ITS WAY THROUGH EUROPE FOR CENTURIES UNTIL IT WOUND UP IN AUSTRIA."
"I REMEMBER. AND THE SAME DAY UNCLE ADOLF ANNEXED THE ENTIRE COUNTRY, HE MADE A BEELINE TO THE HOFBURG PALACE WHERE IT WAS BEING KEPT."
"THAT MANIAC WAS SO INTO MAGICAL MOJO THAT HE SPENT HIS FIRST FEW YEARS IN POWER COLLECTING A BUNCHA MYSTICAL OBJECTS.
"BUT THE SPEAR WAS THE CROWN JEWEL, AND HE KNEW HOW TO USE IT.
"HELL, IT WAS JUST A DAY OR TWO AFTER PEARL THAT HE GOT HELP FROM TOJO AND THAT GUY THE DRAGON KING, TO USE THE SPEAR AND MAKE A BUNCHA J.S.A.ERS FIGHT SOME OF THE B-TEAMERS FROM THE NEW ALL-STAR SQUADRON."
"'B-TEAMERS'? YOU WERE IN THE SQUAD. WE ALL WERE."
"YEAH, WELL, ANY CLUB THAT'D HAVE ME AS A MEMBER...
"ALL WE WANTED TO DO FOR FOUR YEARS WAS TO GO OVER WITH THE REST OF THE TEAM AND KICK THAT RATZI'S ASS ALL THE WAY BACK TO THE SECOND REICH."
"BUT AS LONG AS HE HAD THE SPEAR, OUR MOST POWERFUL MEMBERS WOULD HAVE FALLEN UNDER HIS CONTROL.
"I HAD HEARD OTHER STORIES OFF AND ON OVER THE YEARS... AND WE KNOW THAT THE SPEAR HELPED SEND ALL OF US INTO LIMBO FOR A WHILE...
"...BUT I THOUGHT WE WERE DONE WITH THE WHOLE MESS AFTER THE SPECTRE FINALLY JUST THREW THE THING INTO THE SUN."

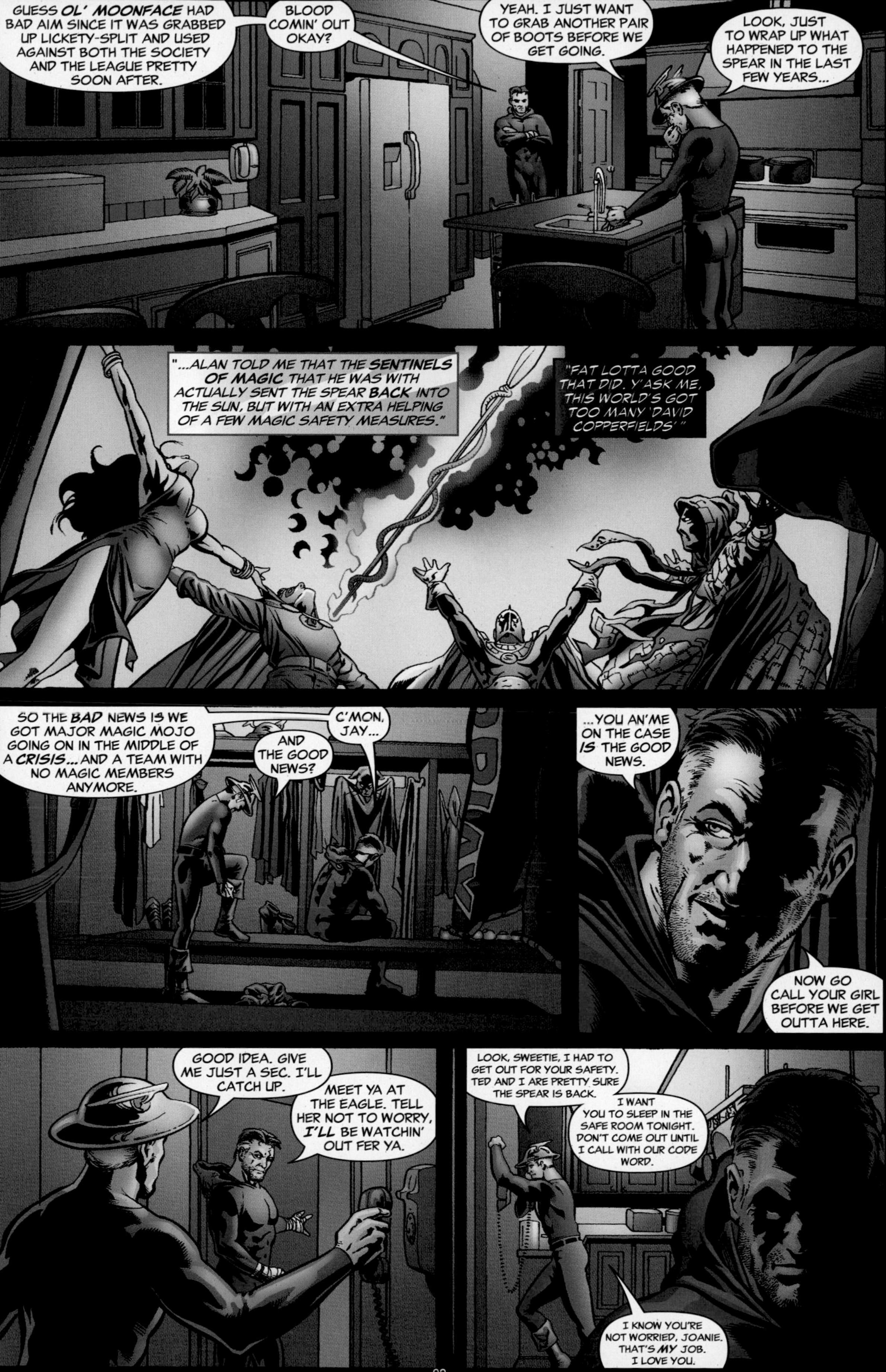
GUESS OL' MOONFACE HAD BAD AIM SINCE IT WAS GRABBED UP LICKETY-SPLIT AND USED AGAINST BOTH THE SOCIETY AND THE LEAGUE PRETTY SOON AFTER.
BLOOD COMIN' OUT OKAY?
YEAH. I JUST WANT TO GRAB ANOTHER PAIR OF BOOTS BEFORE WE GET GOING.
LOOK, JUST TO WRAP UP WHAT HAPPENED TO THE SPEAR IN THE LAST FEW YEARS...
"...ALAN TOLD ME THAT THE SENTINELS OF MAGIC THAT HE WAS WITH ACTUALLY SENT THE SPEAR BACK INTO THE SUN, BUT WITH AN EXTRA HELPING OF A FEW MAGIC SAFETY MEASURES."
"FAT LOTTA GOOD THAT DID. Y'ASK ME, THIS WORLD'S GOT TOO MANY 'DAVID COPPERFIELDS' "
SO THE BAD NEWS IS WE GOT MAJOR MAGIC MOJO GOING ON IN THE MIDDLE OF A CRISIS... AND A TEAM WITH NO MAGIC MEMBERS ANYMORE.
AND THE GOOD NEWS?
C'MON, JAY...
...YOU AN'ME ON THE CASE IS THE GOOD NEWS.
NOW GO CALL YOUR GIRL BEFORE WE GET OUTTA HERE.
GOOD IDEA. GIVE ME JUST A SEC. I'LL CATCH UP.
MEET YA AT THE EAGLE. TELL HER NOT TO WORRY, I'LL BE WATCHIN' OUT FER YA.
LOOK, SWEETIE, I HAD TO GET OUT FOR YOUR SAFETY. TED AND I ARE PRETTY SURE THE SPEAR IS BACK.
I WANT YOU TO SLEEP IN THE SAFE ROOM TONIGHT. DON'T COME OUT UNTIL I CALL WITH OUR CODE WORD.
I KNOW YOU'RE NOT WORRIED, JOANIE. THAT'S MY JOB. I LOVE YOU.

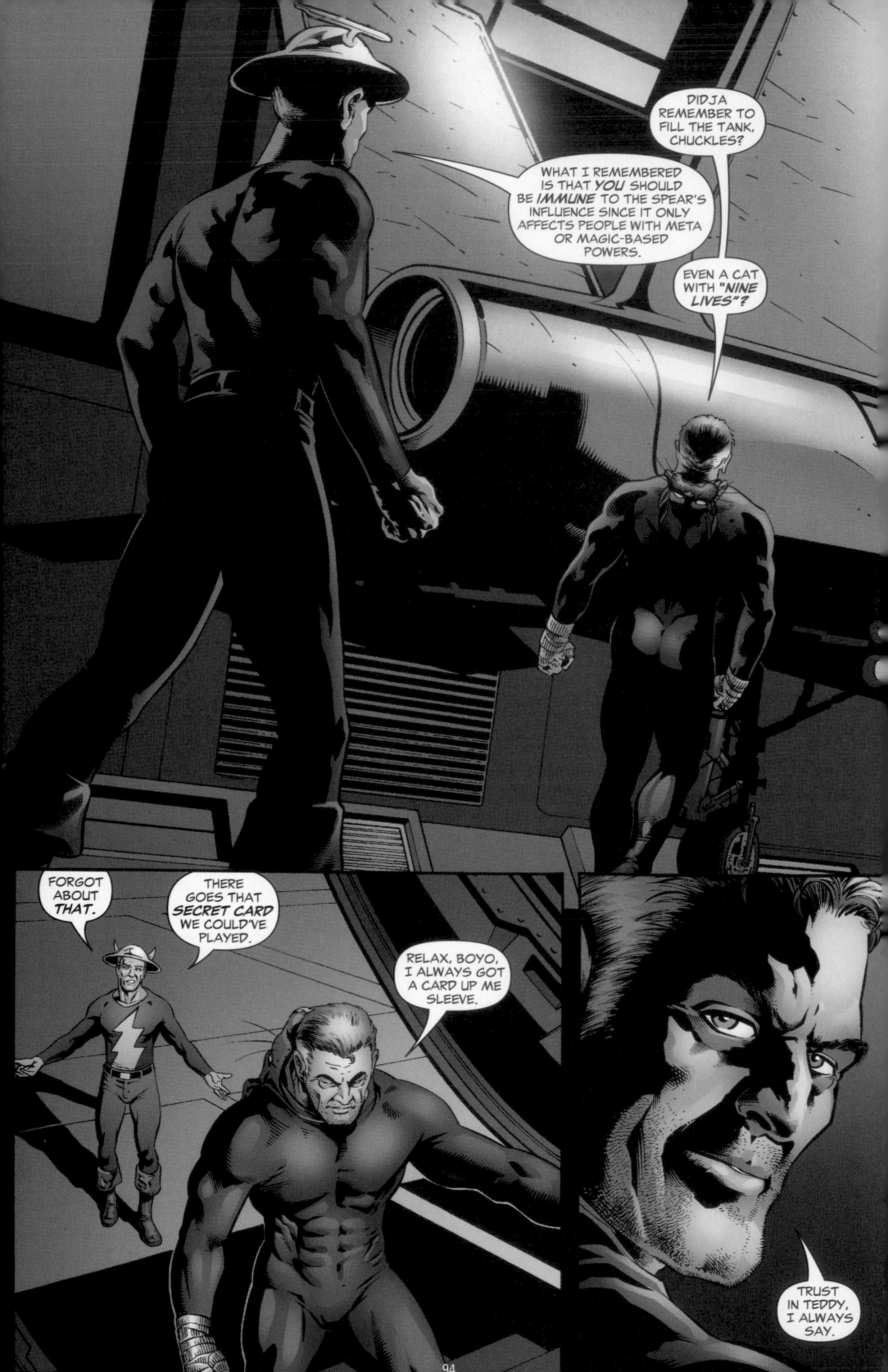
DIDJA REMEMBER TO FILL THE TANK, CHUCKLES?
WHAT I REMEMBERED IS THAT YOU SHOULD BE IMMUNE TO THE SPEAR'S INFLUENCE SINCE IT ONLY AFFECTS PEOPLE WITH META OR MAGIC-BASED POWERS.
EVEN A CAT WITH "NINE LIVES"?
FORGOT ABOUT THAT.
THERE GOES THAT SECRET CARD WE COULD'VE PLAYED.
RELAX, BOYO, I ALWAYS GOT A CARD UP ME SLEEVE.
TRUST IN TEDDY, I ALWAYS SAY.

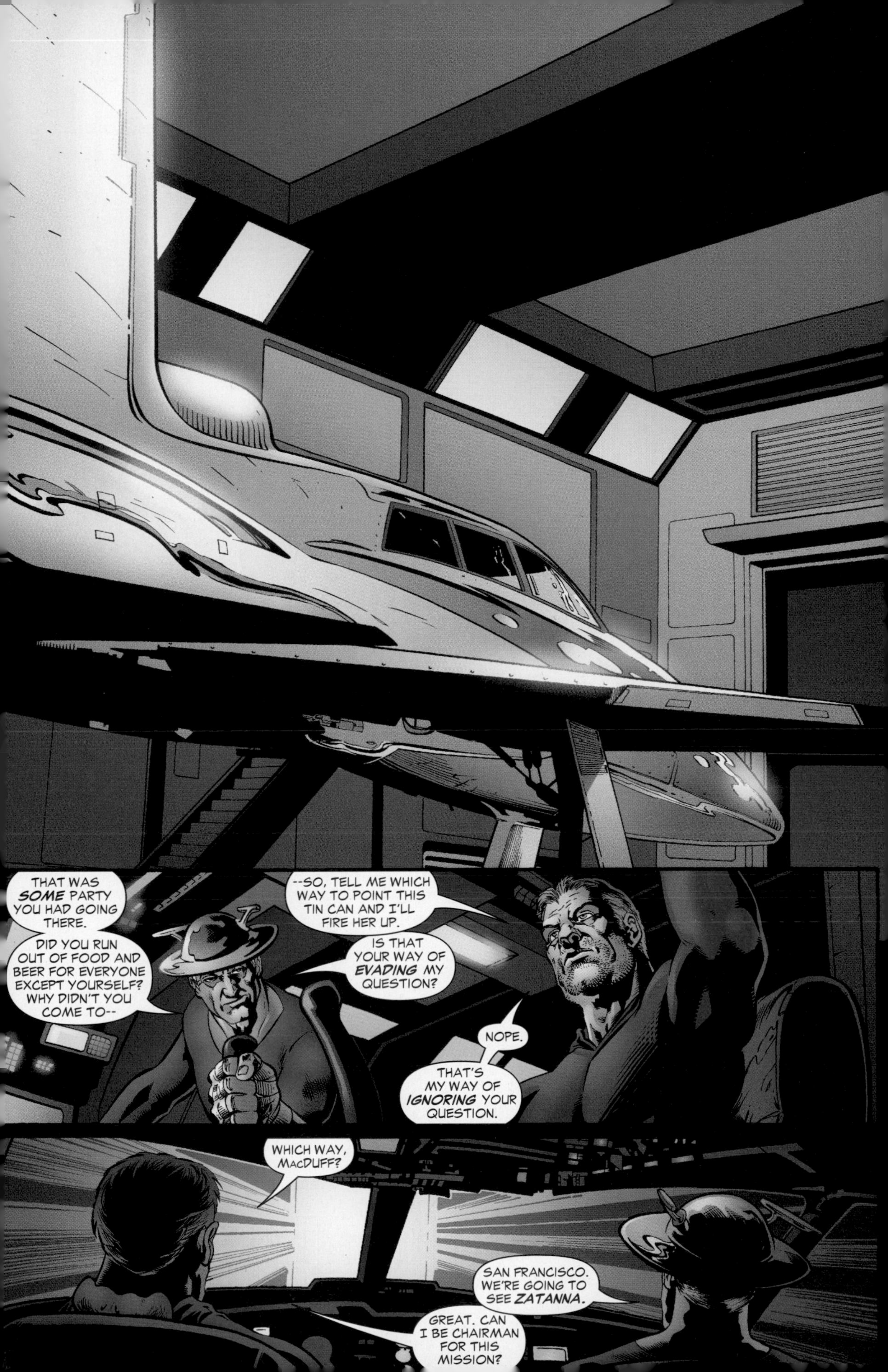
THAT WAS SOME PARTY YOU HAD GOING THERE.
DID YOU RUN OUT OF FOOD AND BEER FOR EVERYONE EXCEPT YOURSELF? WHY DIDN'T YOU COME TO--
--SO, TELL ME WHICH WAY TO POINT THIS TIN CAN AND I'LL FIRE HER UP.
IS THAT YOUR WAY OF EVADING MY QUESTION?
NOPE.
THAT'S MY WAY OF IGNORING YOUR QUESTION.
WHICH WAY, MacDUFF?
SAN FRANCISCO. WE'RE GOING TO SEE ZATANNA.
GREAT. CAN I BE CHAIRMAN FOR THIS MISSION?

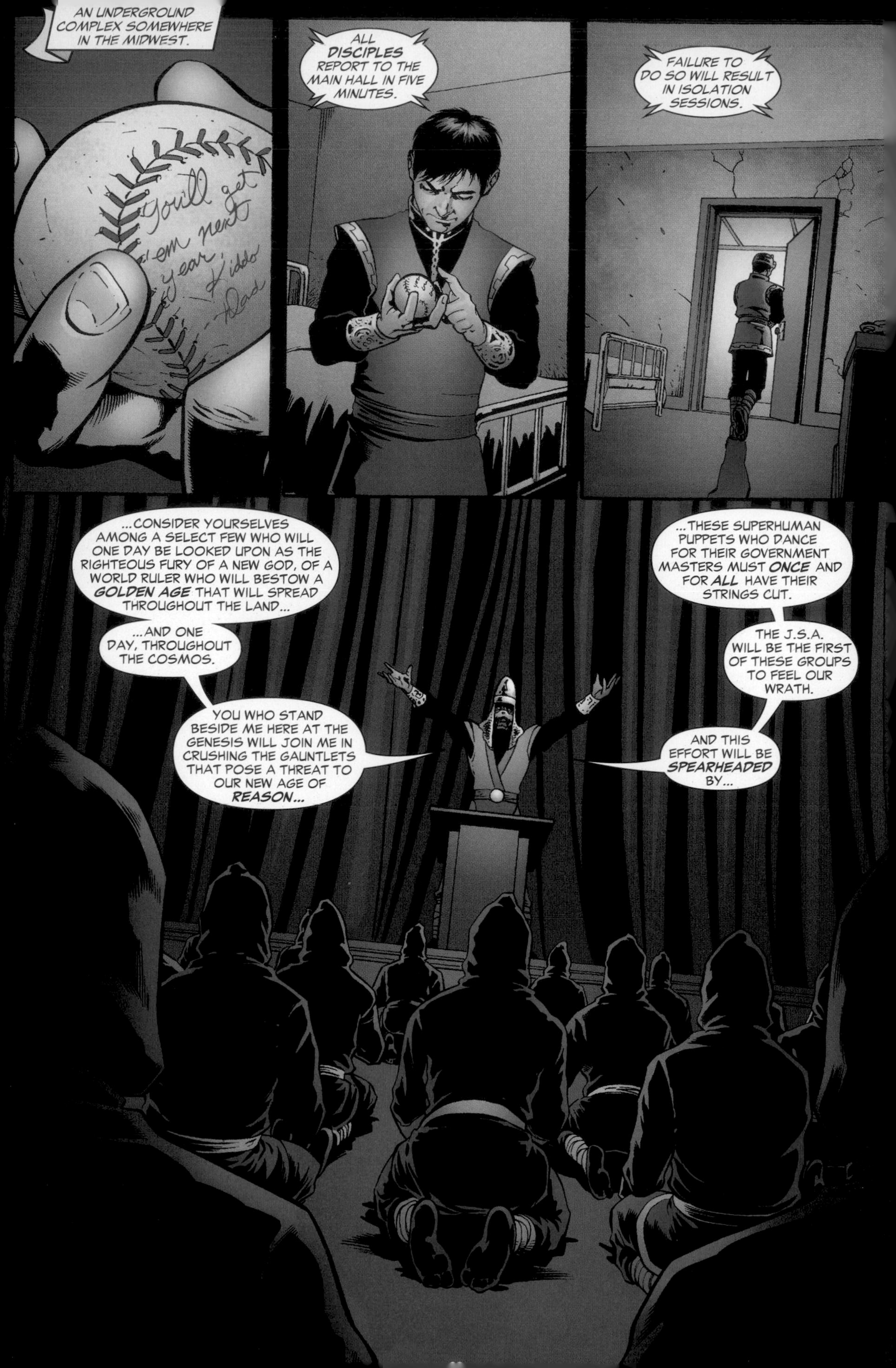
AN UNDERGROUND COMPLEX SOMEWHERE IN THE MIDWEST.
You'll get 'em next year, Kiddo Dad
ALL DISCIPLES REPORT TO THE MAIN HALL IN FIVE MINUTES.
FAILURE TO DO SO WILL RESULT IN ISOLATION SESSIONS.
...CONSIDER YOURSELVES AMONG A SELECT FEW WHO WILL ONE DAY BE LOOKED UPON AS THE RIGHTEOUS FURY OF A NEW GOD, OF A WORLD RULER WHO WILL BESTOW A GOLDEN AGE THAT WILL SPREAD THROUGHOUT THE LAND...
...AND ONE DAY, THROUGHOUT THE COSMOS.
YOU WHO STAND BESIDE ME HERE AT THE GENESIS WILL JOIN ME IN CRUSHING THE GAUNTLETS THAT POSE A THREAT TO OUR NEW AGE OF REASON...
...THESE SUPERHUMAN PUPPETS WHO DANCE FOR THEIR GOVERNMENT MASTERS MUST ONCE AND FOR ALL HAVE THEIR STRINGS CUT.
THE J.S.A. WILL BE THE FIRST OF THESE GROUPS TO FEEL OUR WRATH.
AND THIS EFFORT WILL BE SPEARHEADED BY...

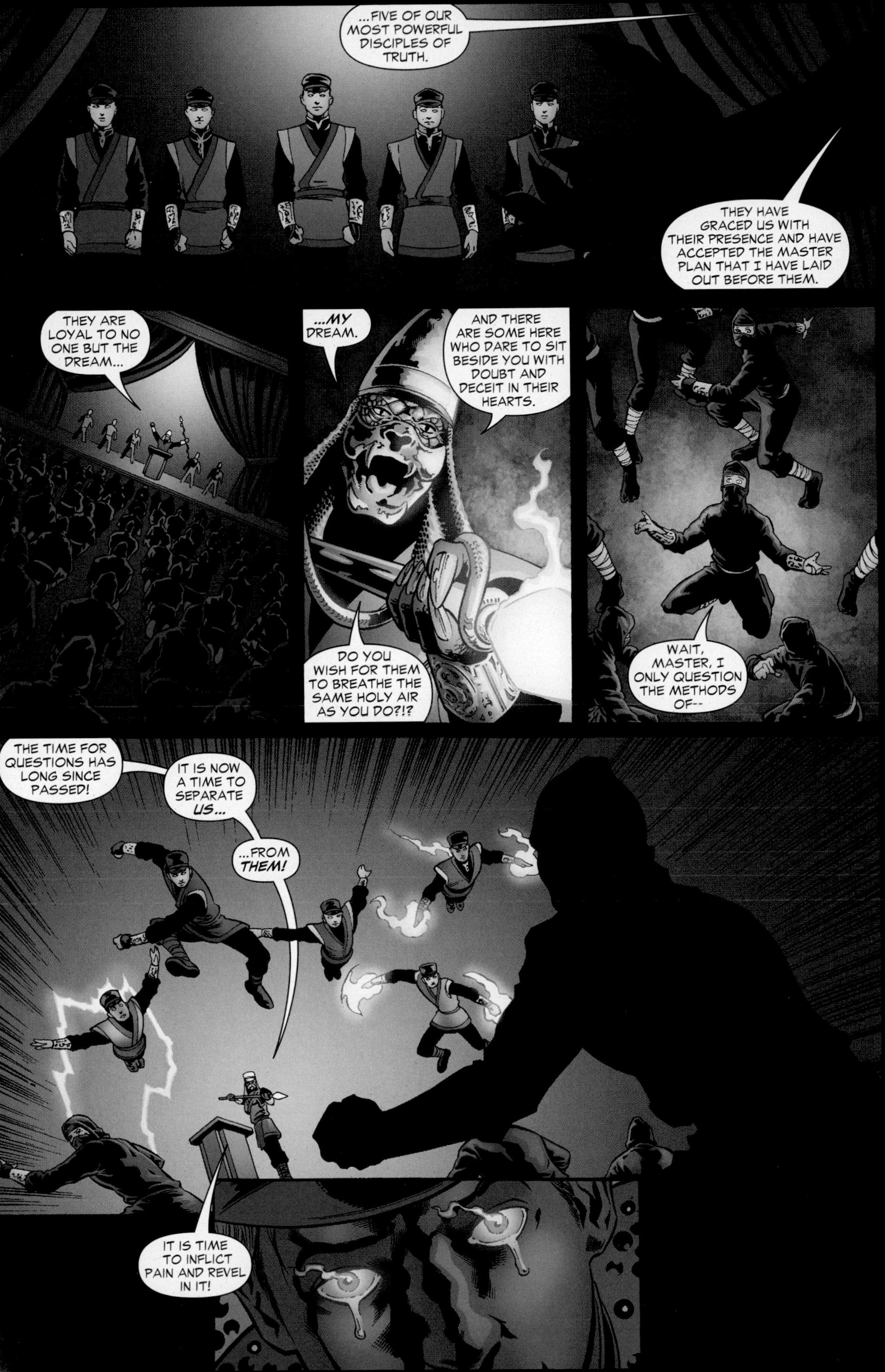
...FIVE OF OUR MOST POWERFUL DISCIPLES OF TRUTH.
THEY HAVE GRACED US WITH THEIR PRESENCE AND HAVE ACCEPTED THE MASTER PLAN THAT I HAVE LAID OUT BEFORE THEM.
THEY ARE LOYAL TO NO ONE BUT THE DREAM...
...MY DREAM.
AND THERE ARE SOME HERE WHO DARE TO SIT BESIDE YOU WITH DOUBT AND DECEIT IN THEIR HEARTS.
DO YOU WISH FOR THEM TO BREATHE THE SAME HOLY AIR AS YOU DO?!?
WAIT, MASTER, I ONLY QUESTION THE METHODS OF--
THE TIME FOR QUESTIONS HAS LONG SINCE PASSED!
IT IS NOW A TIME TO SEPARATE US...
...FROM THEM!
IT IS TIME TO INFLICT PAIN AND REVEL IN IT!

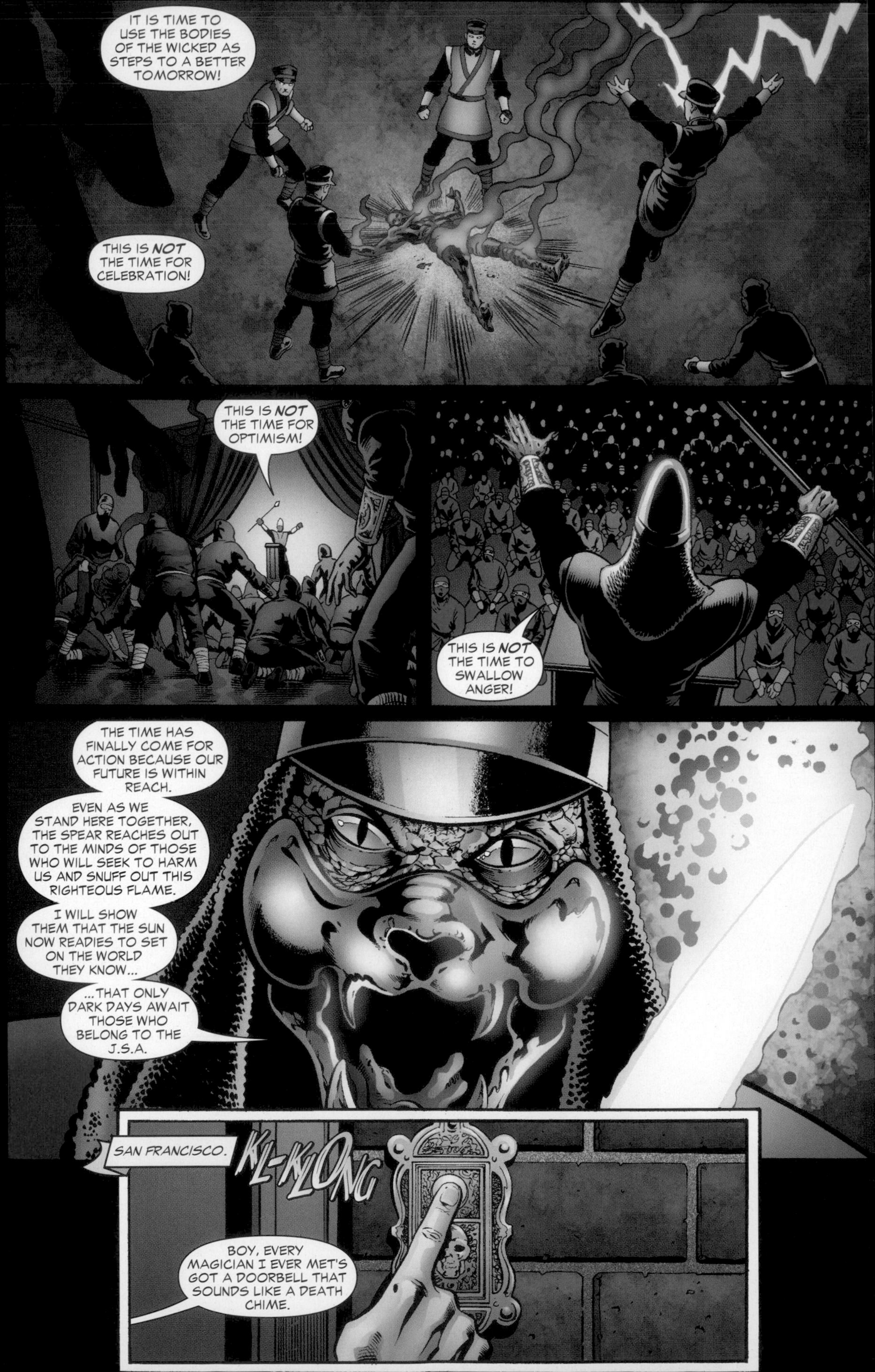
IT IS TIME TO USE THE BODIES OF THE WICKED AS STEPS TO A BETTER TOMORROW!
THIS IS NOT THE TIME FOR CELEBRATION!
THIS IS NOT THE TIME FOR OPTIMISM!
THIS IS NOT THE TIME TO SWALLOW ANGER!
THE TIME HAS FINALLY COME FOR ACTION BECAUSE OUR FUTURE IS WITHIN REACH.
EVEN AS WE STAND HERE TOGETHER, THE SPEAR REACHES OUT TO THE MINDS OF THOSE WHO WILL SEEK TO HARM US AND SNUFF OUT THIS RIGHTEOUS FLAME.
I WILL SHOW THEM THAT THE SUN NOW READIES TO SET ON THE WORLD THEY KNOW...
...THAT ONLY DARK DAYS AWAIT THOSE WHO BELONG TO THE J.S.A.
SAN FRANCISCO.
KL-KLONG
BOY, EVERY MAGICIAN I EVER MET'S GOT A DOORBELL THAT SOUNDS LIKE A DEATH CHIME.

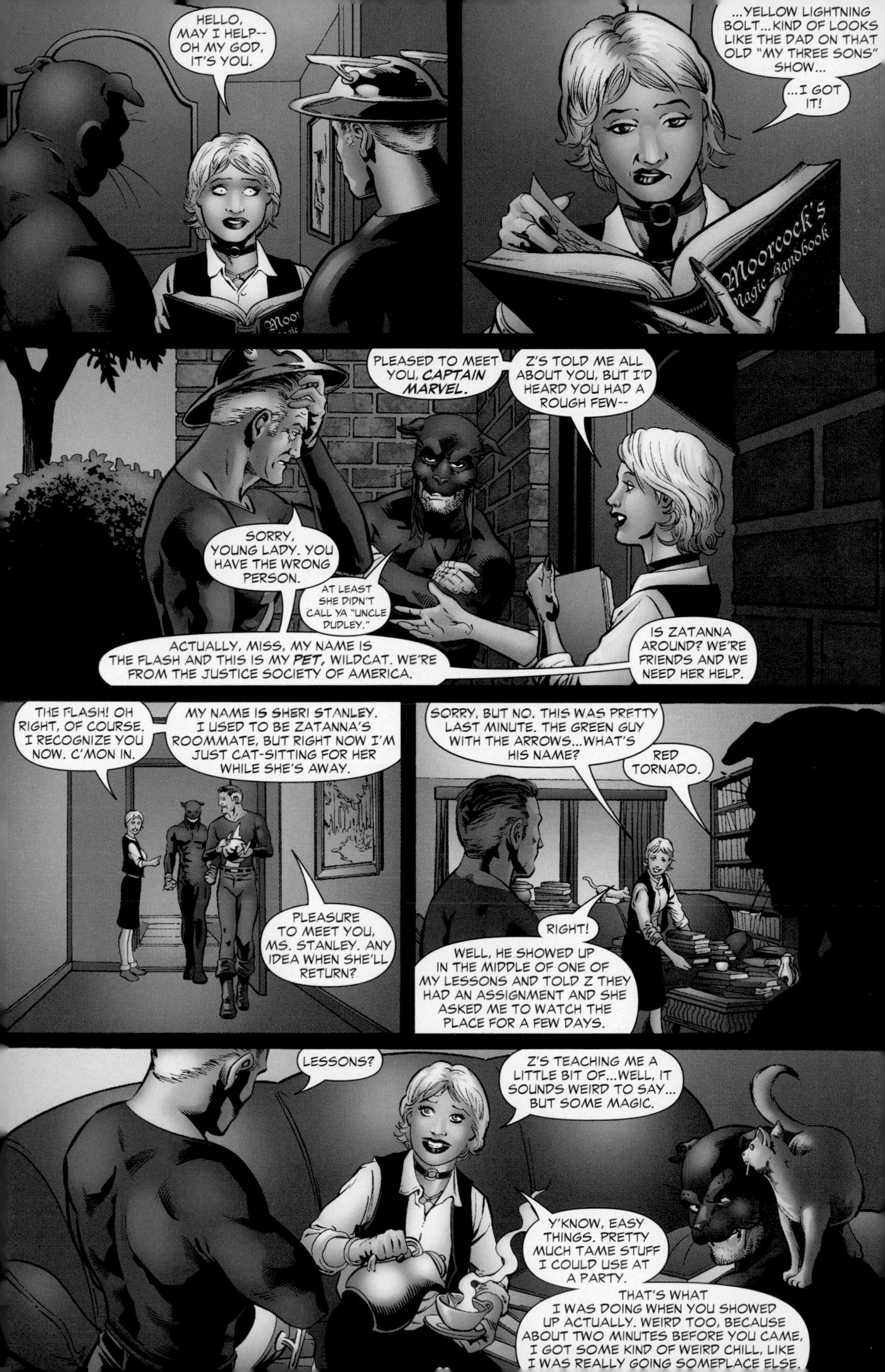
HELLO, MAY I HELP-- OH MY GOD, IT'S YOU.
...YELLOW LIGHTNING BOLT...KIND OF LOOKS LIKE THE DAD ON THAT OLD "MY THREE SONS" SHOW...
...I GOT IT!
Moorcock's Magic Handbook
PLEASED TO MEET YOU, CAPTAIN MARVEL.
Z'S TOLD ME ALL ABOUT YOU, BUT I'D HEARD YOU HAD A ROUGH FEW--
SORRY, YOUNG LADY. YOU HAVE THE WRONG PERSON.
AT LEAST SHE DIDN'T CALL YA "UNCLE DUDLEY."
ACTUALLY, MISS, MY NAME IS THE FLASH AND THIS IS MY PET, WILDCAT. WE'RE FROM THE JUSTICE SOCIETY OF AMERICA.
IS ZATANNA AROUND? WE'RE FRIENDS AND WE NEED HER HELP.
THE FLASH! OH RIGHT, OF COURSE. I RECOGNIZE YOU NOW. C'MON IN.
MY NAME IS SHERI STANLEY. I USED TO BE ZATANNA'S ROOMMATE, BUT RIGHT NOW I'M JUST CAT-SITTING FOR HER WHILE SHE'S AWAY.
PLEASURE TO MEET YOU, MS. STANLEY. ANY IDEA WHEN SHE'LL RETURN?
SORRY, BUT NO. THIS WAS PRETTY LAST MINUTE. THE GREEN GUY WITH THE ARROWS...WHAT'S HIS NAME?
RED TORNADO.
RIGHT!
WELL, HE SHOWED UP IN THE MIDDLE OF ONE OF MY LESSONS AND TOLD Z THEY HAD AN ASSIGNMENT AND SHE ASKED ME TO WATCH THE PLACE FOR A FEW DAYS.
LESSONS?
Z'S TEACHING ME A LITTLE BIT OF...WELL, IT SOUNDS WEIRD TO SAY... BUT SOME MAGIC.
Y'KNOW, EASY THINGS. PRETTY MUCH TAME STUFF I COULD USE AT A PARTY.
THAT'S WHAT I WAS DOING WHEN YOU SHOWED UP ACTUALLY. WEIRD TOO, BECAUSE ABOUT TWO MINUTES BEFORE YOU CAME, I GOT SOME KIND OF WEIRD CHILL, LIKE I WAS REALLY GOING SOMEPLACE ELSE.

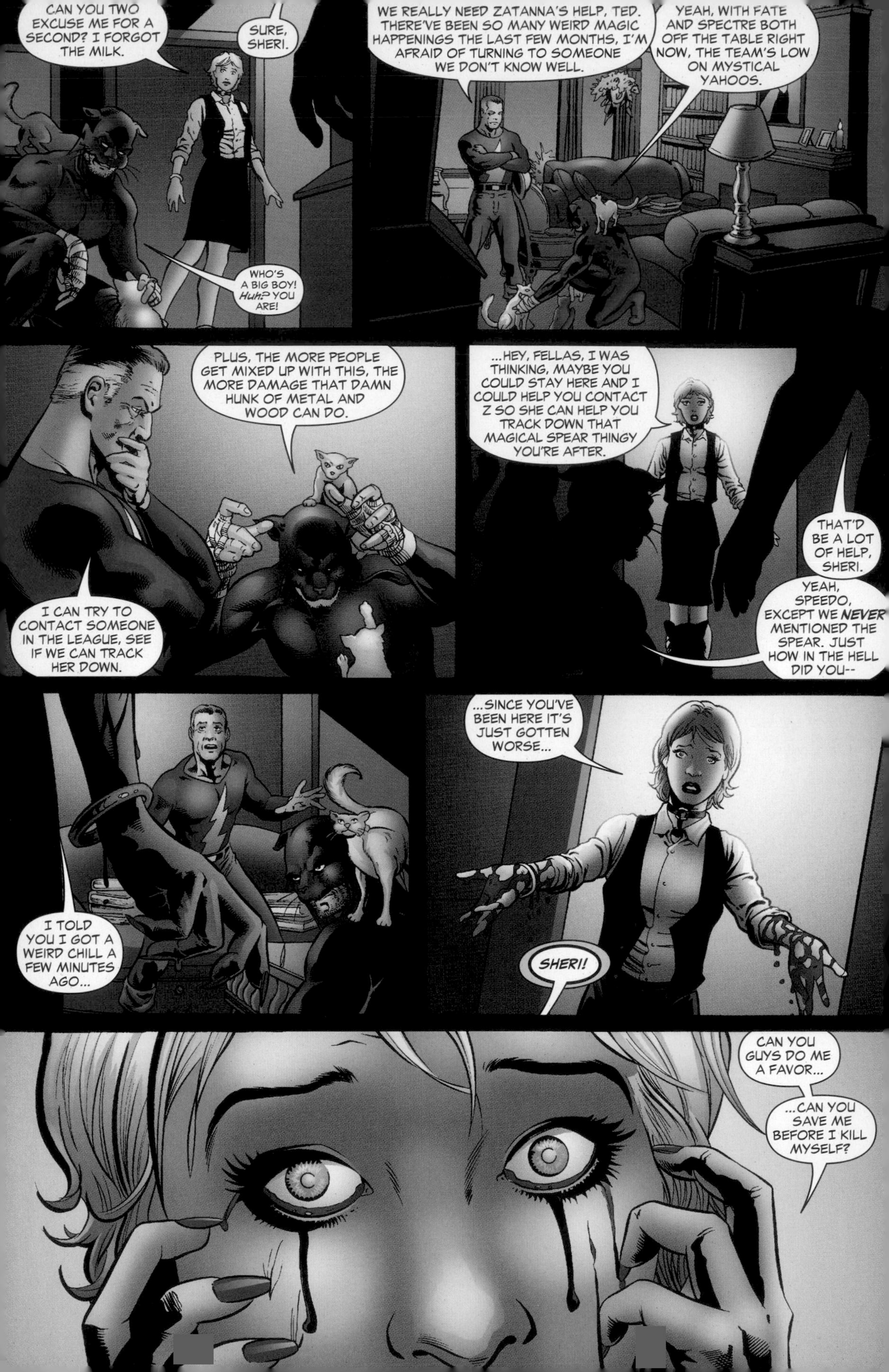

CAN YOU TWO EXCUSE ME FOR A SECOND? I FORGOT THE MILK.
SURE, SHERI.
WHO'S A BIG BOY! *Huh?* YOU ARE!
WE REALLY NEED ZATANNA'S HELP, TED. THERE'VE BEEN SO MANY WEIRD MAGIC HAPPENINGS THE LAST FEW MONTHS, I'M AFRAID OF TURNING TO SOMEONE WE DON'T KNOW WELL.
YEAH, WITH FATE AND SPECTRE BOTH OFF THE TABLE RIGHT NOW, THE TEAM'S LOW ON MYSTICAL YAHOOS.
PLUS, THE MORE PEOPLE GET MIXED UP WITH THIS, THE MORE DAMAGE THAT DAMN HUNK OF METAL AND WOOD CAN DO.
I CAN TRY TO CONTACT SOMEONE IN THE LEAGUE, SEE IF WE CAN TRACK HER DOWN.
...HEY, FELLAS, I WAS THINKING, MAYBE YOU COULD STAY HERE AND I COULD HELP YOU CONTACT Z SO SHE CAN HELP YOU TRACK DOWN THAT MAGICAL SPEAR THINGY YOU'RE AFTER.
THAT'D BE A LOT OF HELP, SHERI.
YEAH, SPEEDO, EXCEPT WE ***NEVER*** MENTIONED THE SPEAR. JUST HOW IN THE HELL DID YOU--
I TOLD YOU I GOT A WEIRD CHILL A FEW MINUTES AGO...
...SINCE YOU'VE BEEN HERE IT'S JUST GOTTEN WORSE...
SHERI!
CAN YOU GUYS DO ME A FAVOR...
...CAN YOU SAVE ME BEFORE I KILL MYSELF?

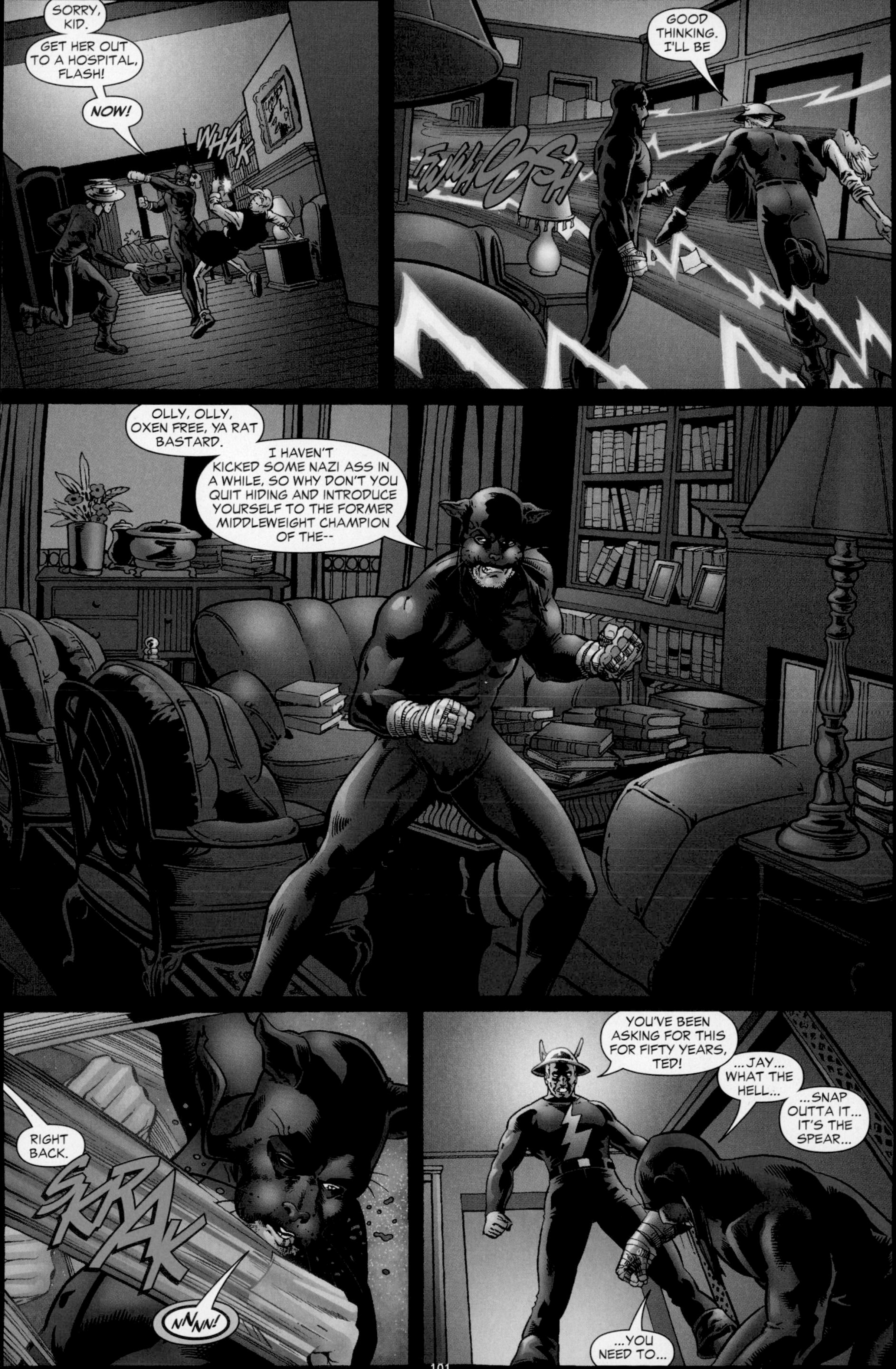
SORRY, KID.
GET HER OUT TO A HOSPITAL, FLASH!
NOW!
WHAK
GOOD THINKING. I'LL BE
FWHOOSH
OLLY, OLLY, OXEN FREE, YA RAT BASTARD.
I HAVEN'T KICKED SOME NAZI ASS IN A WHILE, SO WHY DON'T YOU QUIT HIDING AND INTRODUCE YOURSELF TO THE FORMER MIDDLEWEIGHT CHAMPION OF THE--
RIGHT BACK.
SKRAK
NNNN!
YOU'VE BEEN ASKING FOR THIS FOR FIFTY YEARS, TED!
...JAY... WHAT THE HELL...
...SNAP OUTTA IT... IT'S THE SPEAR...
...YOU NEED TO...

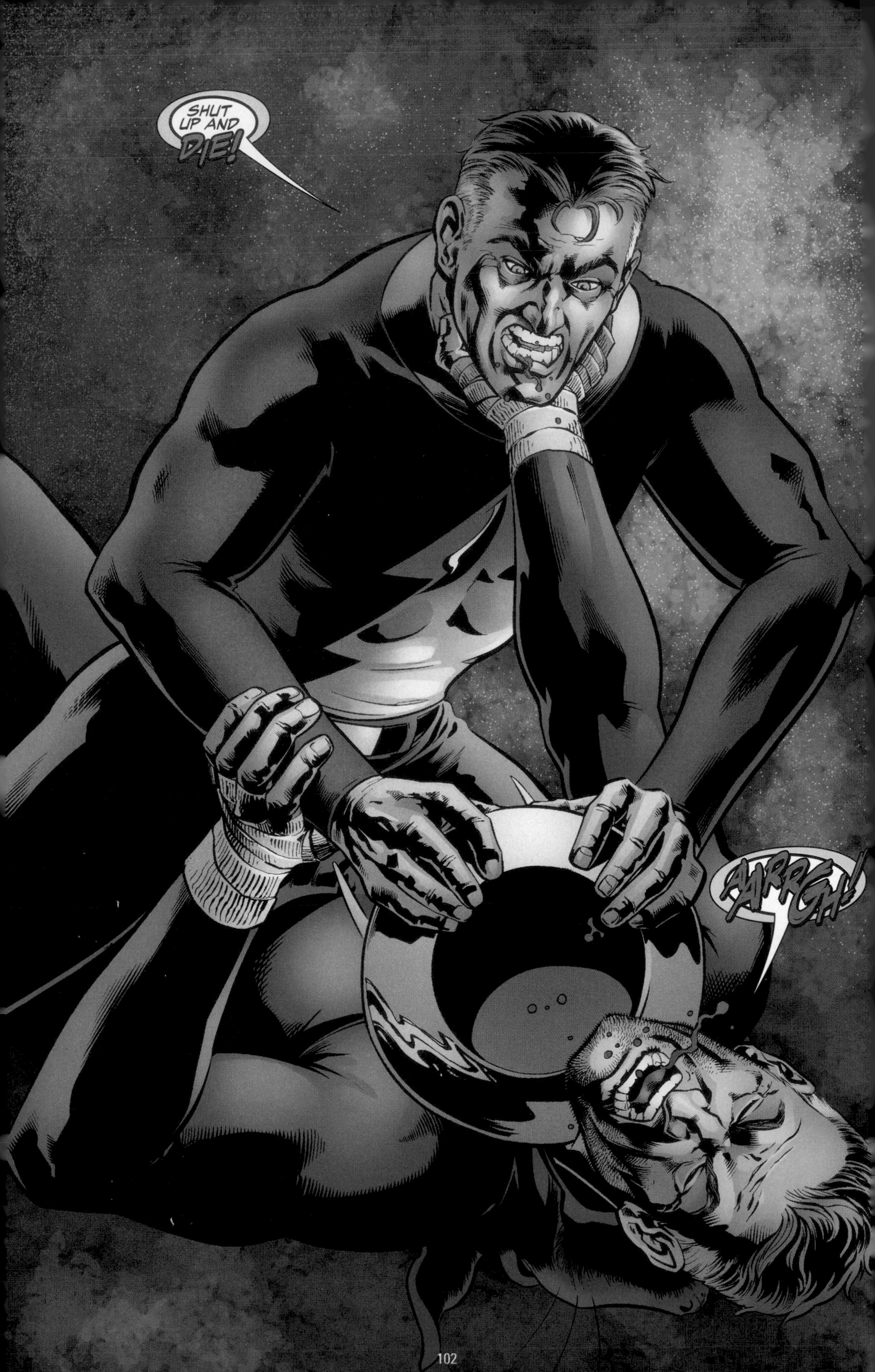
SHUT UP AND DIE!
AARRGH!

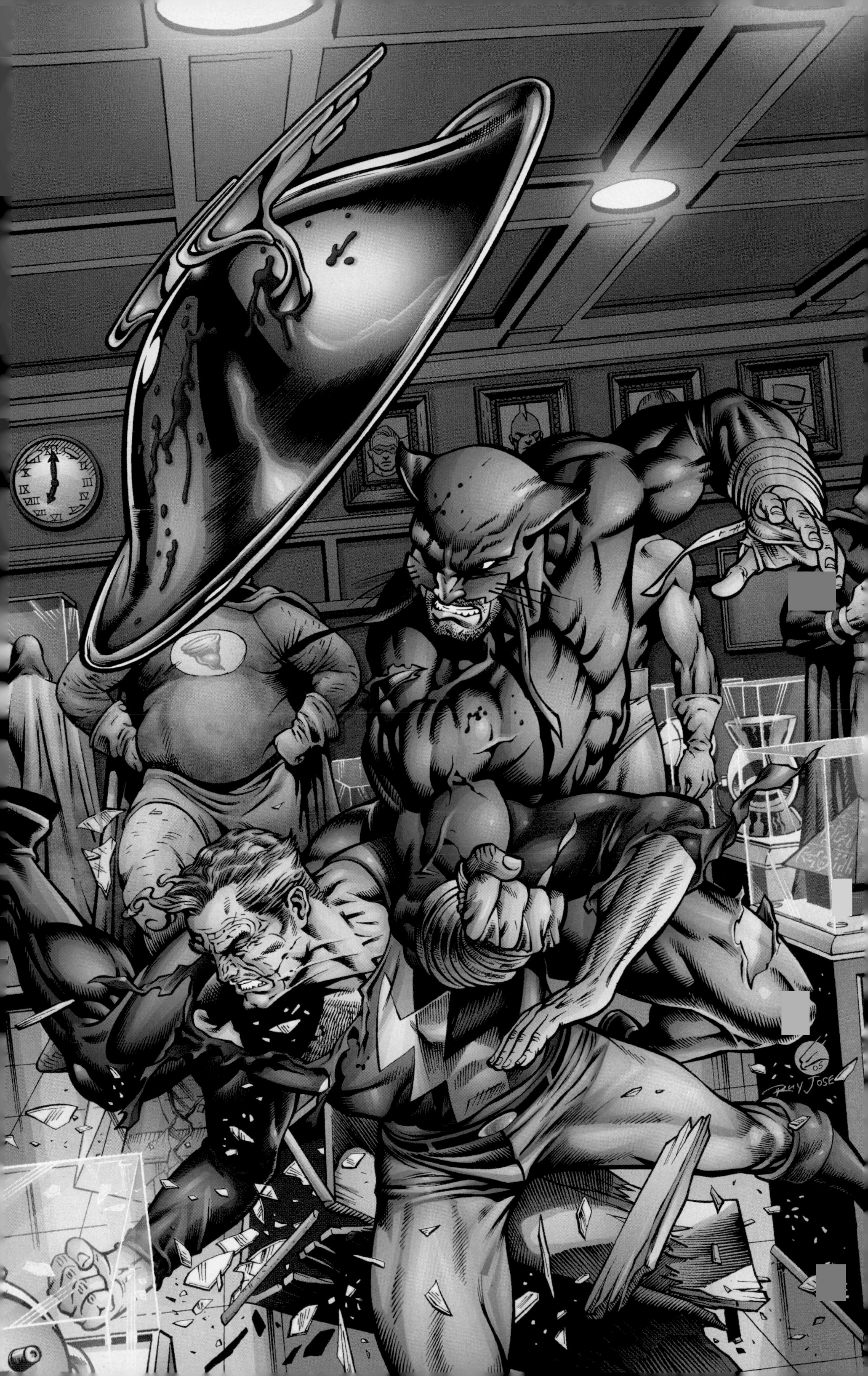
05
RAY JOSE

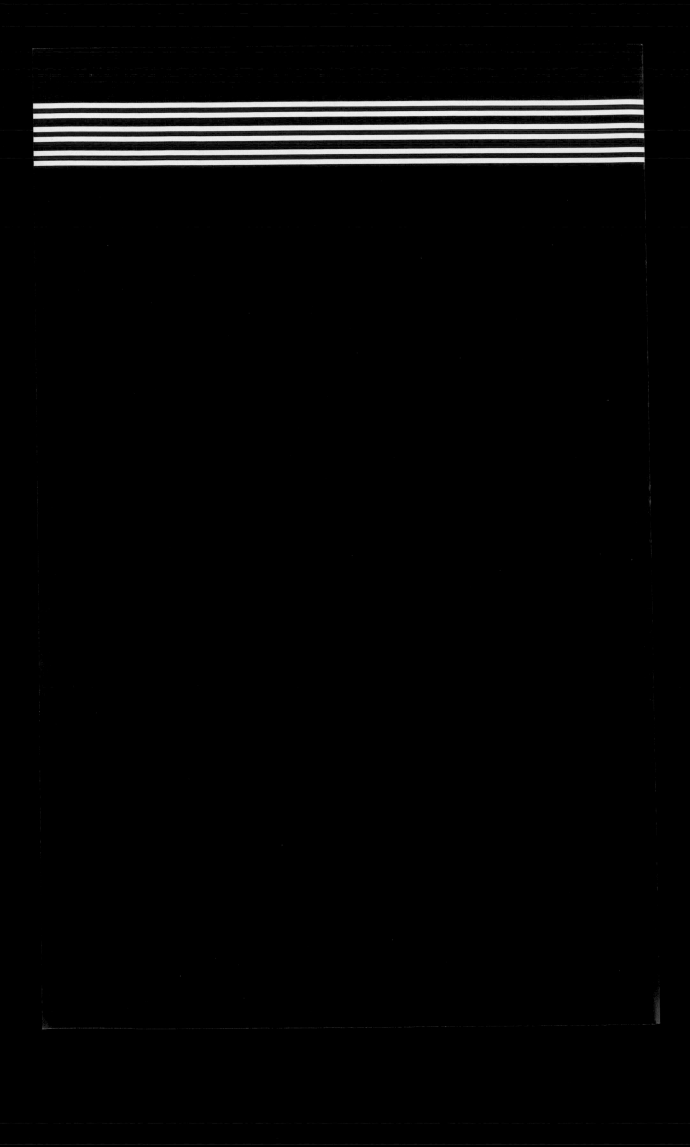

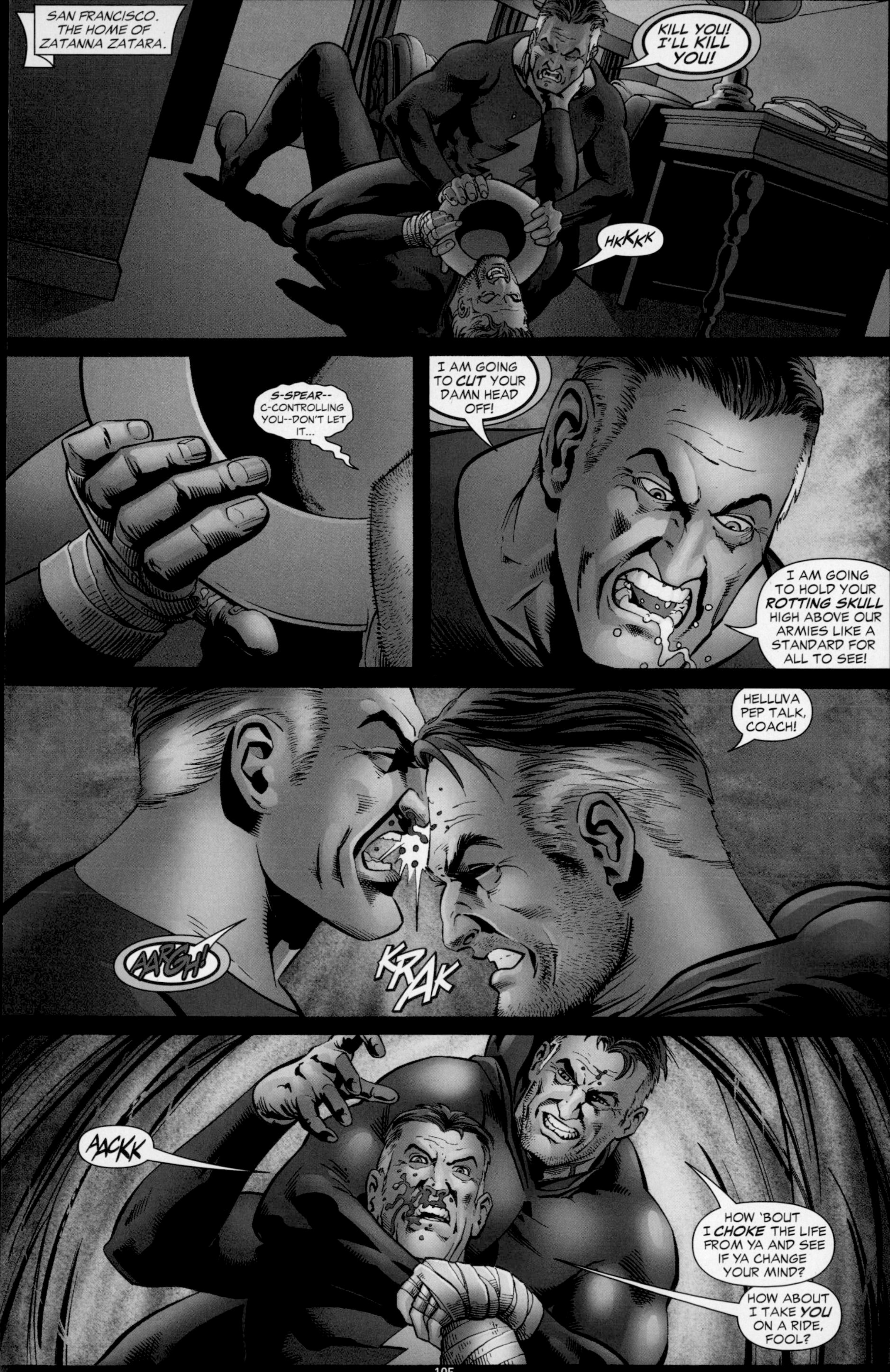
SAN FRANCISCO. THE HOME OF ZATANNA ZATARA.
KILL YOU! I'LL KILL YOU!
HKKKK
S-SPEAR-- C-CONTROLLING YOU--DON'T LET IT...
I AM GOING TO CUT YOUR DAMN HEAD OFF!
I AM GOING TO HOLD YOUR ROTTING SKULL HIGH ABOVE OUR ARMIES LIKE A STANDARD FOR ALL TO SEE!
HELLUVA PEP TALK, COACH!
AARGH!
KRAK
AACKK
HOW 'BOUT I CHOKE THE LIFE FROM YA AND SEE IF YA CHANGE YOUR MIND?
HOW ABOUT I TAKE YOU ON A RIDE, FOOL?

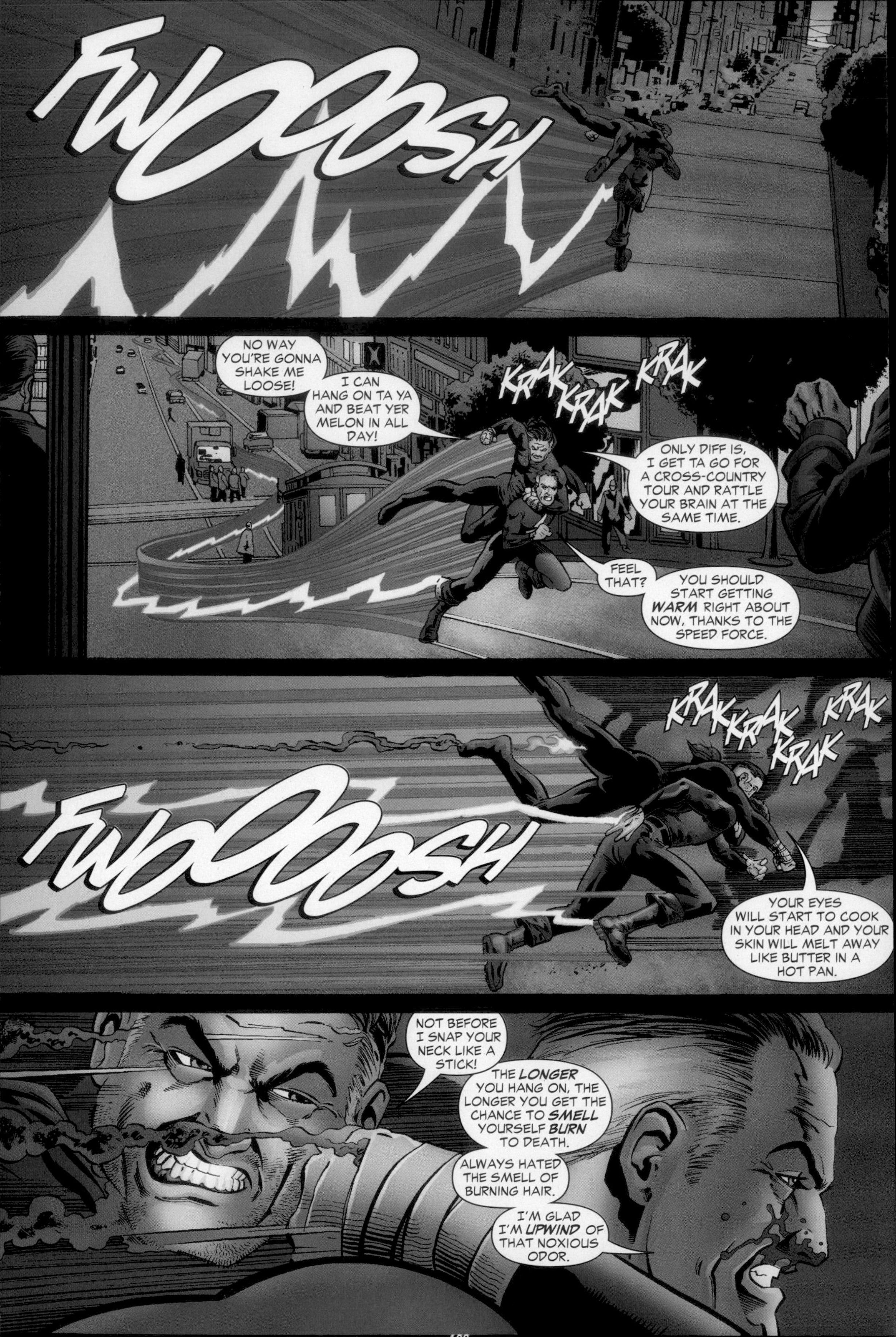
FWOOOSH
NO WAY YOU'RE GONNA SHAKE ME LOOSE!
I CAN HANG ON TA YA AND BEAT YER MELON IN ALL DAY!
KRAK KRAK KRAK KRAK
ONLY DIFF IS, I GET TA GO FOR A CROSS-COUNTRY TOUR AND RATTLE YOUR BRAIN AT THE SAME TIME.
FEEL THAT?
YOU SHOULD START GETTING WARM RIGHT ABOUT NOW, THANKS TO THE SPEED FORCE.
FWOOOSH
KRAK KRAK KRAK KRAK
YOUR EYES WILL START TO COOK IN YOUR HEAD AND YOUR SKIN WILL MELT AWAY LIKE BUTTER IN A HOT PAN.
NOT BEFORE I SNAP YOUR NECK LIKE A STICK!
THE LONGER YOU HANG ON, THE LONGER YOU GET THE CHANCE TO SMELL YOURSELF BURN TO DEATH.
ALWAYS HATED THE SMELL OF BURNING HAIR.
I'M GLAD I'M UPWIND OF THAT NOXIOUS ODOR.

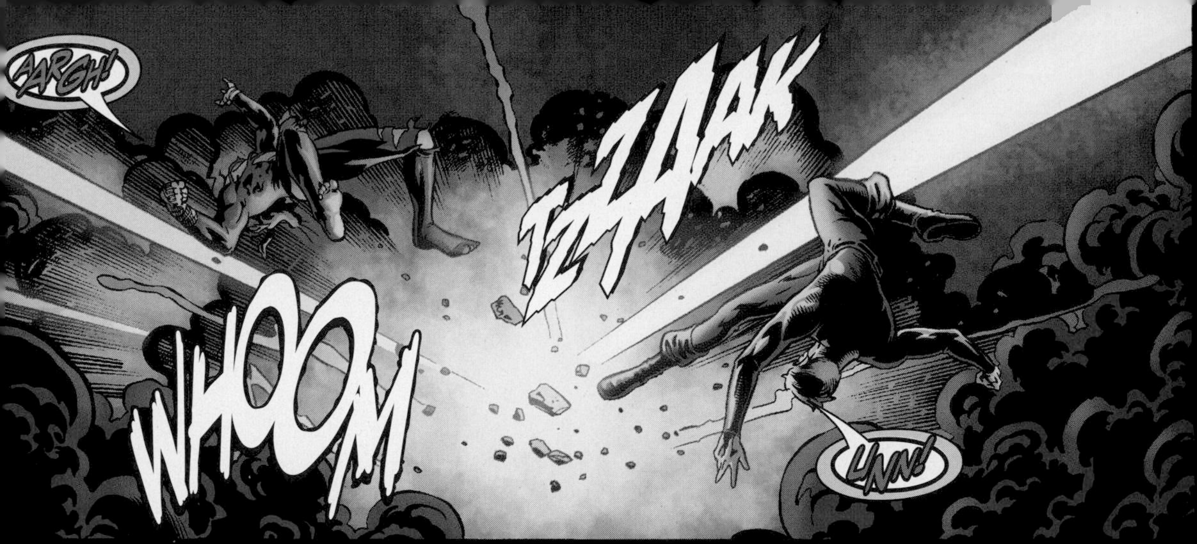
AARGH!
TZZAAK
WHOOM
UNN!

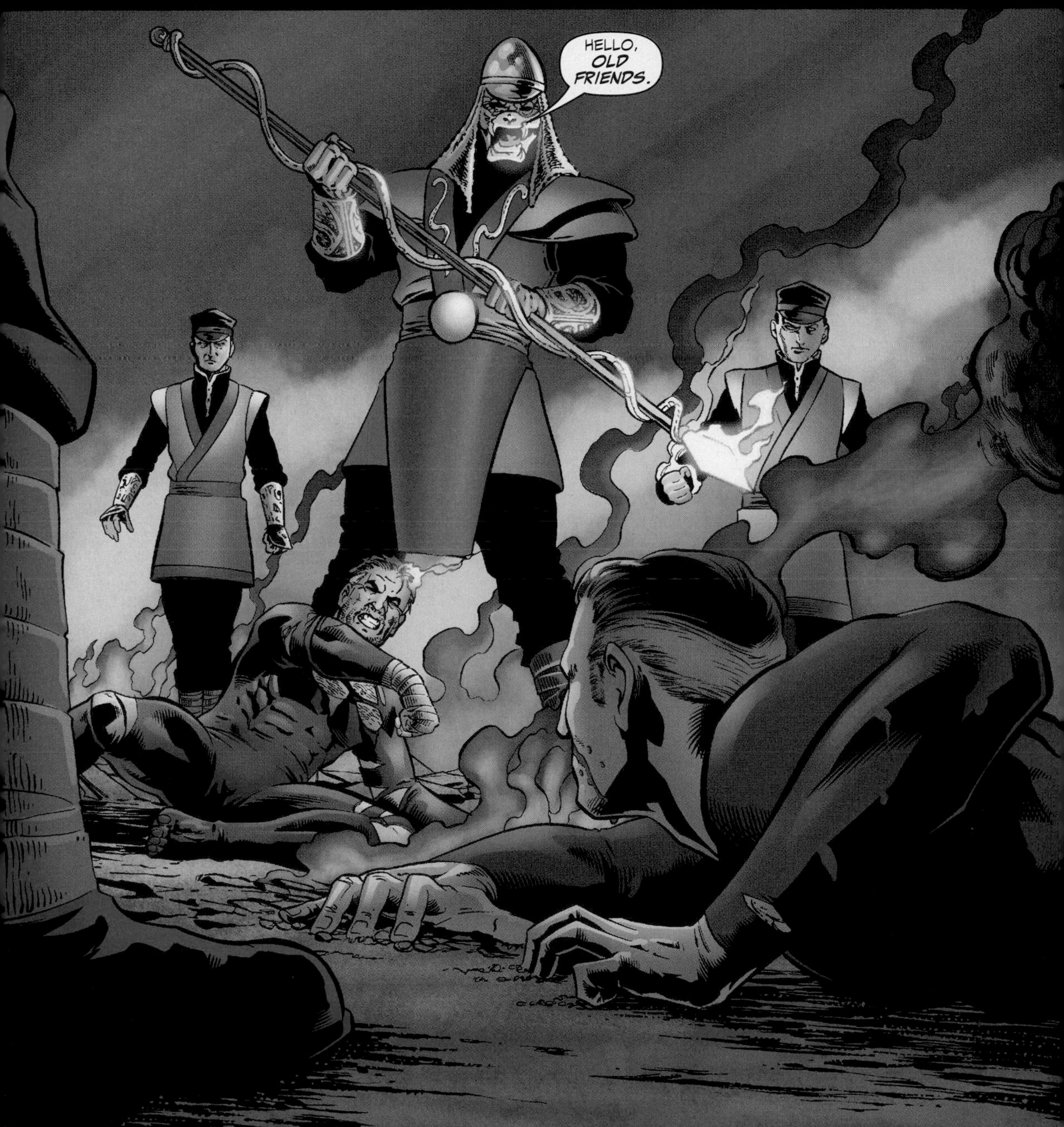
HELLO, OLD FRIENDS.

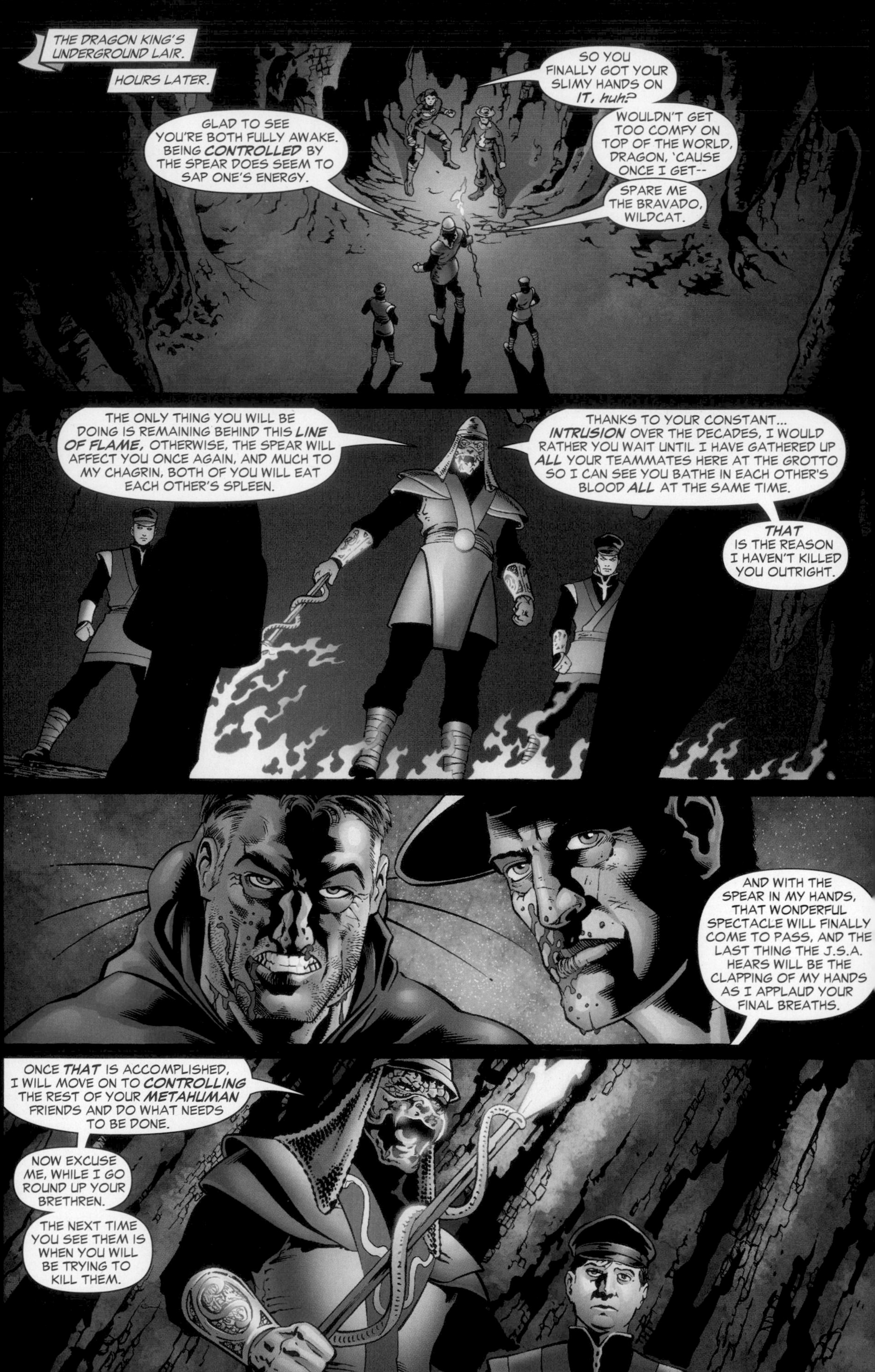
THE DRAGON KING'S UNDERGROUND LAIR.
HOURS LATER.
SO YOU FINALLY GOT YOUR SLIMY HANDS ON IT, huh?
WOULDN'T GET TOO COMFY ON TOP OF THE WORLD, DRAGON, 'CAUSE ONCE I GET--
GLAD TO SEE YOU'RE BOTH FULLY AWAKE. BEING CONTROLLED BY THE SPEAR DOES SEEM TO SAP ONE'S ENERGY.
SPARE ME THE BRAVADO, WILDCAT.
THE ONLY THING YOU WILL BE DOING IS REMAINING BEHIND THIS LINE OF FLAME, OTHERWISE, THE SPEAR WILL AFFECT YOU ONCE AGAIN, AND MUCH TO MY CHAGRIN, BOTH OF YOU WILL EAT EACH OTHER'S SPLEEN.
THANKS TO YOUR CONSTANT... INTRUSION OVER THE DECADES, I WOULD RATHER YOU WAIT UNTIL I HAVE GATHERED UP ALL YOUR TEAMMATES HERE AT THE GROTTO SO I CAN SEE YOU BATHE IN EACH OTHER'S BLOOD ALL AT THE SAME TIME.
THAT IS THE REASON I HAVEN'T KILLED YOU OUTRIGHT.
AND WITH THE SPEAR IN MY HANDS, THAT WONDERFUL SPECTACLE WILL FINALLY COME TO PASS, AND THE LAST THING THE J.S.A. HEARS WILL BE THE CLAPPING OF MY HANDS AS I APPLAUD YOUR FINAL BREATHS.
ONCE THAT IS ACCOMPLISHED, I WILL MOVE ON TO CONTROLLING THE REST OF YOUR METAHUMAN FRIENDS AND DO WHAT NEEDS TO BE DONE.
NOW EXCUSE ME, WHILE I GO ROUND UP YOUR BRETHREN.
THE NEXT TIME YOU SEE THEM IS WHEN YOU WILL BE TRYING TO KILL THEM.

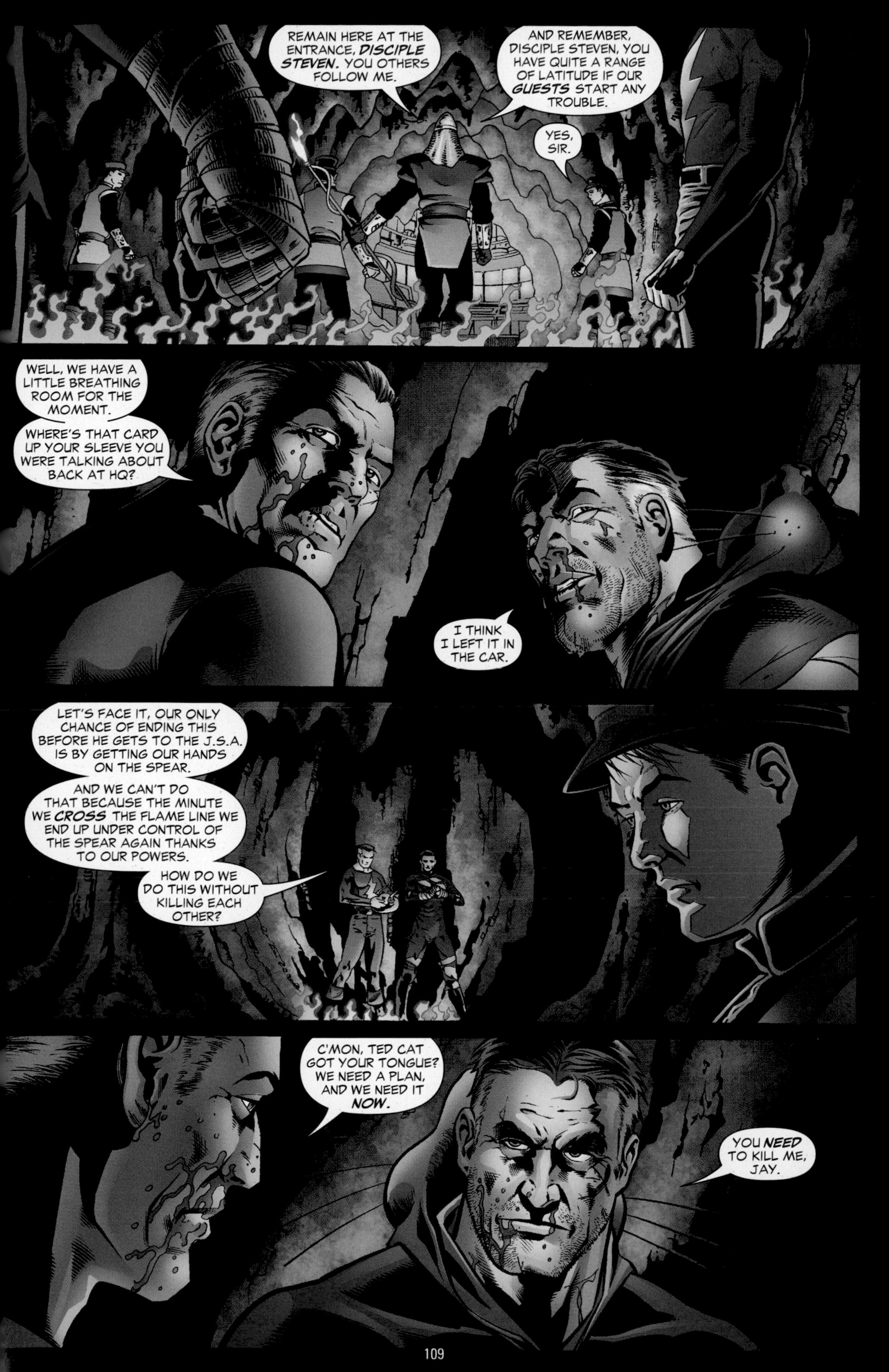
REMAIN HERE AT THE ENTRANCE, DISCIPLE STEVEN. YOU OTHERS FOLLOW ME.
AND REMEMBER, DISCIPLE STEVEN, YOU HAVE QUITE A RANGE OF LATITUDE IF OUR GUESTS START ANY TROUBLE.
YES, SIR.
WELL, WE HAVE A LITTLE BREATHING ROOM FOR THE MOMENT.
WHERE'S THAT CARD UP YOUR SLEEVE YOU WERE TALKING ABOUT BACK AT HQ?
I THINK I LEFT IT IN THE CAR.
LET'S FACE IT, OUR ONLY CHANCE OF ENDING THIS BEFORE HE GETS TO THE J.S.A. IS BY GETTING OUR HANDS ON THE SPEAR.
AND WE CAN'T DO THAT BECAUSE THE MINUTE WE CROSS THE FLAME LINE WE END UP UNDER CONTROL OF THE SPEAR AGAIN THANKS TO OUR POWERS.
HOW DO WE DO THIS WITHOUT KILLING EACH OTHER?
C'MON, TED CAT GOT YOUR TONGUE? WE NEED A PLAN, AND WE NEED IT NOW.
YOU NEED TO KILL ME, JAY.

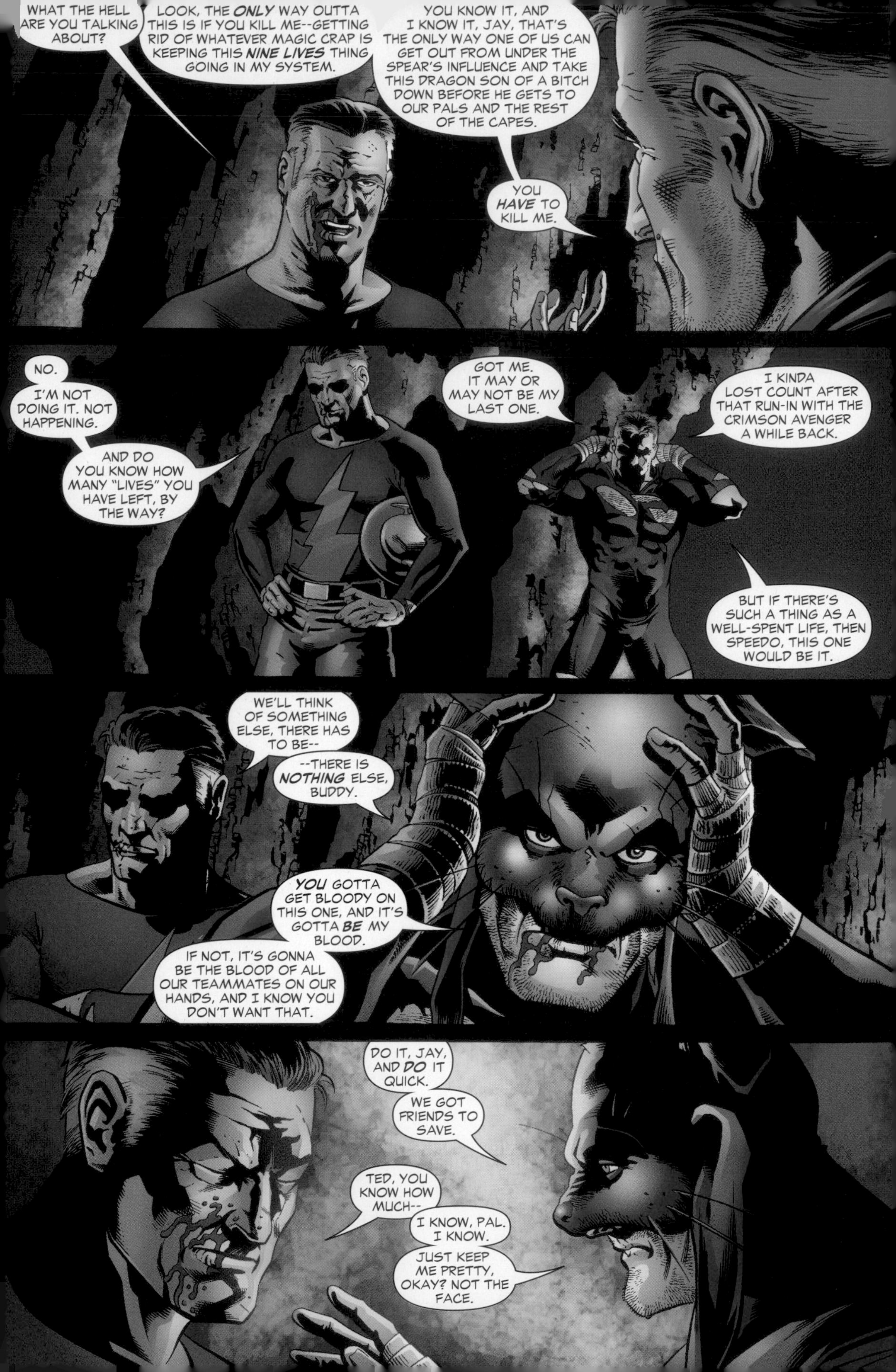
WHAT THE HELL ARE YOU TALKING ABOUT?
LOOK, THE ONLY WAY OUTTA THIS IS IF YOU KILL ME--GETTING RID OF WHATEVER MAGIC CRAP IS KEEPING THIS NINE LIVES THING GOING IN MY SYSTEM.
YOU KNOW IT, AND I KNOW IT, JAY, THAT'S THE ONLY WAY ONE OF US CAN GET OUT FROM UNDER THE SPEAR'S INFLUENCE AND TAKE THIS DRAGON SON OF A BITCH DOWN BEFORE HE GETS TO OUR PALS AND THE REST OF THE CAPES.
YOU HAVE TO KILL ME.
NO.
I'M NOT DOING IT. NOT HAPPENING.
AND DO YOU KNOW HOW MANY "LIVES" YOU HAVE LEFT, BY THE WAY?
GOT ME. IT MAY OR MAY NOT BE MY LAST ONE.
I KINDA LOST COUNT AFTER THAT RUN-IN WITH THE CRIMSON AVENGER A WHILE BACK.
BUT IF THERE'S SUCH A THING AS A WELL-SPENT LIFE, THEN SPEEDO, THIS ONE WOULD BE IT.
WE'LL THINK OF SOMETHING ELSE, THERE HAS TO BE--
--THERE IS NOTHING ELSE, BUDDY.
YOU GOTTA GET BLOODY ON THIS ONE, AND IT'S GOTTA BE MY BLOOD.
IF NOT, IT'S GONNA BE THE BLOOD OF ALL OUR TEAMMATES ON OUR HANDS, AND I KNOW YOU DON'T WANT THAT.
DO IT, JAY, AND DO IT QUICK.
WE GOT FRIENDS TO SAVE.
TED, YOU KNOW HOW MUCH--
I KNOW, PAL. I KNOW.
JUST KEEP ME PRETTY, OKAY? NOT THE FACE.

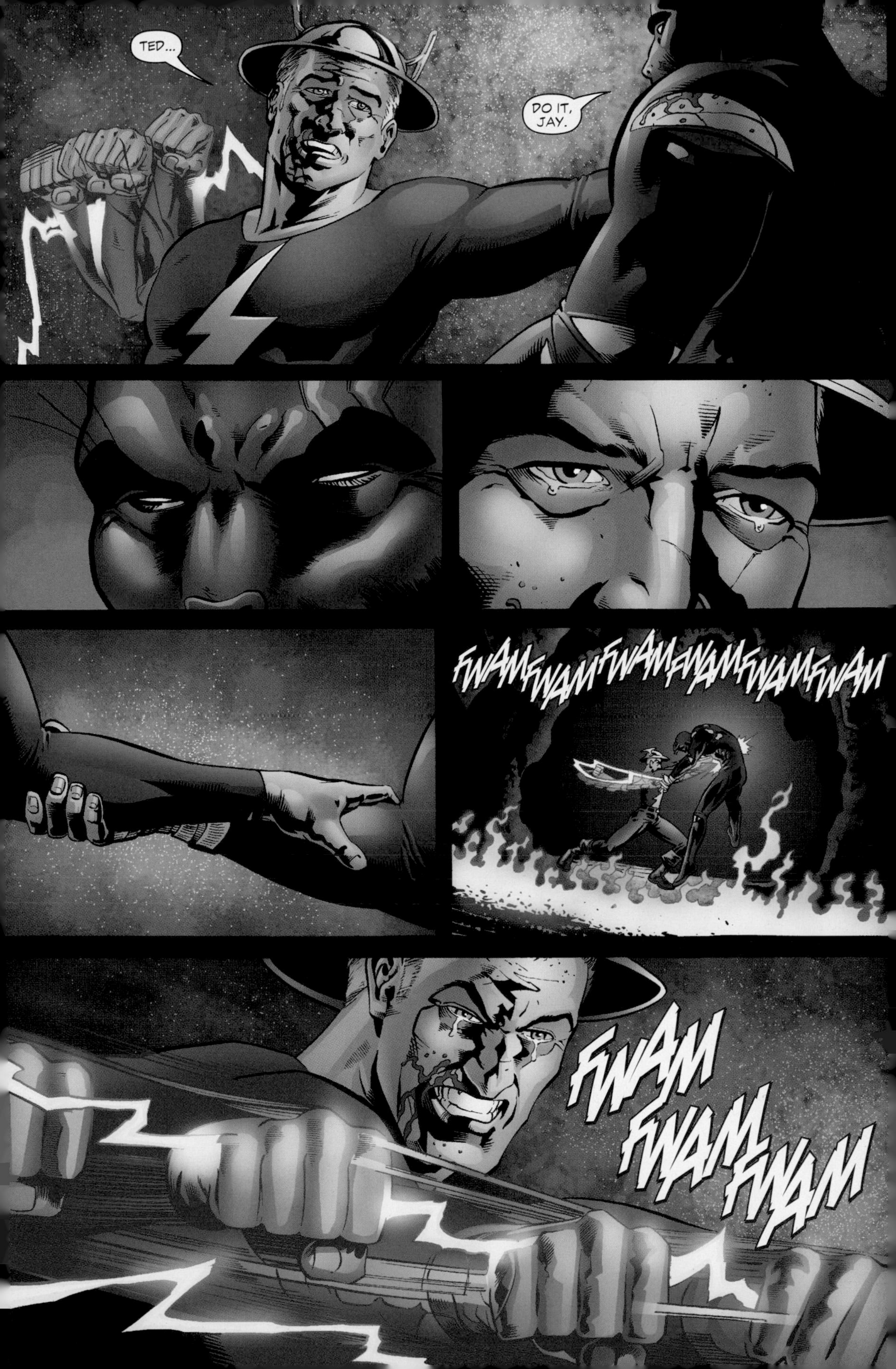
TED...
DO IT, JAY.
FWAM FWAM FWAM FWAM FWAM FWAM
FWAM
FWAM
FWAM

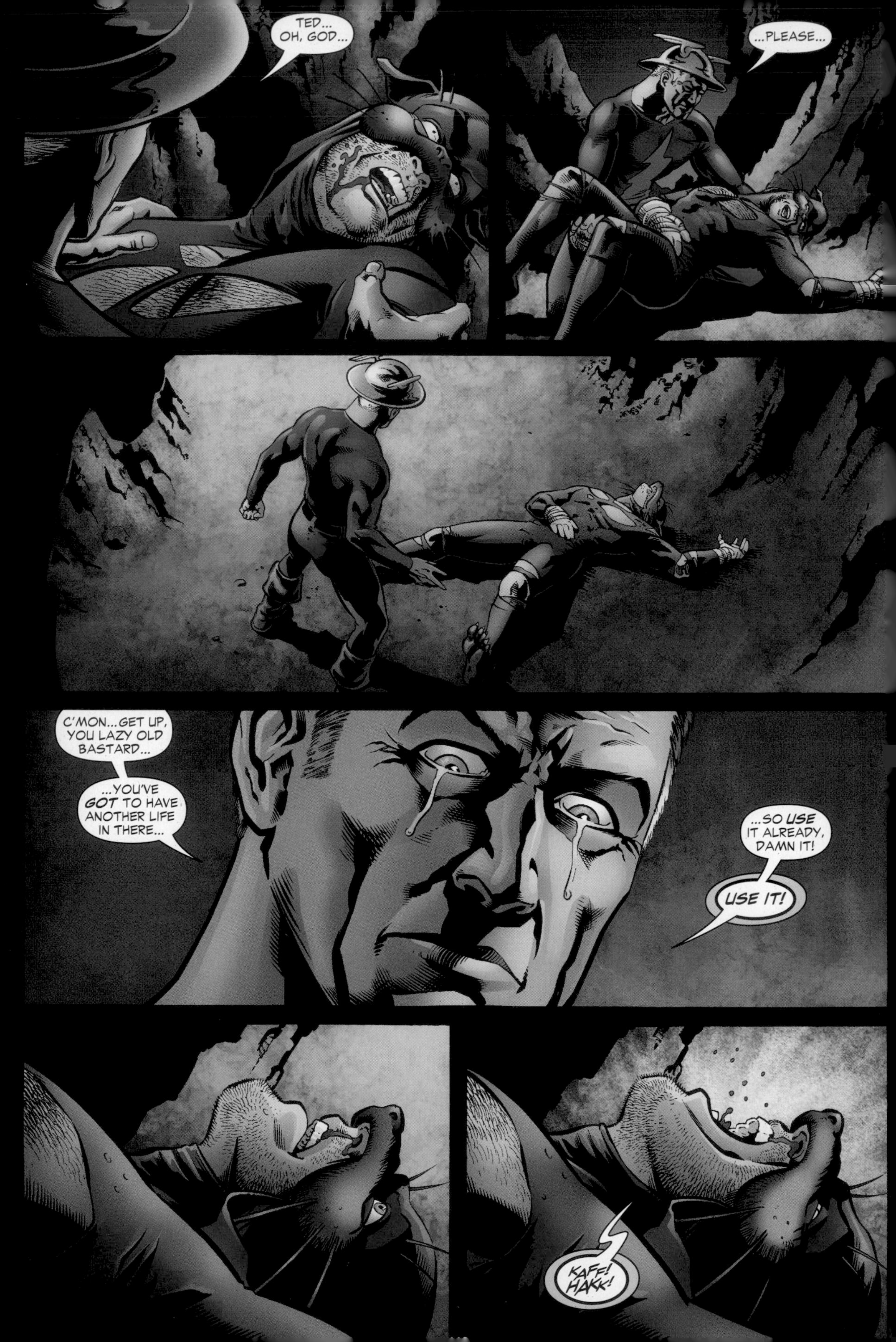
TED... OH, GOD...
...PLEASE...
C'MON...GET UP, YOU LAZY OLD BASTARD...
...YOU'VE GOT TO HAVE ANOTHER LIFE IN THERE...
...SO USE IT ALREADY, DAMN IT!
USE IT!
KAFF! HAKK!

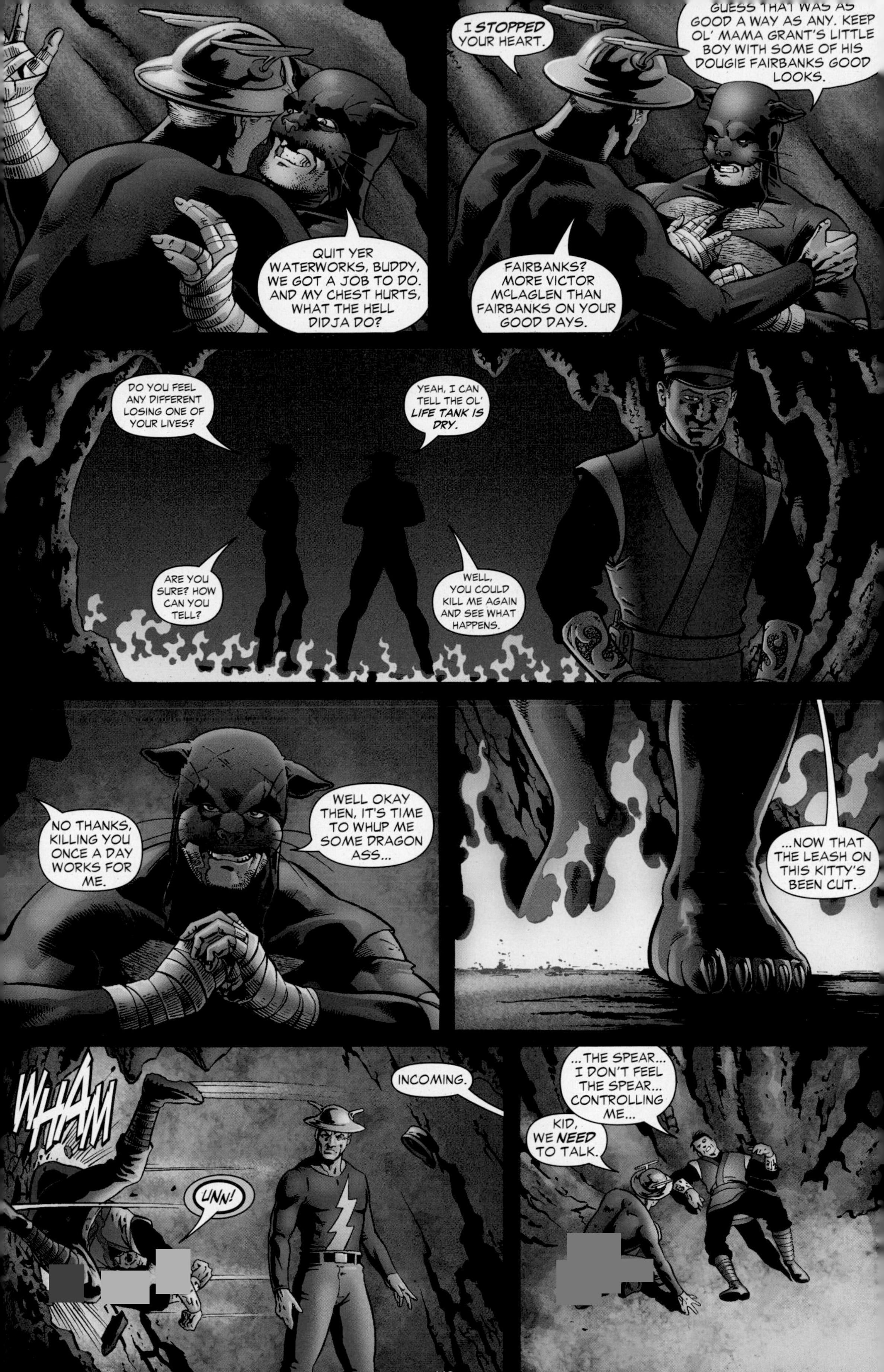
QUIT YER WATERWORKS, BUDDY, WE GOT A JOB TO DO. AND MY CHEST HURTS, WHAT THE HELL DIDJA DO?
I STOPPED YOUR HEART.
GUESS THAT WAS AS GOOD A WAY AS ANY. KEEP OL' MAMA GRANT'S LITTLE BOY WITH SOME OF HIS DOUGIE FAIRBANKS GOOD LOOKS.
FAIRBANKS? MORE VICTOR McLAGLEN THAN FAIRBANKS ON YOUR GOOD DAYS.
DO YOU FEEL ANY DIFFERENT LOSING ONE OF YOUR LIVES?
YEAH, I CAN TELL THE OL' LIFE TANK IS DRY.
ARE YOU SURE? HOW CAN YOU TELL?
WELL, YOU COULD KILL ME AGAIN AND SEE WHAT HAPPENS.
NO THANKS, KILLING YOU ONCE A DAY WORKS FOR ME.
WELL OKAY THEN, IT'S TIME TO WHUP ME SOME DRAGON ASS...
...NOW THAT THE LEASH ON THIS KITTY'S BEEN CUT.
WHAM
UNN!
INCOMING.
...THE SPEAR... I DON'T FEEL THE SPEAR... CONTROLLING ME...
KID, WE NEED TO TALK.

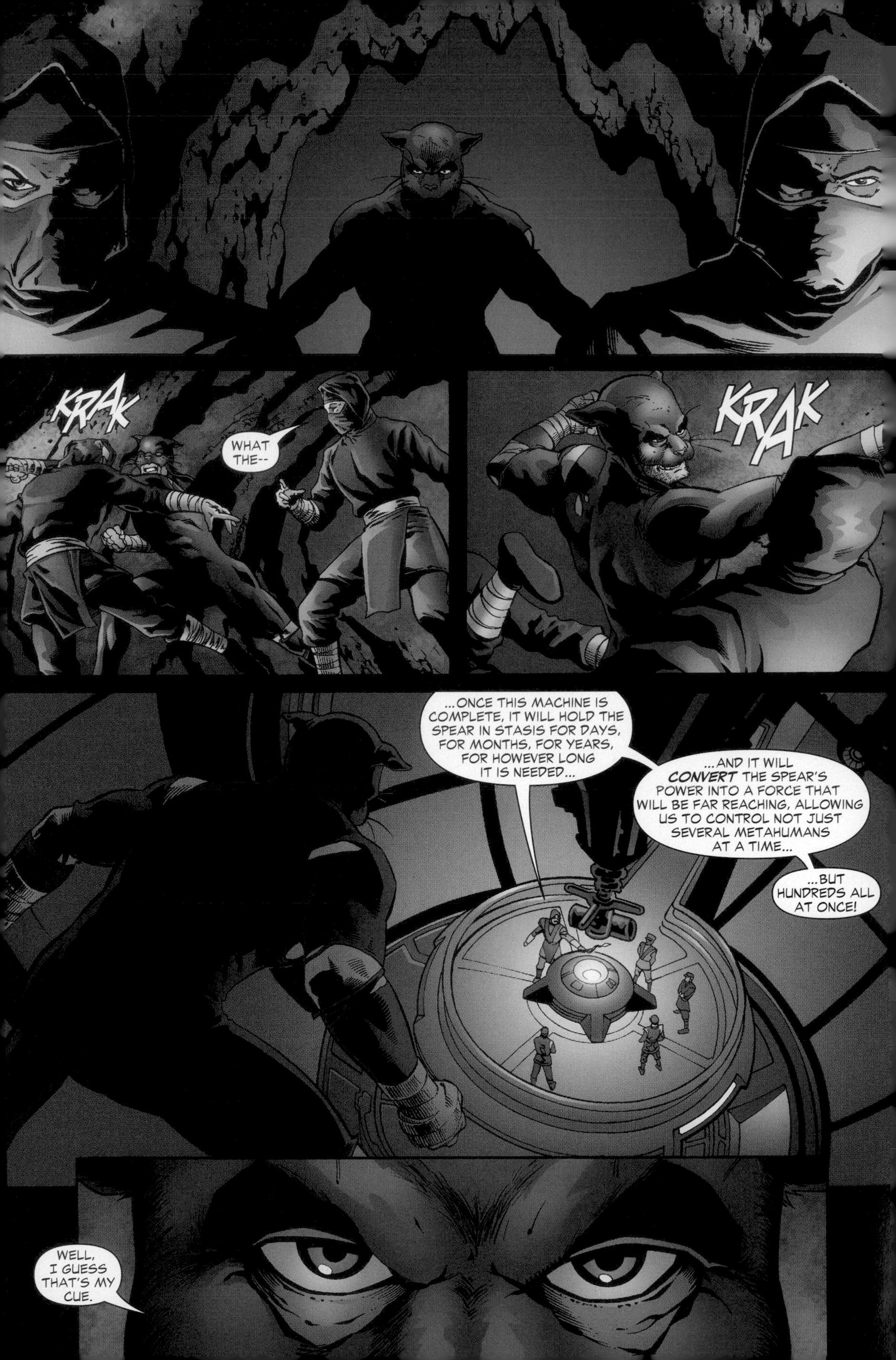
KRAK
WHAT THE--
KRAK
...ONCE THIS MACHINE IS COMPLETE, IT WILL HOLD THE SPEAR IN STASIS FOR DAYS, FOR MONTHS, FOR YEARS, FOR HOWEVER LONG IT IS NEEDED...
...AND IT WILL CONVERT THE SPEAR'S POWER INTO A FORCE THAT WILL BE FAR REACHING, ALLOWING US TO CONTROL NOT JUST SEVERAL METAHUMANS AT A TIME...
...BUT HUNDREDS ALL AT ONCE!
WELL, I GUESS THAT'S MY CUE.

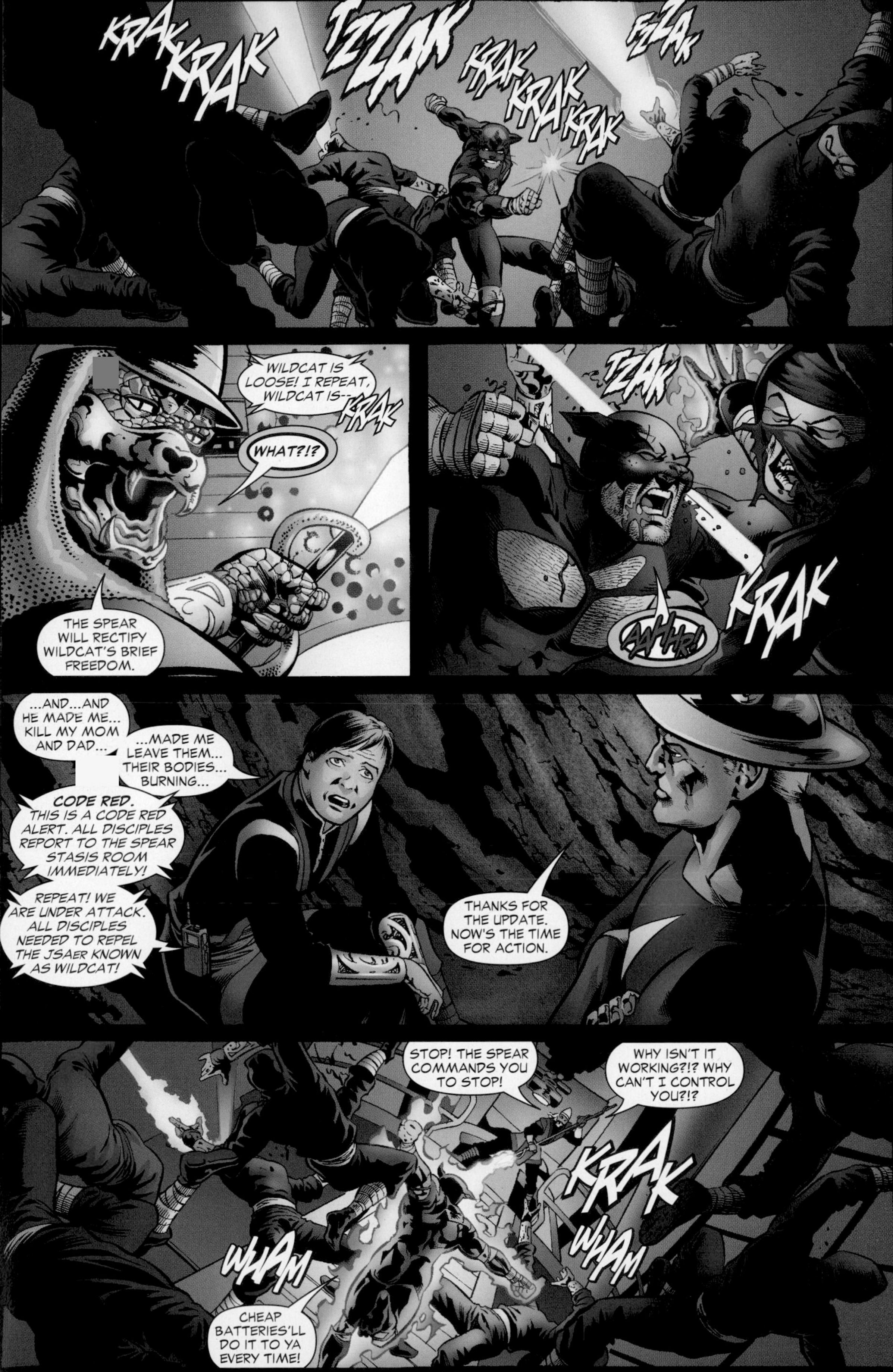
KRAK KRAK
TZZAK
KRAK KRAK KRAK
FZZAK
WILDCAT IS LOOSE! I REPEAT, WILDCAT IS--
KRAK
WHAT?!?
THE SPEAR WILL RECTIFY WILDCAT'S BRIEF FREEDOM.
TZZAK
AAHHR!
KRAK
...AND...AND HE MADE ME... KILL MY MOM AND DAD...
...MADE ME LEAVE THEM... THEIR BODIES... BURNING...
CODE RED. THIS IS A CODE RED ALERT. ALL DISCIPLES REPORT TO THE SPEAR STASIS ROOM IMMEDIATELY!
REPEAT! WE ARE UNDER ATTACK. ALL DISCIPLES NEEDED TO REPEL THE JSAER KNOWN AS WILDCAT!
THANKS FOR THE UPDATE. NOW'S THE TIME FOR ACTION.
STOP! THE SPEAR COMMANDS YOU TO STOP!
WHY ISN'T IT WORKING?!? WHY CAN'T I CONTROL YOU?!?
KRAK
WHAM
WHAM
CHEAP BATTERIES'LL DO IT TO YA EVERY TIME!

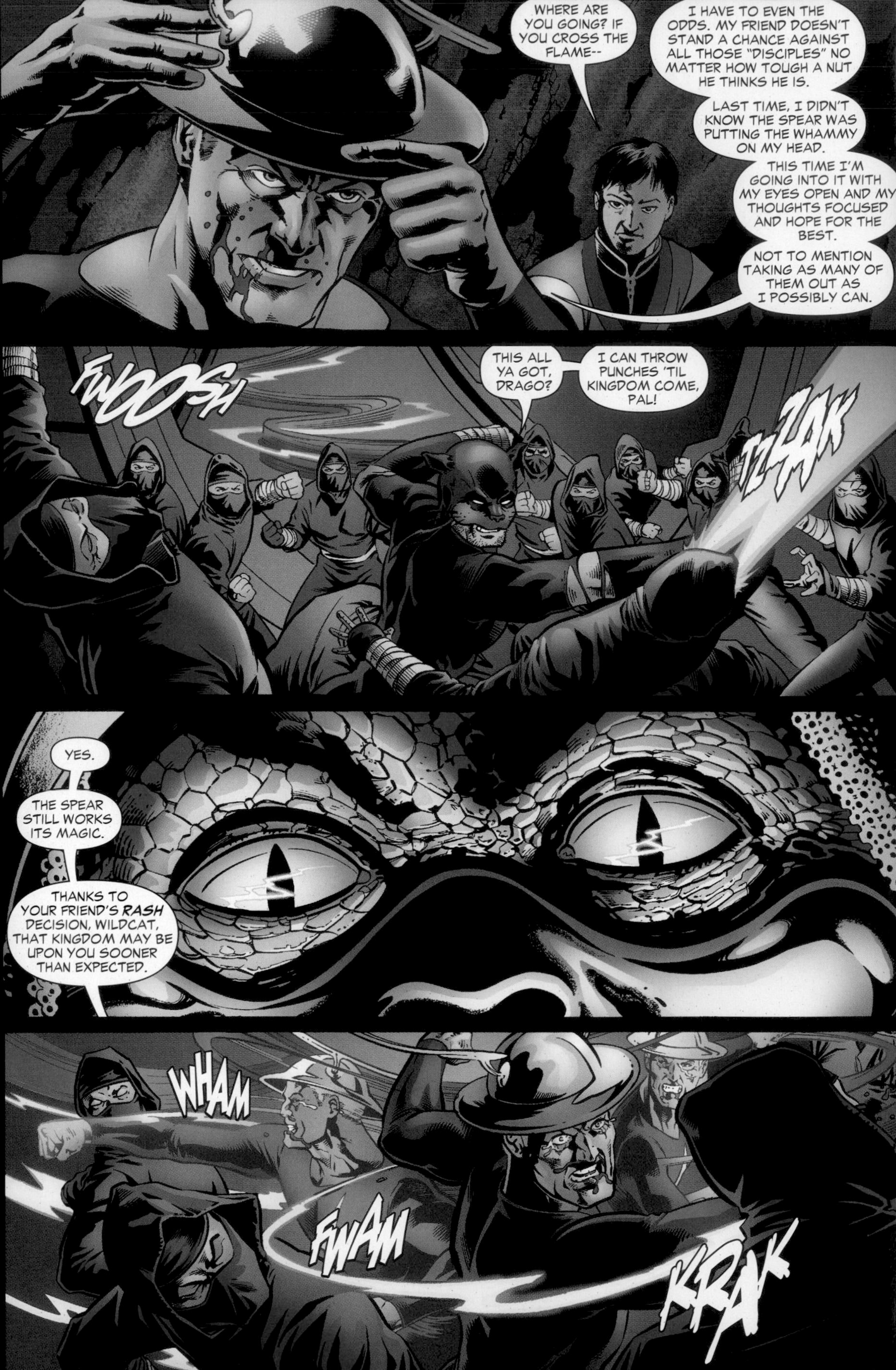
WHERE ARE YOU GOING? IF YOU CROSS THE FLAME--
I HAVE TO EVEN THE ODDS. MY FRIEND DOESN'T STAND A CHANCE AGAINST ALL THOSE "DISCIPLES" NO MATTER HOW TOUGH A NUT HE THINKS HE IS.
LAST TIME, I DIDN'T KNOW THE SPEAR WAS PUTTING THE WHAMMY ON MY HEAD.
THIS TIME I'M GOING INTO IT WITH MY EYES OPEN AND MY THOUGHTS FOCUSED AND HOPE FOR THE BEST.
NOT TO MENTION TAKING AS MANY OF THEM OUT AS I POSSIBLY CAN.
FWOOSH
THIS ALL YA GOT, DRAGO?
I CAN THROW PUNCHES 'TIL KINGDOM COME, PAL!
TZZAK
YES.
THE SPEAR STILL WORKS ITS MAGIC.
THANKS TO YOUR FRIEND'S *RASH* DECISION, WILDCAT, THAT KINGDOM MAY BE UPON YOU SOONER THAN EXPECTED.
WHAM
FWAM
KRAK

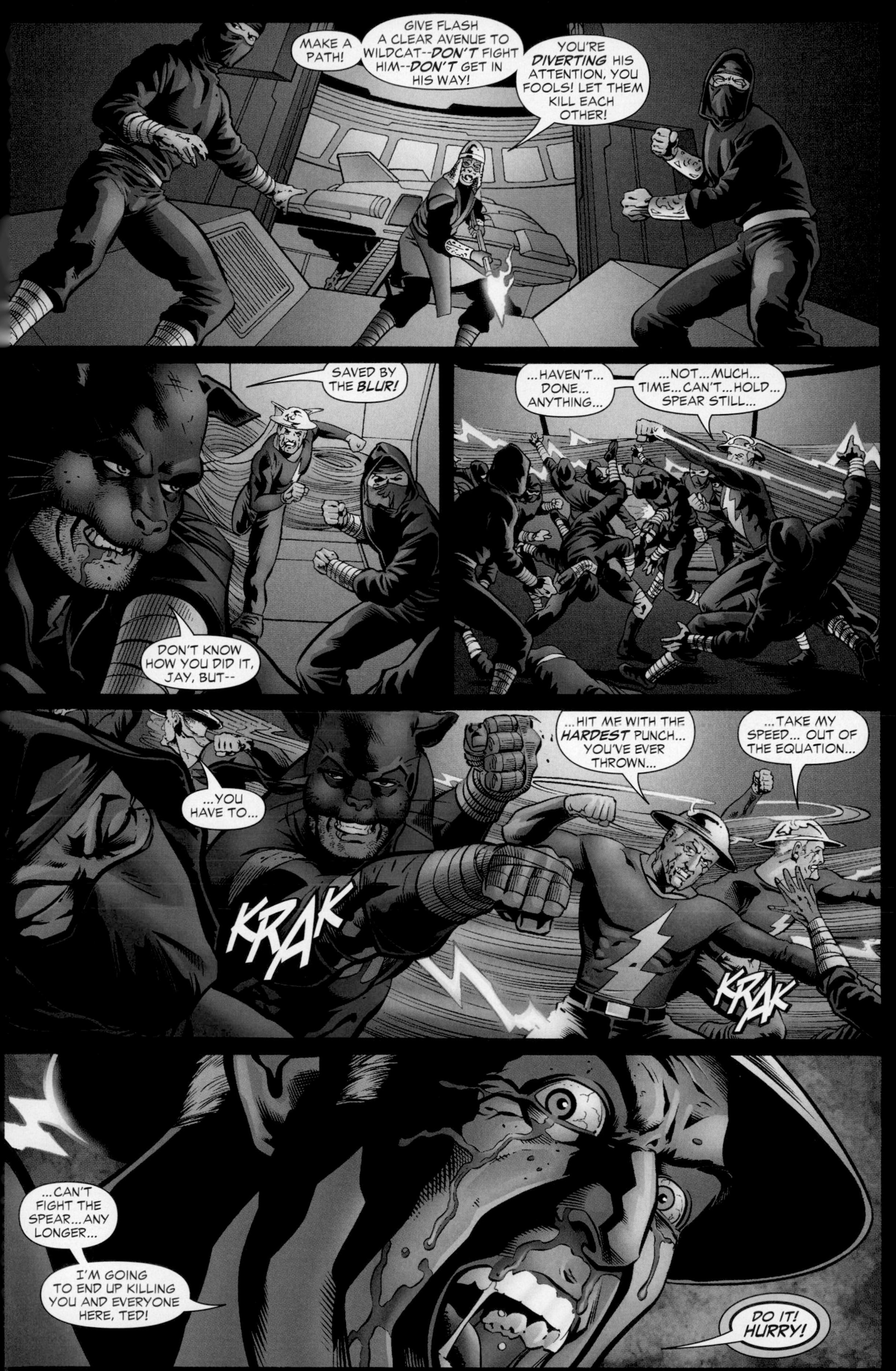
MAKE A PATH!
GIVE FLASH A CLEAR AVENUE TO WILDCAT--DON'T FIGHT HIM--DON'T GET IN HIS WAY!
YOU'RE DIVERTING HIS ATTENTION, YOU FOOLS! LET THEM KILL EACH OTHER!
SAVED BY THE BLUR!
DON'T KNOW HOW YOU DID IT, JAY, BUT--
...HAVEN'T... DONE... ANYTHING...
...NOT...MUCH... TIME...CAN'T...HOLD... SPEAR STILL...
...YOU HAVE TO...
...HIT ME WITH THE HARDEST PUNCH... YOU'VE EVER THROWN...
...TAKE MY SPEED... OUT OF THE EQUATION...
KRAK
KRAK
...CAN'T FIGHT THE SPEAR...ANY LONGER...
I'M GOING TO END UP KILLING YOU AND EVERYONE HERE, TED!
DO IT! HURRY!

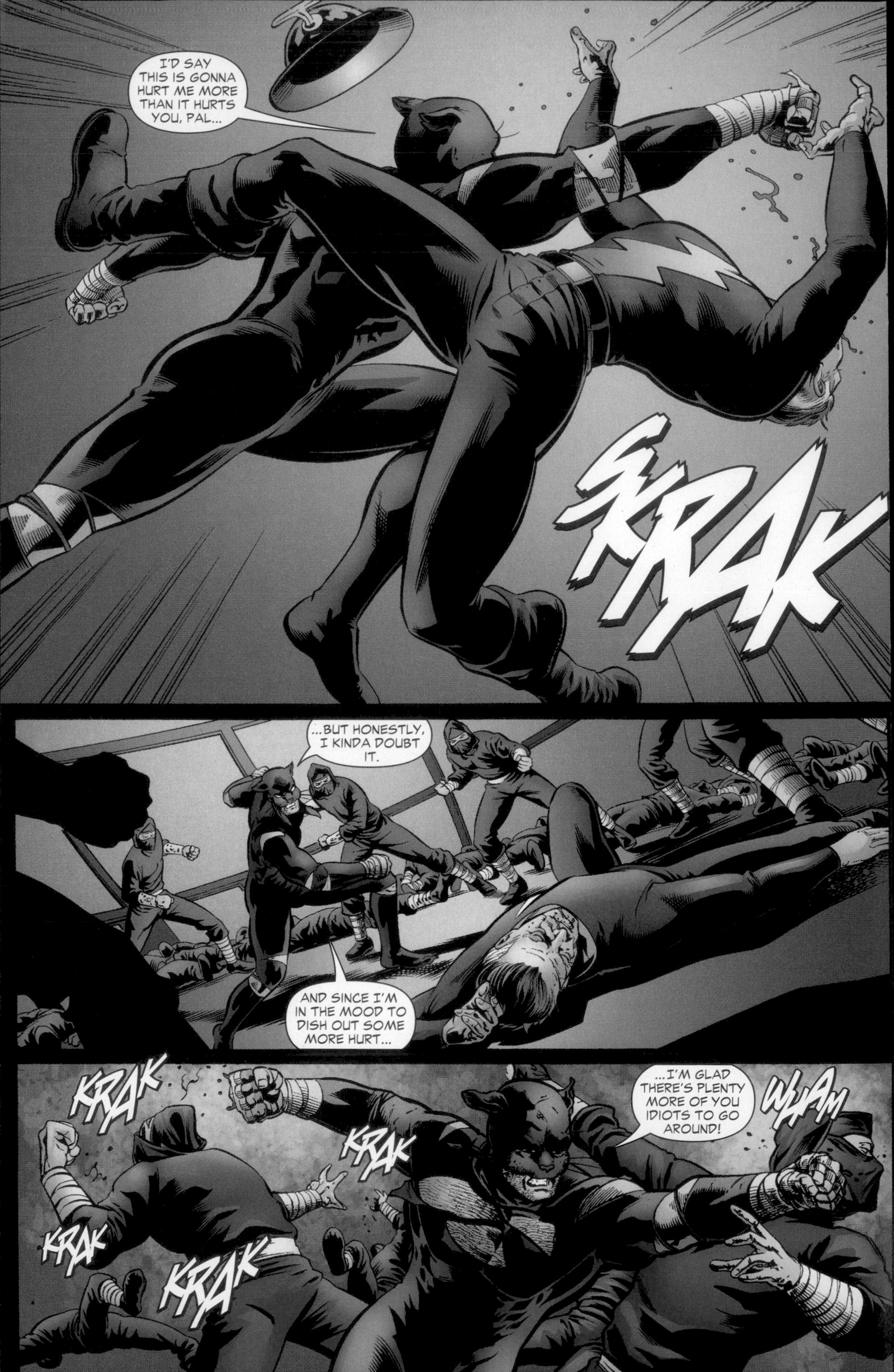

I'D SAY THIS IS GONNA HURT ME MORE THAN IT HURTS YOU, PAL...
SKRAK
...BUT HONESTLY, I KINDA DOUBT IT.
AND SINCE I'M IN THE MOOD TO DISH OUT SOME MORE HURT...
KRAK
KRAK
...I'M GLAD THERE'S PLENTY MORE OF YOU IDIOTS TO GO AROUND!
WHAM
KRAK
KRAK

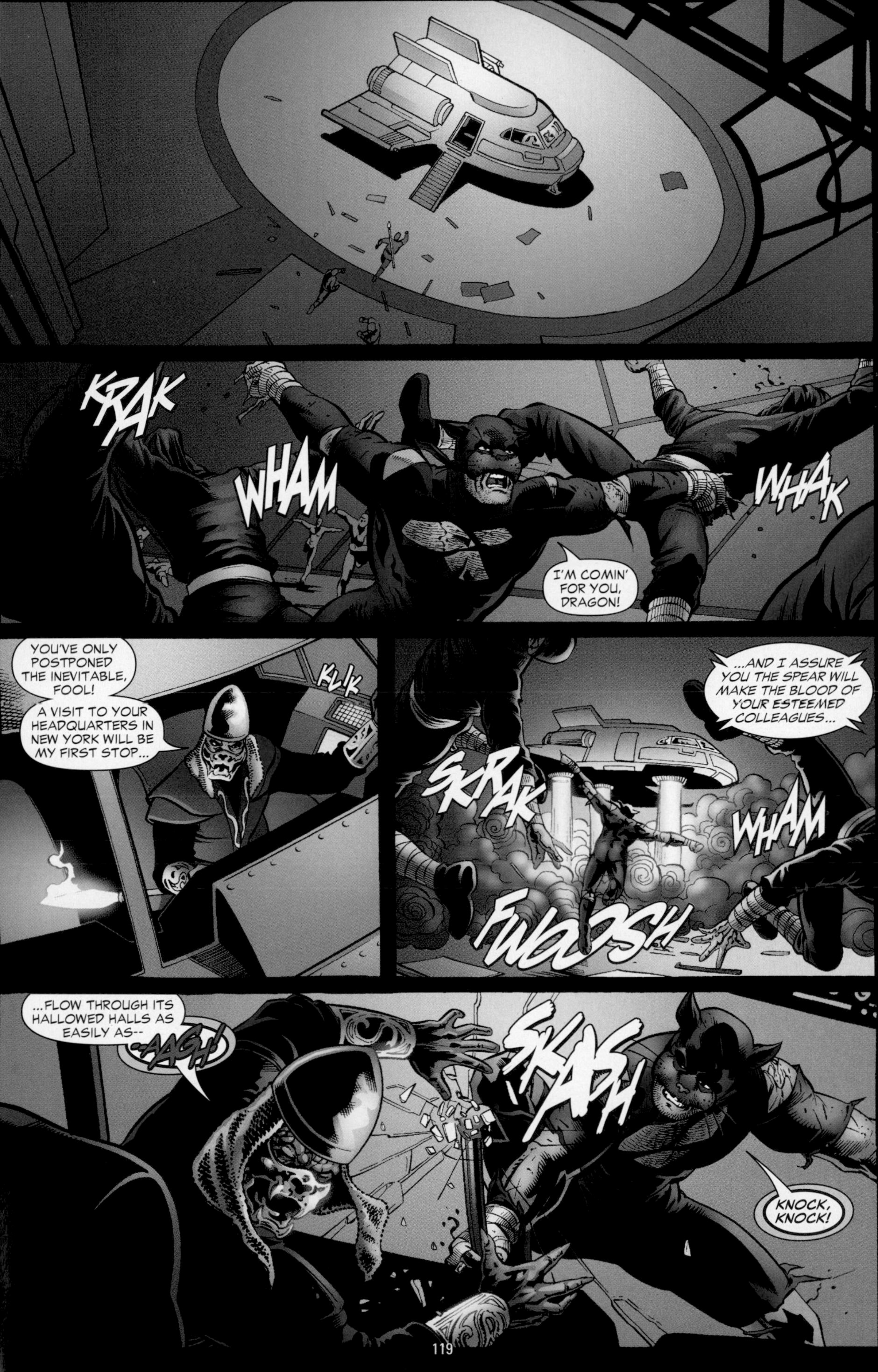
KRAK
WHAM
WHAK
I'M COMIN' FOR YOU, DRAGON!
YOU'VE ONLY POSTPONED THE INEVITABLE, FOOL!
A VISIT TO YOUR HEADQUARTERS IN NEW YORK WILL BE MY FIRST STOP...
KLIK
...AND I ASSURE YOU THE SPEAR WILL MAKE THE BLOOD OF YOUR ESTEEMED COLLEAGUES...
SKRAK
WHAM
FWOOSH
...FLOW THROUGH ITS HALLOWED HALLS AS EASILY AS--
--AAGH!
SKASH
KNOCK, KNOCK!

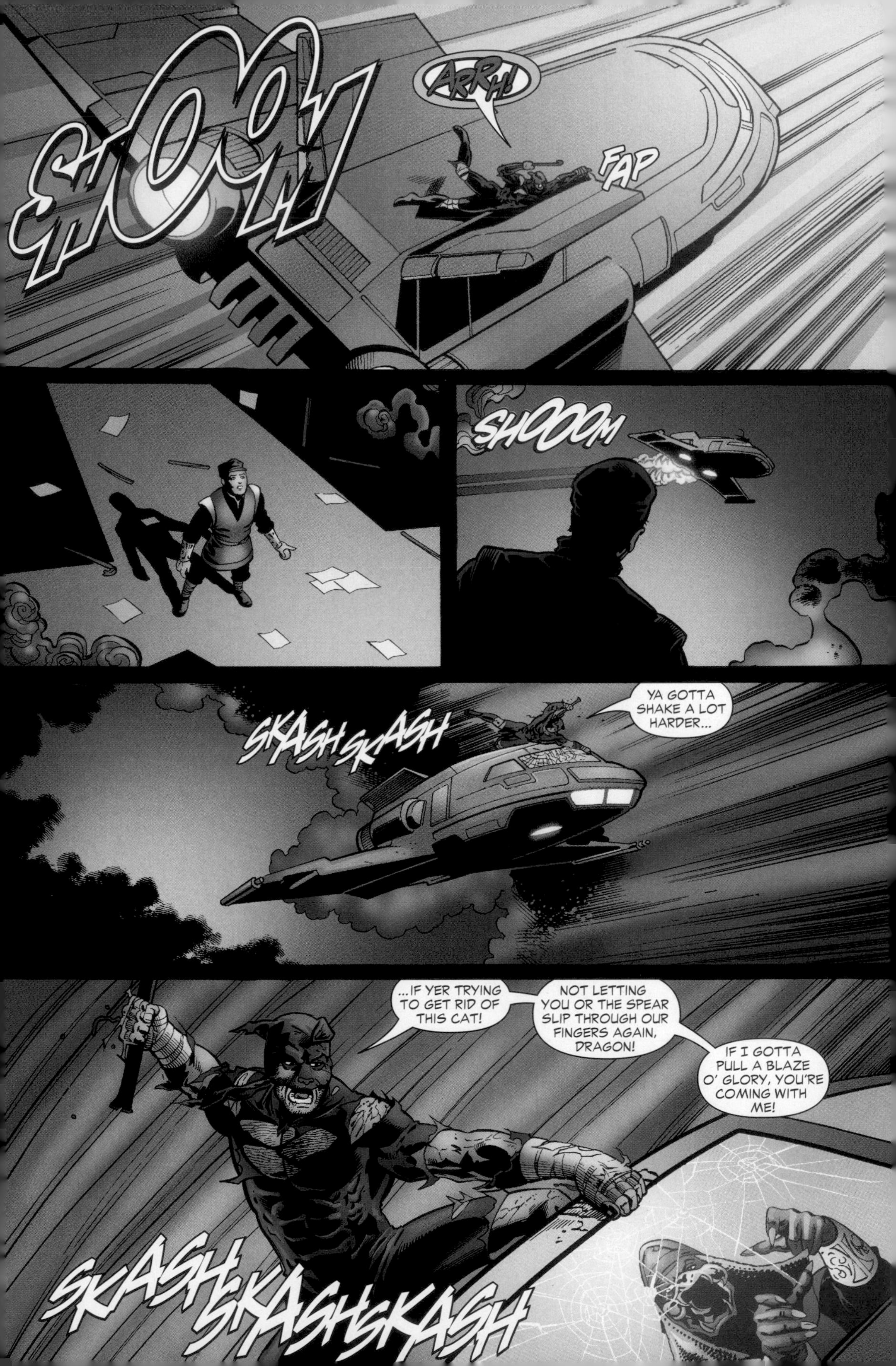
SHOOM
ARRH!
FAP
SHOOOM
SKASH SKASH
YA GOTTA SHAKE A LOT HARDER...
...IF YER TRYING TO GET RID OF THIS CAT!
NOT LETTING YOU OR THE SPEAR SLIP THROUGH OUR FINGERS AGAIN, DRAGON!
IF I GOTTA PULL A BLAZE O' GLORY, YOU'RE COMING WITH ME!
SKASH SKASH SKASH

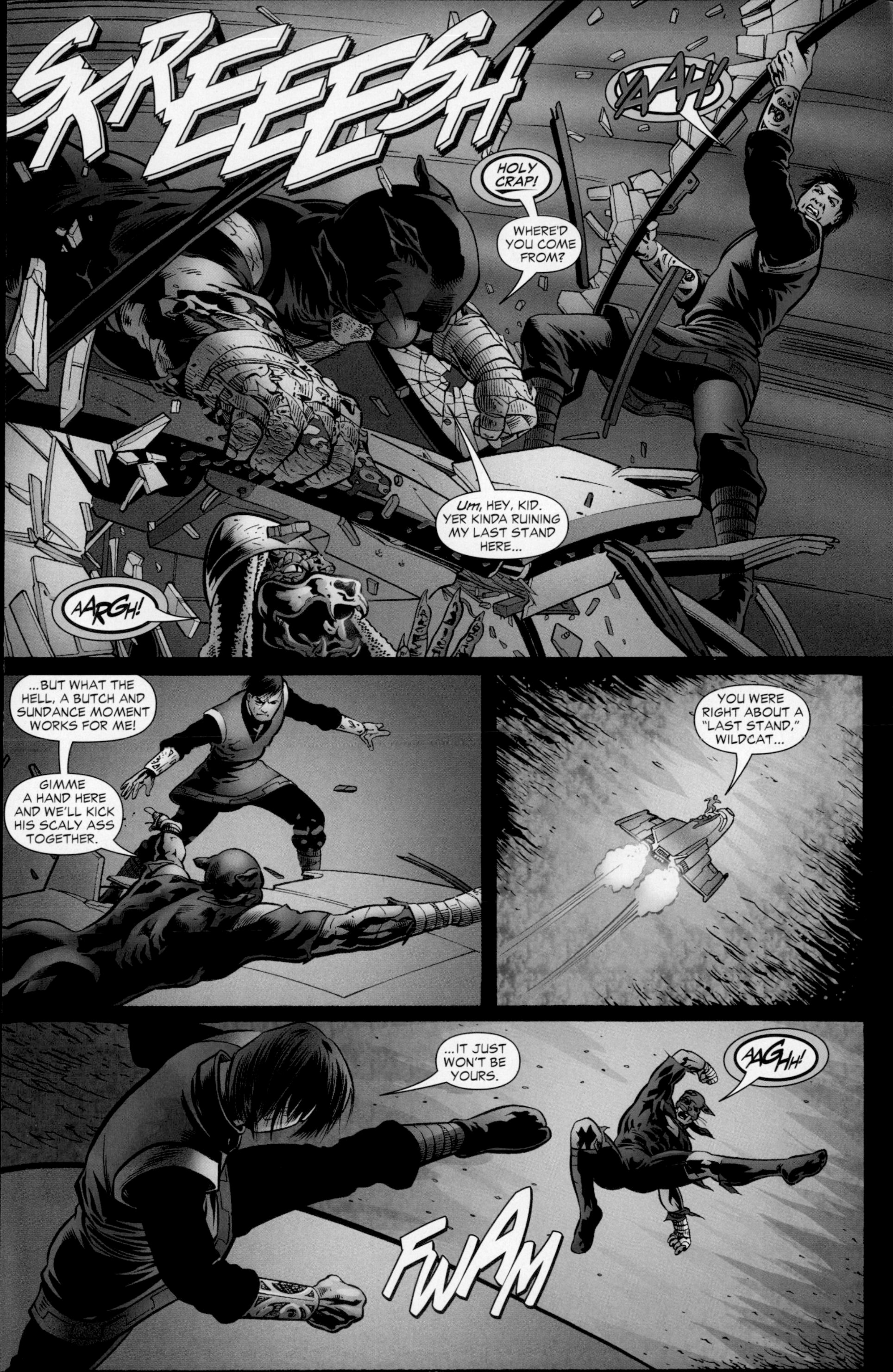
SKREEESH
YAAH!
HOLY CRAP!
WHERE'D YOU COME FROM?
Um, HEY, KID. YER KINDA RUINING MY LAST STAND HERE...
AARGH!
...BUT WHAT THE HELL, A BUTCH AND SUNDANCE MOMENT WORKS FOR ME!
GIMME A HAND HERE AND WE'LL KICK HIS SCALY ASS TOGETHER.
YOU WERE RIGHT ABOUT A "LAST STAND," WILDCAT...
...IT JUST WON'T BE YOURS.
AAGHH!
FWAM

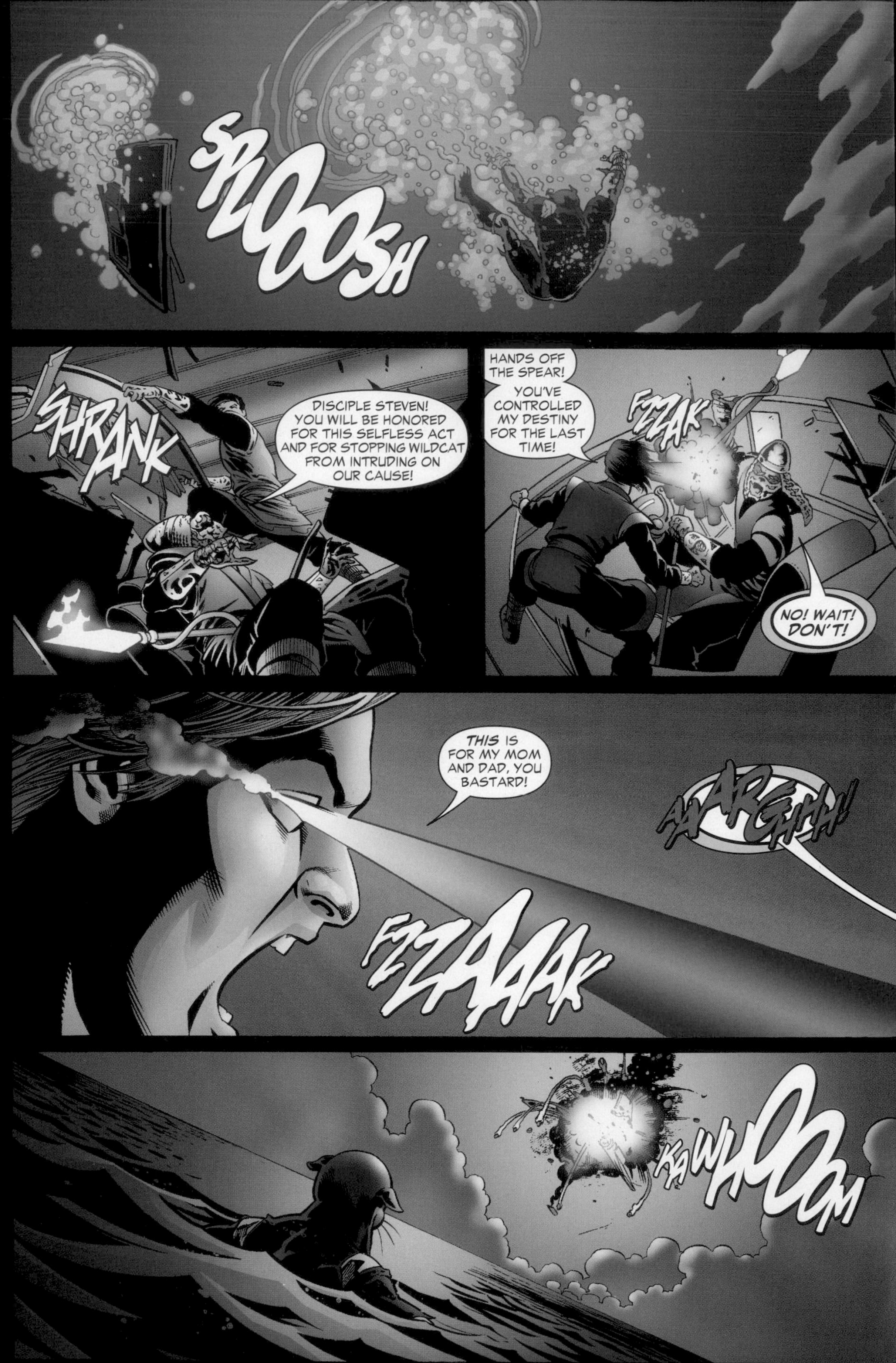
SPLOOOOSH
SHRANK
DISCIPLE STEVEN! YOU WILL BE HONORED FOR THIS SELFLESS ACT AND FOR STOPPING WILDCAT FROM INTRUDING ON OUR CAUSE!
HANDS OFF THE SPEAR!
YOU'VE CONTROLLED MY DESTINY FOR THE LAST TIME!
FZZAK
NO! WAIT! DON'T!
THIS IS FOR MY MOM AND DAD, YOU BASTARD!
AAARGHHH!
FZZAAAK
KA-WHOOOM

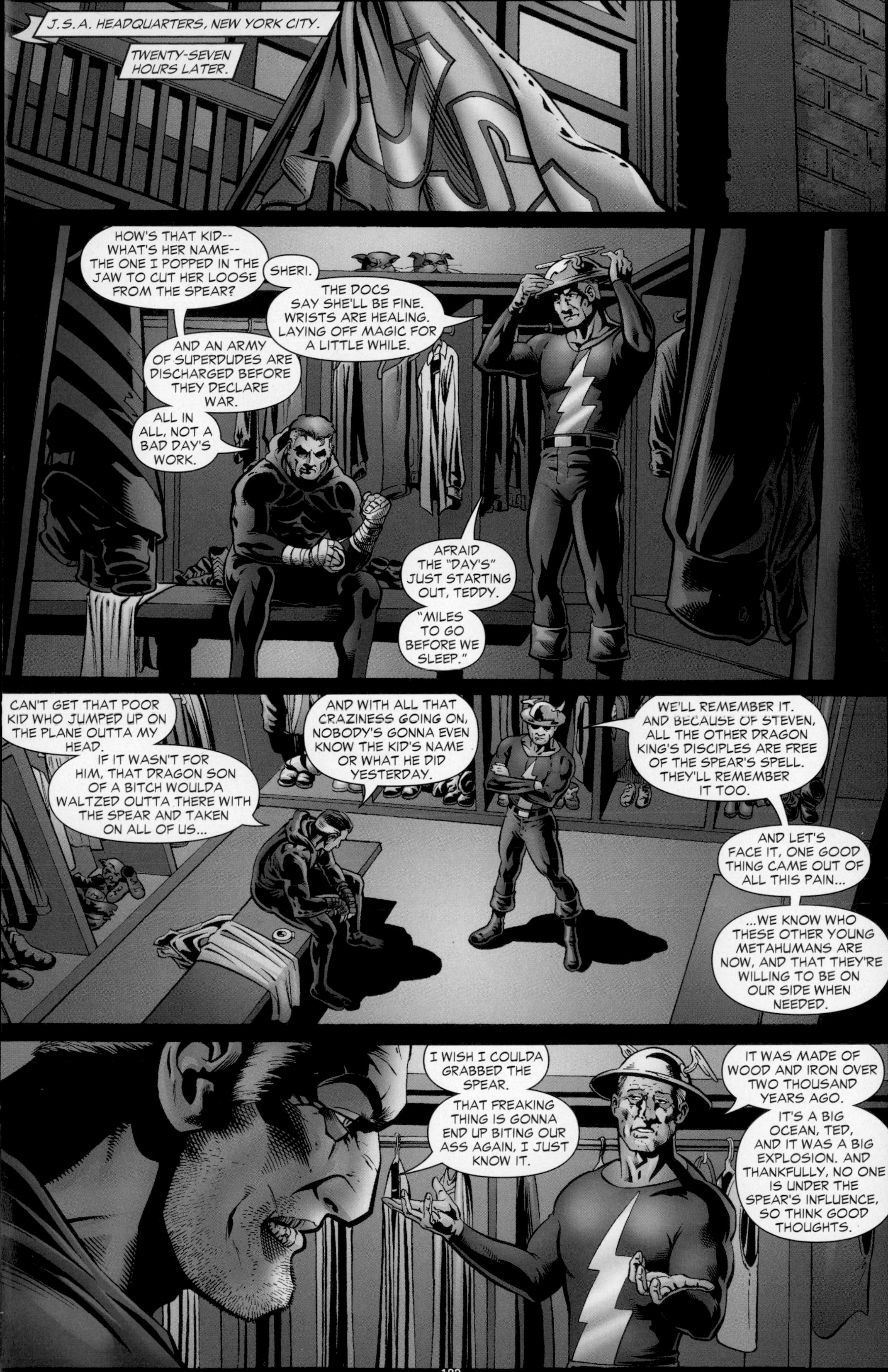

J.S.A. HEADQUARTERS, NEW YORK CITY.
TWENTY-SEVEN HOURS LATER.
HOW'S THAT KID-- WHAT'S HER NAME-- THE ONE I POPPED IN THE JAW TO CUT HER LOOSE FROM THE SPEAR?
SHERI.
THE DOCS SAY SHE'LL BE FINE. WRISTS ARE HEALING. LAYING OFF MAGIC FOR A LITTLE WHILE.
AND AN ARMY OF SUPERDUDES ARE DISCHARGED BEFORE THEY DECLARE WAR.
ALL IN ALL, NOT A BAD DAY'S WORK.
AFRAID THE "DAY'S" JUST STARTING OUT, TEDDY.
"MILES TO GO BEFORE WE SLEEP."
CAN'T GET THAT POOR KID WHO JUMPED UP ON THE PLANE OUTTA MY HEAD.
IF IT WASN'T FOR HIM, THAT DRAGON SON OF A BITCH WOULDA WALTZED OUTTA THERE WITH THE SPEAR AND TAKEN ON ALL OF US...
AND WITH ALL THAT CRAZINESS GOING ON, NOBODY'S GONNA EVEN KNOW THE KID'S NAME OR WHAT HE DID YESTERDAY.
WE'LL REMEMBER IT. AND BECAUSE OF STEVEN, ALL THE OTHER DRAGON KING'S DISCIPLES ARE FREE OF THE SPEAR'S SPELL. THEY'LL REMEMBER IT TOO.
AND LET'S FACE IT, ONE GOOD THING CAME OUT OF ALL THIS PAIN...
...WE KNOW WHO THESE OTHER YOUNG METAHUMANS ARE NOW, AND THAT THEY'RE WILLING TO BE ON OUR SIDE WHEN NEEDED.
I WISH I COULDA GRABBED THE SPEAR.
THAT FREAKING THING IS GONNA END UP BITING OUR ASS AGAIN, I JUST KNOW IT.
IT WAS MADE OF WOOD AND IRON OVER TWO THOUSAND YEARS AGO.
IT'S A BIG OCEAN, TED, AND IT WAS A BIG EXPLOSION. AND THANKFULLY, NO ONE IS UNDER THE SPEAR'S INFLUENCE, SO THINK GOOD THOUGHTS.

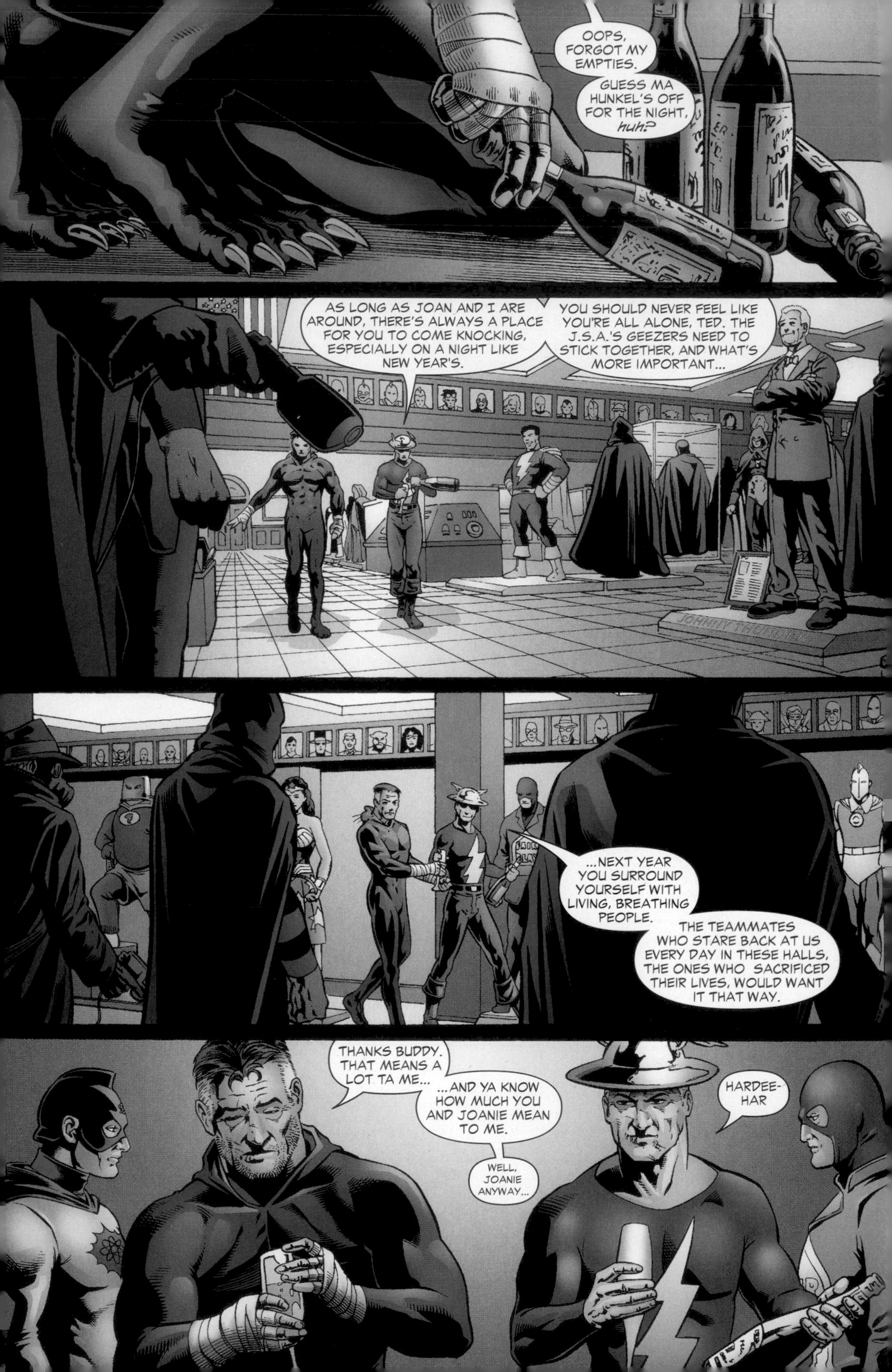
OOPS, FORGOT MY EMPTIES.
GUESS MA HUNKEL'S OFF FOR THE NIGHT, *huh?*
AS LONG AS JOAN AND I ARE AROUND, THERE'S ALWAYS A PLACE FOR YOU TO COME KNOCKING, ESPECIALLY ON A NIGHT LIKE NEW YEAR'S.
YOU SHOULD NEVER FEEL LIKE YOU'RE ALL ALONE, TED. THE J.S.A.'S GEEZERS NEED TO STICK TOGETHER, AND WHAT'S MORE IMPORTANT...
...NEXT YEAR YOU SURROUND YOURSELF WITH LIVING, BREATHING PEOPLE.
THE TEAMMATES WHO STARE BACK AT US EVERY DAY IN THESE HALLS, THE ONES WHO SACRIFICED THEIR LIVES, WOULD WANT IT THAT WAY.
THANKS BUDDY. THAT MEANS A LOT TA ME...
...AND YA KNOW HOW MUCH YOU AND JOANIE MEAN TO ME.
WELL, JOANIE ANYWAY...
HARDEE-HAR

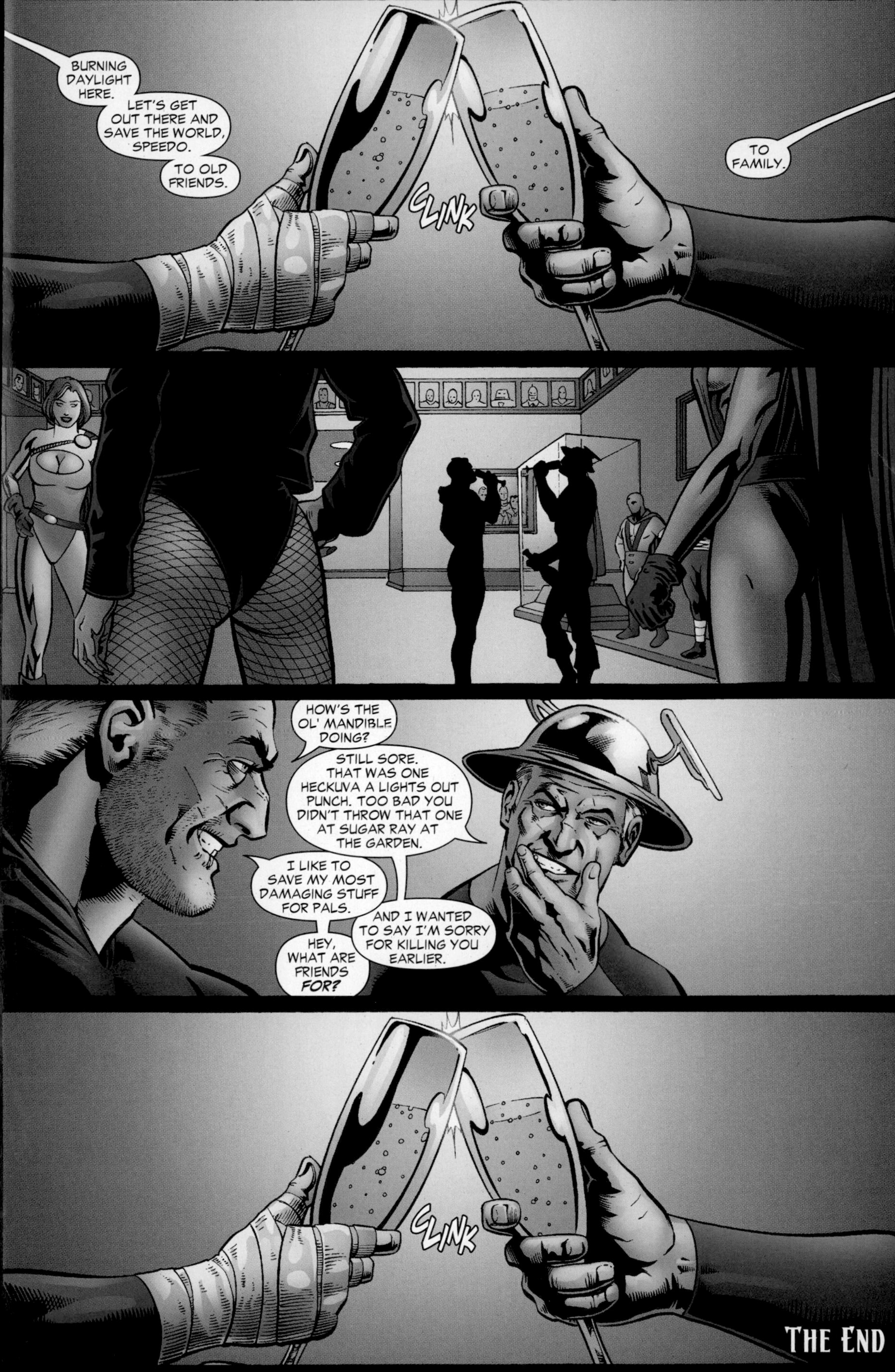
BURNING DAYLIGHT HERE.
LET'S GET OUT THERE AND SAVE THE WORLD, SPEEDO.
TO OLD FRIENDS.
TO FAMILY.
CLINK
HOW'S THE OL' MANDIBLE DOING?
STILL SORE. THAT WAS ONE HECKUVA A LIGHTS OUT PUNCH. TOO BAD YOU DIDN'T THROW THAT ONE AT SUGAR RAY AT THE GARDEN.
I LIKE TO SAVE MY MOST DAMAGING STUFF FOR PALS.
AND I WANTED TO SAY I'M SORRY FOR KILLING YOU EARLIER.
HEY, WHAT ARE FRIENDS FOR?
CLINK
THE END

DON'T MISS THESE OTHER GREAT TITLES FROM AROUND THE DCU!

SUPERMAN:
BIRTHRIGHT

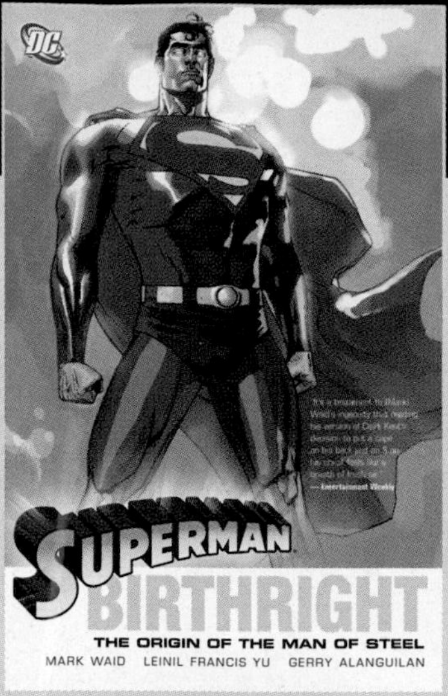
SUPERMAN
BIRTHRIGHT
THE ORIGIN OF THE MAN OF STEEL
MARK WAID LEINIL FRANCIS YU GERRY ALANGUILAN

MARK WAID
LEINIL FRANCIS YU
GERRY ALANGUILAN

BATMAN:
DARK VICTORY

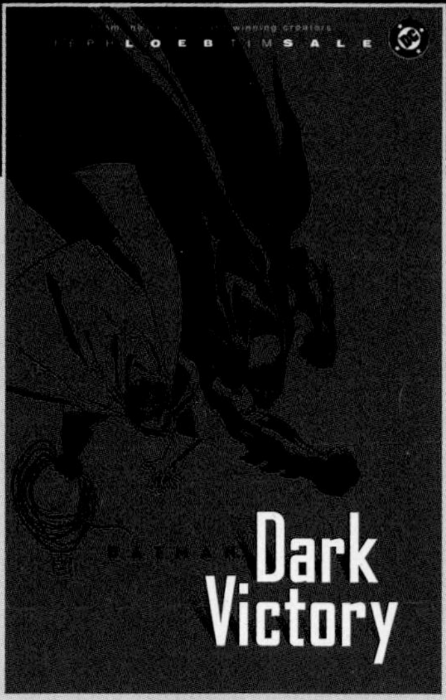
Dark Victory

JEPH LOEB
TIM SALE

WONDER WOMAN:
GODS AND MORTALS

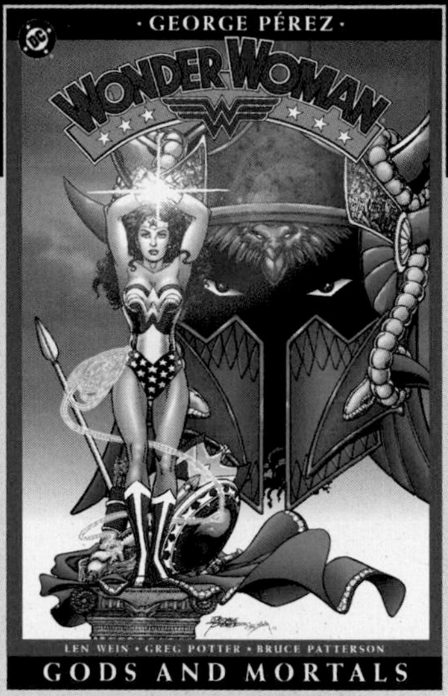
· GEORGE PÉREZ ·
WONDER WOMAN
LEN WEIN • GREG POTTER • BRUCE PATTERSON
GODS AND MORTALS

GEORGE PÉREZ
LEN WEIN/GREG POTTER
BRUCE PATTERSON

GREEN LANTERN:
NO FEAR

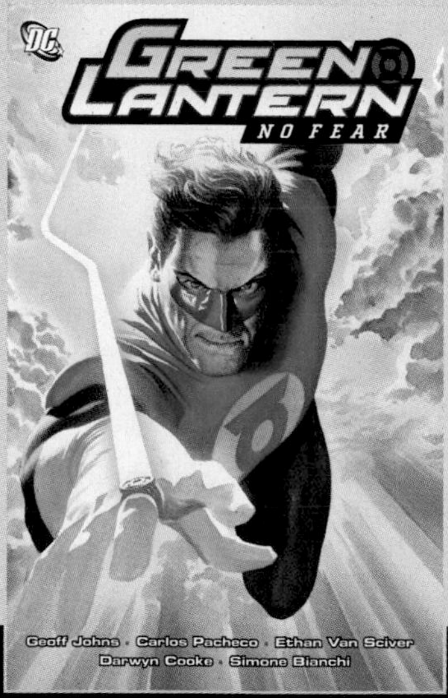
GREEN LANTERN
NO FEAR
Geoff Johns · Carlos Pacheco · Ethan Van Sciver
Darwyn Cooke · Simone Bianchi

GEOFF JOHNS
CARLOS PACHECO
ETHAN VAN SCIVER

GREEN ARROW:
QUIVER

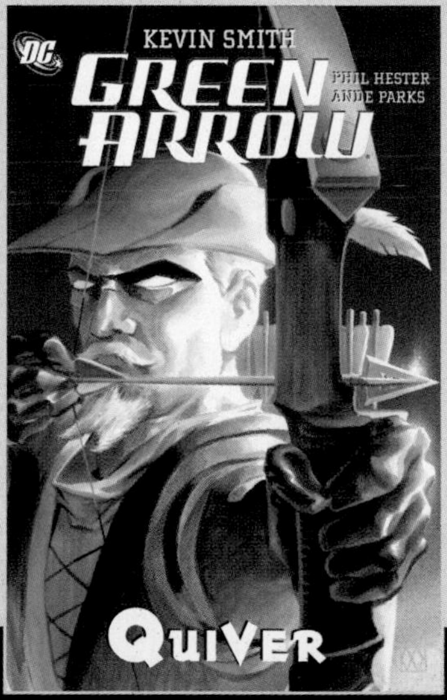
KEVIN SMITH
GREEN ARROW
PHIL HESTER
ANDE PARKS
QUIVER

KEVIN SMITH
PHIL HESTER
ANDE PARKS

TEEN TITANS:
A KID'S GAME

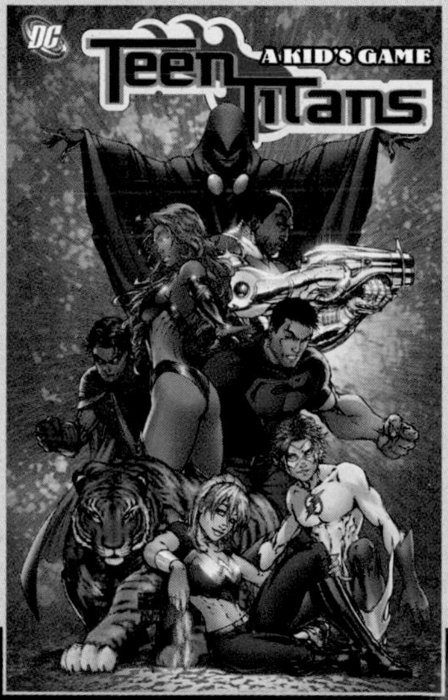
A KID'S GAME
Teen Titans

GEOFF JOHNS
MIKE McKONE

SEARCH THE GRAPHIC NOVELS SECTION OF
www.DCCOMICS.com
FOR ART AND INFORMATION ON ALL OF OUR BOO

READ MORE ADVENTURES OF YOUR FAVORITE HEROES IN THESE COLLECTIONS FROM DC COMICS:

KINGDOM COME

THE GREATEST SUPER HERO EPIC OF TOMORROW!
KINGDOM COME
Mark WAID
Alex ROSS

Mark Waid and **Alex Ross** deliver a grim tale of youth versus experience, tradition versus change and what defines a hero. KINGDOM COME is a riveting story pitting the old guard — Superman, Batman, Wonder Woman and their peers — against a new uncompromising generation.

WINNER OF FIVE EISNER AND HARVEY AWARDS, INCLUDING BEST LIMITED SERIES AND BEST ARTIST

IDENTITY CRISIS

NEW YORK TIMES BEST-SELLING AUTHOR OF THE ZERO GAME
BRAD MELTZER
RAGS MORALES MICHAEL BAIR
IDENTITY CRISIS
Introduction by JOSS WHEDON, creator of BUFFY THE VAMPIRE SLAYER and FIREFLY

BRAD MELTZER
RAGS MORALES
MICHAEL BAIR

CRISIS ON INFINITE EARTHS

CRISIS
ON INFINITE EARTHS
MARV WOLFMAN
& GEORGE PÉREZ

MARV WOLFMAN
GEORGE PÉREZ

DC: THE NEW FRONTIER VOLUME 1

DC: The New Frontier
BY DARWYN COOKE WITH DAVE STEWART

DARWYN COOKE
DAVE STEWART

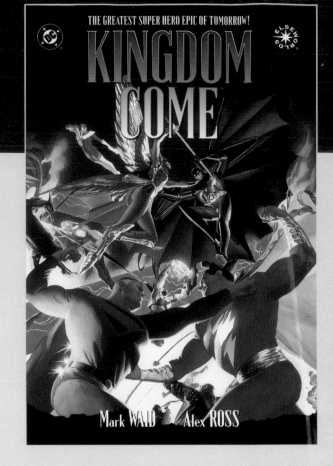

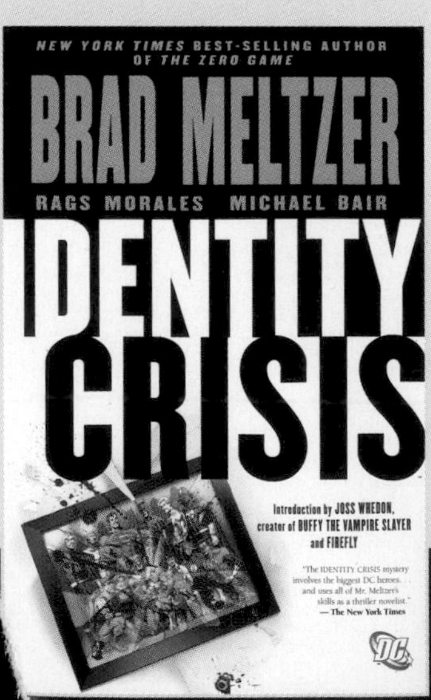